PREVAIL UNTIL THE BITTER END

A volume in the series
Battlegrounds: Cornell Studies in Military History
edited by David J. Silbey

A list of titles in this series is available at www.cornellpress.cornell.edu.

Prevail until the Bitter End

Germans in the Waning Years of World War II

Alexandra Lohse

Cornell University Press

Ithaca and London

First published 2021 by Cornell University Press

Printed in the United States of America

Library of Congress Cataloging-in-Publication Data

Names: Lohse, Alexandra, author.
Title: Prevail until the bitter end : Germans in the waning years of
    World War II / Alexandra Lohse.
Description: Ithaca [New York] : Cornell University Press, 2021. |
    Series: Battlegrounds : Cornell studies in military history |
    Includes bibliographical references and index.
Identifiers: LCCN 2021008202 (print) | LCCN 2021008203 (ebook) |
    ISBN 9781501759390 (hardcover) | ISBN 9781501759406 (epub) |
    ISBN 9781501759413 (pdf)
Subjects: LCSH: World War, 1939–1945—Germany—Public opinion. |
    Public opinion—Germany—History—20th century. | Germany—
    History—1933–1945. | National socialism—Public opinion. |
    Germans—Attitudes.
Classification: LCC D810.P85 G44 2021 (print) | LCC D810.P85 (ebook) |
    DDC 940.53/43—dc23
LC record available at https://lccn.loc.gov/2021008202
LC ebook record available at https://lccn.loc.gov/2021008203

For Sabine, Tine, and the guys

Contents

ACKNOWLEDGMENTS

I owe this book to the expertise, support, and kindness of so many people. I am humbled by their generosity and pleased to finally say my thanks for their many contributions to this project. Its shortcomings are the only thing to which I lay sole claim.

First and foremost, I wish to thank Richard Breitman. This book would not have been conceived or executed without him. His patience and dedication continue to astound me, and I look forward to having him ask me what is next. I am also thankful to Eric Lohr and Max Paul Friedman for their guidance during this project's earlier iterations.

I am grateful for the institutional support I received from my professional home, the Mandel Center for Advanced Holocaust Studies, including the Independent Staff Research Fellowship that helped me carry this project across the finish line. Of course, the views expressed in this book are mine and do not represent those of the United States Holocaust Memorial Museum (USHMM), its officers, or employees.

It is such a privilege to work among the many brilliant scholars and fellows who populate the Mandel Center. I am particularly indebted to my friends in the Mandel Writing Group, whose feedback, encouragement, and comradery were invaluable. Thank you, Kierra Crago-Schneider, Betsy Anthony, Rebecca Carter-Chand, Katherine White, Sara Brinegar, Dallas Michelbacher, and Jake Newsome. A special thanks to Steve Feldman for his support in shepherding this project toward publication.

Laura Hilton's research on rumors has broadened my thinking and has been inspiring throughout this process. I would also like to acknowledge April Shelford, Amanda Harrison, Katie Lampadarios, Nick Underwood, Scott Blair, Rob Williams, Katrin Paehler, Ed Westermann, Jürgen Matthäus, and many others who offered good cheer and support over many years. A very special thanks to Matt Lantry for sharing his research with me and for providing notes on an early draft of this project.

I am indebted to the patience and expertise of staff at many archives and libraries in the United States, Germany, and the United Kingdom. I would like to thank the staff at the USHMM library and archives, in particular, for years of support. I owe a special debt of gratitude to Stephen Tyas for sharing his pioneering research and expertise of the Combined Services Detailed Interrogation Centre (CSDIC) files with me many years ago at the National Archives in Kew. I would also like to extend a heartfelt thanks to Emily Andrew and David J. Silbey at Cornell University Press for their support and to the anonymous readers whose feedback allowed me to see this book with fresh eyes.

My mother, Sabine, and my sister, Christine, have been my greatest supporters from day one, and no one will be more excited to have this book on their shelves. Thank you. For making all my days good, even the bad ones when the words just would not come, I would like to thank Rudi and Maddie. Without them, none of this would have been possible. Lauren was a source of calm and encouragement when I needed it most. I would like to thank Michael for the courage to embark on this project. And more than anything, I would like to thank Chris for the courage to finish it. I do not know how I would have done it without him, and I am so glad I did not have to.

List of Abbreviations

BA-BA	Bundesarchiv-Bildarchiv, Koblenz, Germany
BA-MA	Bundesarchiv-Militärarchiv, Freiburg, Germany
BBC	British Broadcasting Corporation
CIA	Central Intelligence Agency
CMF	Central Mediterranean Forces
CSDIC	Combined Services Detailed Interrogation Centre
Gestapo	Geheime Staatspolizei (Secret State Police)
IWM	Imperial War Museum, London, UK
MI5	Military Intelligence, Section 5
MI6	Military Intelligence, Section 6
NARA	National Archives and Records Administration, College Park, MD, USA
NCO	noncommissioned officer
NSDAP	Nationalsozialistische Deutsche Arbeiterpartei (National Socialist German Workers' Party or commonly Nazi Party)
OSS	Office of Strategic Services

POW   prisoner of war
RAD   Reicharbeitsdienst (Reich Labor Service)
SD   Sicherheitsdienst des Reichsführers-SS (Security Service of
            the SS)
SS   Schutzstaffel ("Protection Squadron")
TNA   the National Archives, Kew, UK
USHMM   United States Holocaust Memorial Museum, Washington,
            DC, USA
Waffen-SS   military branch of the SS ("Armed-SS")

Introduction

The World at War

The war had swept Lieutenant Metzenthien along European shores for five long years before Allied forces captured him at Toulon on August 15, 1944. He still remembered what "a world at peace looked like," but it bore little resemblance to what he had seen during his recent travels that had taken him from Russia in the East to France in the West. The world at war was a world upended, and Metzenthien had found his fellow countrymen unmoored from the values and norms he recognized. In conversations with his cellmates, he complained bitterly about the conduct of "our young chaps" in France who had treated the country as "one vast restaurant" and had "stuffed and stuffed themselves, till all at once they'd been taken unawares." He understood why the French had "every reason to hate us. . . . I can tell you the whole French people hates us like poison. Some poor devils had to put up with a lot from us."[1] Metzenthien was equally incensed about the German occupation forces and administrators in Poland, "chaps who [rose] in the Party, and the bastards [had] never set eyes on a foreign country before." Now they had come to plunder under the cover of war: "No one wanted to fight, they all wanted to make money and send [foodstuffs] home to Germany. You've only got to look at the type of chap in the [prisoner of war (POW)] camps here to realize that we're on the decline."[2]

But if Metzenthien abhorred his countrymen's greed and callousness abroad, he admired their courage at the home front under fire. In his cell, he agonized over memories of the "hellish things" he had witnessed on home visits to a country that he barely recognized. Recalling the harrowing aftermath of an air raid on Leipzig, he admitted, "I felt quite faint at what I saw there—there were bodies that had fallen all over the streets, lying and sitting, and women and children screaming, piles of dead."[3] On his last trip to his hometown of Hamburg in May 1942, he had dragged his suitcase through rubble-strewn streets, past wrecked buildings and ramshackle tents that haphazardly sheltered tens of thousands of bombing victims living under "terrible conditions." He had spent his final night home crammed into an underground shelter with hundreds of people while Allied bombers wreaked from above: "What a night, women and children yelling and crying and praying to heaven." Abruptly recalled to Bordeaux the following morning, he had passed the burning Hamburg harbor, where "some fires were two days old," before arriving at the train station: "God, what a sight. All the wretched people who had been bombed out during the night's raid, about 4,000 of them were standing there in pajamas, in broad daylight at 5 o'clock in the afternoon, shivering and howling."[4] Several days later, "a wire arrived . . . to say that my house had been bombed, my wife and children [were] safe but everything we possessed had been lost. And I never got any more leave either to make up for it."[5] Still, as he reflected on the war's rising tolls from captivity, Metzenthien was confident that the home front would hold: "I tell you, it's alright if we go on fighting to the last man and the last inhabitant because the German nation has nothing more to lose, it has lost everything already. I'm amazed at the high morale of the people of Hamburg; naturally they grumble and curse, but they stand up to their fate. . . . The enemy, if it comes to that, will have to pay heavily for every inch of ground he wins in Germany. Artillery can't do any damage to our possessions—they are all gone already."[6]

Metzenthien hoped "that the war should end quickly," but he expected it to drag on for many years to come.[7] In his cell, he traded jokes set some twenty years in the future in which Germans looked up the meaning of unknown terms like "peace" or "butter" in old dictionaries, only to learn that such things had existed long ago, "before the time of the Führer."[8] Underlying the banter was the implicit assumption that Germans were facing indefinite war, not imminent defeat, in the fall of 1944. This was not for lack of information. Metzenthien had witnessed firsthand the ruinous failures of the German air force, the crippling material shortages in several theaters of war, and the calamities of the home front under fire. He knew of the hostility and outrage that the Germans had stoked all over occupied Europe. In captivity, he learned from news and propaganda materials of the Russian advances toward the Baltic states, of Allied armies pushing up north through Italy, and of their progress across western Europe following the landings at Normandy. The news of their arrival at Germany's western borders in September 1944 shocked him as deeply as the sight of German women and children entombed in the ruins of the Reich: "If anybody had said to me at the beginning of the war that the Americans would ever be knocking on the gates of Aachen I should have packed him straight off to a lunatic asylum."[9] Metzenthien also learned about the abdication of Germany's Romanian, Finnish, and Bulgarian allies in August and September 1944, a rapid succession of "betrayals" that outraged German combatants and civilians alike.[10] And yet, although as he professed, he did not "see what we ought to do exactly," he maintained that "we'll come out alright, we must do. Everything may be shot to bits but I tell you on our own soil we won't yield a single step."[11] Palpably frustrated by his captors' failure to grasp that "the political attitude of the German" fueled "his power of resistance," he railed that "these stupid English have never yet succeeded in realizing what National Socialism is. They're scared stiff of our so-called Gestapo methods, but they remain in complete ignorance of our real way of going about things."[12] As he instructed his cellmate:

> You should have told [the Interrogating Officer] that it's not a question of National Socialism or the Führer but the fact that Germany has become great again. You have to thrust that simple fact under their noses, because so far they haven't realized the truth of it. That's the thing that really matters. It doesn't matter if it's the Führer or a Müller or a Schubert, and we might have had Communism or Socialism, never mind. The fact is, no one else did it, and because one man did what no one else could, that's why we are grateful to the Führer, and that's what makes every German a Nazi . . . his love and pride for his country.[13]

Metzenthien's enduring confidence in the resolve of the militarized national community and the legitimacy of its cause was not singular. Nor was his intransigence exceptional. In the fifth year of the war, Allied observers routinely encountered among the growing numbers of captured German soldiers, sailors, and airmen proclamations of dogged faith in a coming and deserved German victory. It was a strikingly dissonant response to mounting evidence of Germany's untenable military situation and was all the more confounding when voiced by men like Metzenthien who spoke about their world cogently and who openly reviled the wanton corruption and destruction that had flourished under Nazism. How could such men nonetheless believe the Nazi regime capable of turning the tide and achieving victory against all odds? Why did they continue to mount a defense of an empire already lost? What accounted for their remarkable determination to "go on fighting to the last man and the last inhabitant" and to follow Adolf Hitler's regime into a doom that was becoming apparent from nearly every other vantage point?

This book charts the roughly twenty-seven months that lay between the destruction of the German Sixth Army at Stalingrad in January 1943 and Germany's unconditional surrender in May 1945, revisiting these and other persistent questions about the nature and endurance of popular support for the Nazi regime. Mobilized for "total war," German civilians and military personnel experienced an unparalleled convergence of military, economic, political, and social crises. The precipitous escalation of emergency conditions fostered widespread discontent and disillusionment with the Nazi regime and forced some people to question the purpose and likely outcome of the conflagration. But few Germans were willing to relinquish their investment in National Socialism and the war altogether, and many continued to believe the Nazi regime capable of salvaging Germany's rapidly deteriorating situation.

Even in retreat, Germany's militarized national community unleashed ferocious energies, staving off defeat for two and a half years and continuing its systematic murder campaigns against European Jews, Slavs, and others. Rumors about mass atrocities circulated widely among German military and civilian populations just as they embarked on total mobilization and gave rise to a grim corollary, the specter of Jewish vengeance that haunted the German popular imagination in the final war years and beyond. *Prevail until the Bitter End: Germans in the Waning Years of World War II* examines the conception of such notions under the crisis conditions of the final war years. It asks how members of the militarized national community interpreted their experiences at the intersection of extreme violence perpetrated by them and against them.[14] How did they respond to the war's rising tolls and receding fortunes? What were their visions and expectations for the future? What impact did the war's descending trajectory have on people's relationship with the Nazi regime, and what did National Socialism in decline mean to those mobilized in its defense?

This book probes popular responses to the violent dissolution of the Third Reich from an inclusive perspective that considers German military and civilian populations as integral members of Germany's wartime society (*Kriegsgesellschaft*). By 1943, both Nazi and Allied policies increasingly blurred dividing lines, treating all Germans as combatants and rendering the final war years the most lethal and grueling phase of their war. Between mid-1944 and 1945, when Germans were outgunned and outnumbered by rapidly advancing Russian and Anglo-US forces and facing cataclysmic aerial attacks against urban and industrial centers, Germans suffered some several hundred thousand military and civilian casualties each month. In the final year of the war, more Germans died than in the nearly five-year period preceding it.[15]

Importantly, many of the ravages of the final war years were not the result of Allied escalation of military violence, including against civilians, but were self-inflicted, the direct and intentional consequence of Nazi policies. Believing itself encircled by enemies without and infiltrated by enemies within, the Nazi regime orchestrated the all-or-nothing existential struggle that formed the very core of its worldview, insisting that the German nation fight and triumph as one by sheer force of will. Total mobilization included the deployment of ever younger and older cohorts of men to the front. Simultaneously, the militarization of civilian society proceeded with the drafting of women, children, and the elderly into labor and auxiliary services. The Nazi regime's chaotic efforts to raise an effective civil defense culminated in the establishment of its people's militia (Volkssturm, or "People's Storm") in October 1944 as a last stand against invading enemy armies.[16] Moreover, in their attempt to fully mobilize all national resources, Nazi authorities issued spates of directives, laws, and regulations that aimed to control all aspects of life in wartime. Noncompliance and nonconformity were punished with increasingly draconian sentences as authorities intensified their persecution of alleged saboteurs, deserters, and defeatists in the ranks of the military and of the general population alike. The Nazi persecution of alleged enemies within escalated dramatically after the failed assassination and coup attempt against Hitler on July 20, 1944. Moreover, in the final months of the war, German wartime society became subject to a grassroots campaign of "German-on-German terror" as fanatical Nazis turned against waning soldiers and civilians for their refusal to go down fighting.[17] The regime and its most ardent followers enacted their "total defeat in 1945," as historian Nicholas Stargardt recently put it, "in the process expending and exhausting all the moral and physical reserves of German society."[18]

Under the combined impact of these conditions, Germans with and without uniforms came to live and fight total war. Their experiences were not identical, but they became increasingly comparable, if Metzenthien's reflections on the embattled home front are at all indicative. Indeed, *Prevail until the Bitter End* shows that in the final war years, many German civilian and military combatants purposely attempted to forge themselves into the militarized national community of Nazi lore. As the home front transformed into the final battlefield, German forces gave equal weight to the wartime contributions of civilians, while many civilians identified as active participants in an existential struggle of their nation, their actions and experiences spanning the entire spectrum between wartime complicity and victimhood. For many, it was an article of faith that Germany would outlast its enemies in the unfolding war of attrition if front and home front fought in concert. As one soldier serving in the East put the commonly expressed sentiment in a letter in September 1944, "There must not be a single German shirking at the home front or the front. That's the only way to win this war. So, the motto for us: Persist until the bitter end."[19]

Paradoxically, German total mobilization occurred against the context of social, political, economic, and military dissolution. With Germany's military situation rapidly deteriorating and its war economy collapsing by late 1944, the Nazi regime increasingly lacked the means to enforce its policies at home and abroad. As the world inhabited by Germans contracted and fractured at once, new spaces opened for popular apathy, disobedience, or even defiance, a full range of responses to escalating crisis conditions. This inquiry is based largely on sources that were generated in the newly created fissures of the German wartime society. These include more than two thousand transcripts of surreptitiously recorded discussions among German POWs in

Western captivity, like those that registered Lieutenant Metzenthien's reflections.[20] These records were created by the Combined Services Detailed Interrogation Centre, or CSDIC, a British intelligence collaborative founded in 1939 by the directors of intelligence for the army, air force, and navy in conjunction with members of the security services (MI5 and MI6).[21] Conceived initially for the systematic interrogation of German POWs, the CSDIC soon shifted its focus to the surreptitious recording and transcription of discussions among prisoners in the presumed privacy of their detention cells. The first CSDIC facility was located in the Tower of London and featured cells equipped with hidden listening devices connected to recording equipment. The CSDIC employed the same methods when it moved to Trent Park, on the outskirts of London. In addition to the facilities of CSDIC (UK), consisting of surveillance camps at Trent Park, Latimer House, and Milton Park, the organization eventually operated mobile units under the auspices of CSDIC (Middle East) in North Africa and CSDIC (West) in France and later Germany.

The British Prisoner of War Department prescreened German and Italian prisoners in transition camps and transferred those believed to harbor valuable intelligence to a CSDIC facility or "cage" for interrogation and surveillance.[22] High-ranking German prisoners were routinely taken to England for interrogation, and many of them spent the entire war there. By contrast, most rank-and-file prisoners were processed and later imprisoned outside of the United Kingdom. Initially, the organization prioritized technical and tactical information. However, in the later war years, at the urging of the US Office of Strategic Services (OSS), the precursor to the Central Intelligence Agency (CIA), it shifted its focus to a broader range of subjects. Most prisoners arrived at a CSDIC facility mere days or weeks after capture, undergoing during their stay several rounds of interrogations in which CSDIC officers often needled the detainees to elicit unguarded responses. Numerous CSDIC transcripts in which inmates complained to their cellmates about such provocations suggest this was a successful tactic. CSDIC officers also supplied inmates with propaganda and news materials and occasionally plied them with treats and even alcohol to stimulate discussions in the cells. German-language specialists monitored inmate conversations and recorded and transcribed those they deemed relevant. Many of them were not native English speakers, and their transcriptions contain Briticisms, sometimes misused, that can sound awkward and anachronistic to modern ears. My translations of the German-language originals would have undoubtedly smoothed some of the rough edges and seemingly strange word choices. However, I wanted to minimize introducing current-day styles to these unique historical records. Instead, I chose to work predominantly with slightly edited English-language translations, which communicate so much about the time and place in which these records were created.

Most of the recorded conversations fell into broad topical categories, which included "secret weapons; comparisons of Allied and enemy equipment; bombing of German and enemy occupied territory; food generally and enemy rations; Allied rations; battle or service reminiscence; economic conditions on the [German] home front; politics; religion; frivolous or purely personal matters."[23] Many CSDIC transcripts touch on several of these categories and often contain POWs' broader reflections about the world at war. Moreover, in their discussions, many prisoners not only revealed glimpses of their own experiences and observations but also spoke at length about the experiences and outlooks of their comrades in arms and of their families and friends back home. Prisoners were transferred to regular POW camps as soon as CSDIC officers deemed their secrets revealed.[24]

By war's end, more than ten thousand German prisoners had passed through CSDIC facilities, and the agency had issued some seventeen thousand transcripts of their conversations, distributing up to ninety copies of each report to more than twelve intelligence agencies, including the OSS, after 1943. Transcripts ranged in length from half a page to several dozen pages. Most were recorded between 1943 and 1945, when Britain received the largest influx of prisoners, principally from the western and southern European theaters of war, although many, like Metzenthien, had witnessed conditions in various theaters over the course of a long war. By comparison, the CSDIC issued only five thousand interrogation reports during the same period.[25] The last CSDIC facility operated in Bad Nenndorf, in postwar Germany, between June 1945 and July 1947.

The CSDIC privileged surreptitious monitoring because it promised to yield more "unfiltered" and "authentic" intelligence than interrogations alone. The agency worked diligently to conceal the true nature of its operation from its subjects, and evidence suggests it did so successfully. There are numerous transcripts in which prisoners boasted about misleading interrogators, only to inadvertently reveal the information while chatting with fellow prisoners. Metzenthien, for instance, speculated in his cell that "the main idea of these interrogations seems to be political, not military . . . they're trying to get all they can out of us—because in the military field they knew a lot." He then proceeded to coach his cellmate for his next interrogation, a discussion that likely would not have occurred if the men knew of their continuous surveillance.[26] Discussions of atrocities and war crimes were rare but did occur.[27] CSDIC agents also recorded self-purported perpetrators or eyewitnesses discussing their efforts to conceal their involvement from their captors, another indicator that many prisoners were unaware of the true nature of the CSDIC operation.[28]

While it is likely that all major enemy powers engaged in surreptitious monitoring of their prisoners during World War II, the British operation was exceptionally sophisticated and extensive.[29] Today, CSDIC transcripts offer rare glimpses into the concerns and preoccupations of German soldiers, airmen, and sailors in Western captivity, with a level of detail and frankness rarely found in other sources generated during this period of the war. Since the transcripts' declassification, scholars have analyzed them for insights into the behaviors and mentalities of German combatants, exploring, for instance, the spectrum between situational and ideological explanations for the ferocious violence they unleashed until final defeat.[30] Among others, their studies have further dismantled the myth of a "clean Wehrmacht," the exculpatory fiction that the regular German armed forces had waged conventional warfare, while the Schutzstaffel (SS) alone perpetrated genocidal violence and other war crimes. *Prevail until the Bitter End* shows that such myths were not merely opportunistic postwar creations. Rather, Germans intentionally forged strands of this persistent narrative in the later war years. They found a receptive audience among the general population preoccupied with its own suffering and unwilling to reckon with German-perpetrated atrocities in the violent end phase of the war and beyond.

CSDIC transcripts circumscribe a relatively narrow sample of subjects, and this might be a good time to discuss what this book is not. It is not a comprehensive study of popular opinion in German wartime society, or of the German military, and not even of German POWs. It cannot be, although in privileging linguistic concision over conceptual precision, I speak of "Germans," "German combatants," and "German society" throughout. Importantly, though, none of the ideas and perceptions featured here are singular or exceptional within the larger source base. Rather, they are reflective of larger thought patterns that transcended divisions in German wartime society. The prisoners represented here had served in southern and western Europe at the time of their capture, although many, like Metzenthien, had witnessed conditions in various theaters over the course of a long war. Still, relatively few POWs spoke of firsthand experiences on the eastern front, site of many of the most brutal battles and atrocities that define our understanding of World War II today. Instead, the experiences of those who "stuffed and stuffed" themselves in France well into 1944, and of their vocal critics, are bound to be overrepresented here. At the same time, I show that hearsay, rumors, and speculations about the East circulated widely, even among the civilians and combatants who had never been deployed there.

The same is true for nearly all other theaters of war. Increasingly weary of official propaganda, German civilians considered their deployed soldiers, sailors, and airmen a most reliable source of information about the war and clamored for their accounts and impressions in letters and in conversations during home leave, which some were granted as late as 1944. Letters and home visits maintained strong bonds between military and civilian populations throughout the war, and disruptions to mail delivery or canceled home leave caused popular resentment and anger whenever they occurred. Metzenthien, for instance, still complained in captivity about his foreshortened final home visit, for which he was never granted makeup leave.[31] Around the same time, Frau M. Müller in Kirchberg voiced her grievance that the armed forces' "ban on leave" (*Urlaubssperre*) was unevenly applied only to the rank and file of the field army, while members of the home army got to enjoy vacations even in late 1944. She wrote, "Today I came home from work, and I think I've been struck by lightning because Erich Weber is already back on home leave. And when one passes by them, they laugh and mock. Oh dear, soon I will burst with anger. One person keeps getting leave, and another person can merely look on. All you hear is proclamations of the 'ban on leave,' but those fine lords keep coming home."[32]

Bitter complaints about the inequities of the burdens of war were increasingly common as the German war effort deteriorated. They were disseminated widely beyond people's immediate circle of trusted family and friends and thus reverberated throughout wartime society.[33] It was therefore no coincidence, for example, that stories about the slothful "young chaps" in western Europe circulated not only among eyewitnesses like Metzenthien but throughout Germany's wartime society more broadly. As Frau Chr. Jansen from Niederbieber wrote in a letter from September 1944: "The attitude among the civilian population regarding the Western front soldier is not very good, and I too believe that if the Eastern front soldiers had stood in the West, there would not have been the [Anglo-US] breakthrough. Things would have turned out differently if the soldiers from the East had been deployed [in the] West."[34] Similar sentiments were echoed by Frau Maria Lakowsky from Koblenz who wrote in a scathing indictment: "Those guys spent three years lounging and luxuriating and resting in France, all the while sending heavy packages back home, and now they can't even manage to hold the front. That is infuriating."[35] While not impossible, it is unlikely that either Jansen or Lakowsky had ever visited occupied France.[36] But they certainly would have heard accounts about it from their deployed husbands, brothers, or sons. They may have heard stories and rumors from the wives or sisters of soldiers stationed in France, the envied beneficiaries of those parcels of plunder. Regardless of the precise origin of their information, that these women had not seen France with their own eyes did not stop them from opining strongly and in great detail on the events unfolding there.

Germany's rumor mill churned incessantly, generating a wartime discourse that transcended front, home front, and even Allied prison fences. It molded prevalent perceptions of the Nazi regime in decline and generated common reactions toward the crisis conditions of the final war years. The shared "linguistic landscape" of this period encompassed fictional and factual elements and allowed Germans to incorporate their own personal experiences while also assuming the experiences of others as part of their wartime narrative.[37] In order to trace common and divergent themes in the stories Germans told about their war, and for the purposes of gauging morale among German military and civilian populations in the later war years, I draw on additional intelligence materials generated by a number of German and Allied agencies. These include comprehensive OSS surveillance reports in which Allied moles sent to live among German POWs, albeit not in CSDIC facilities, analyze group dispositions and preoccupations. Foreign agents also infiltrated German civilian society, and their reports add nuance and outside perspective to the "secret situation reports" produced by the Nazi Security Service (Sicherheitsdienst des Reichsführers-SS, or SD) to gauge the "mood and attitudes" on the German home front. Finally, I incorporate eyewitness accounts from diaries and letters as well as more comprehensive censorship reports based on German wartime mail intercepted by the Allies, specifically

through the British Broadcasting Corporation (BBC), and especially by Wehrmacht censors.

By bringing voices from the front, the home front, and captivity into conversation with one another, this book shows that actual wartime conversations happened not only within but across these spaces. No matter where they
lived or fought, Germans told surprisingly similar stories to make sense of
their world in crisis. Also, whether at home, in the field, or in POW camps,
they cast themselves as active participants in a shared wartime experience.
For instance, around the time of Metzenthien's capture, Wehrmacht censors
intercepted a letter from August 1944, in which a soldier by the name of Er-
brich, stationed in the East, reflected on the mass deployment of hundreds
of thousands of German civilians to build field entrenchments and fortifications along Germany's borders. Like Metzenthien, he took great pride in
the resolve of the home front to fight, marveling, "We are living in an astound-
ing time. You can really call this a popular uprising. The entire nation is rushing to our country's borders to protect it from the invasion of an overwhelming
enemy. 'People rise up, storm break loose.' The poet's words have become reality. The nation's willingness to self-sacrifice will grant us victory."[38]

Voices from the home front could be equally fanatic. Not surprisingly, this
was true especially for youths, who had spent their formative years under more
than a decade of National Socialism, and some five years at war. For instance,
Fräulein Anny Dolle eagerly vowed to support the war effort in an intercepted letter from Saarbrücken to the East, in September 1944: "Before we
can celebrate victory, I want to contribute my part. At the West Wall we all
go build fortifications. Our hometown will be defended until the last man. . . .
Our entire company is going tomorrow, Sunday, shovel in hand. We want to
make things a little easier for our soldiers. Now I can finally actively participate in this war. . . . [N]ow that the fight is about our home territory, of
course we participate. Let's get going!"[39]

To be sure, such home-front fervor was rare in the fifth year of the war.
As German military setbacks mounted, Nazi morale monitors frequently bemoaned the fact that "it is impossible to ignore that the home front is
marked by a general despondency."[40] Moreover, they feared that home-front
war weariness would sap the resolve of the front, where the troops' outlook
was already "negatively impacted by the recent stresses and by deep worry
about the fate of loved ones back home."[41] Still, like Metzenthien, Nazi authorities observed that while Germans habitually "grumbled and cursed"

about the growing burdens and sacrifices of the war, their outlook largely remained "bleak but hopeful."[42]

Many Germans remained committed until the bitter end to a war they deemed legitimate toward a victory they deemed their due. For instance, in mid-September 1944, Frau Ruth Kuschmann in Karwin, in Upper Silesia, pledged her determination to carry on in a letter to Private H. Siebert. Painfully aware of an overwhelming enemy force advancing from all sides, she nonetheless believed that Germans were bound by faith and duty to continue the war: "Terrible battles are raging at the moment. I am really anxious to know how the war will turn out. Things are as critical in the East as they are in the West. But what's the point in thinking about it all. The only thing we can do is remain steadfast in our faith in victory and to continue to do our duty until the end. We must not waver."[43] In the final war years, Germans rarely reflected on the origins of the conflagration. If they did, they framed it not as a brutal war of German conquest and extermination but rather as it had been portrayed in Nazi propaganda, as a preemptive stance against foreign aggression. This official version resonated powerfully under the crisis conditions of the final war period when many believed that a German victory was the nation's just deserts. As Fräulein Wendt wrote from Berlin in September 1944, "It is simply impossible that all those many, many sacrifices for the life and future of our nation were for naught. Of course, the current situation is very, very bitter. But even so, I still have absolute faith that we will be able to withstand the violent advance of the enemy. Even if it takes a miracle; if there is any justice in the world, a miracle will happen."[44]

Even at the precipice of privation and loss, the humdrum of everyday life at the German home front continued. In the later war years, when many Germans strained to secure basic necessities like food, clothing, or shelter, their daily struggles fueled widespread discontent. Germans from all walks of life freely aired their grievances and resentments against the Nazi regime and the ineffective party and state apparatus. Importantly, they frequently imbued the challenges and burdens of everyday life in wartime with the same urgency with which they discussed the latest military developments. Their preoccupation with everyday matters also helped insulate them from a self-reckoning with the suffering Germans had wrought elsewhere.

The stories that Germans told themselves about their world at war suggest that "the war" was a physical setting but also a mind-set expressed through a shared "linguistic landscape" that framed their observations and colored their expectations. For those who inhabited it literally or figuratively, the world at war was a world apart where anything could, and indeed did, happen. Perhaps this also helps account for Germans' enduring faith in a coming "miracle" that would bring about a final victory. Their reflections suggest that under the conditions of war, regular categories of analysis and judgment were recalibrated to encompass the previously unfathomable. Metzenthien, for instance, told of a world of jarring extremes, in which Germany had ascended to destined greatness and plunged to catastrophic lows. It was populated by German fighters succumbing to greed and sloth abroad while their women and children endured near-apocalyptic horrors at the home front. Metzenthien's stories featured triumphs and travesties that hit many of the major fault lines of wartime culture, including class, gender, and race. If they defied reason, they nonetheless seemed plausible to him and many of his peers when set within the world at war.

Prevail until the Bitter End features a range of German military and civilian perspectives to show how even radically different wartime experiences unfolded within the shared reality of the war. Moving chronologically from January 1943 through May 1945, the individual chapters are organized around important milestones on the road to "total defeat," exploring reactions of German civilians and military personnel to wartime policies and events that marked the war's transition from global conquest to domestic crisis. Chapter 1 examines popular reactions to the German defeat at Stalingrad, perceived as a turning point by contemporaries and historians alike, and to the Nazi regime's efforts to harness the nation's collective force of will to the point of self-annihilation. Chapter 2 examines how the early "totalizing measures" amplified popular resentments of the failures and corruptions of the Nazi state and party apparatus. Chapter 3 explores popular reactions to rumors and eyewitness accounts of mass atrocities in eastern Europe. In tracing the transformation of how Germans related to the fallible Nazi regime and its floundering war effort, these chapters tell the story of two parallel developments: On the one hand, there were growing popular doubts and disillusionment with the German political and military leadership. On the other hand, there was the rise of a peculiar confidence common to both German forces and civilians even in the later war years. As some Germans began to glimpse the awesome forces stacked against them, they nonetheless maintained a stubborn, almost defiant confidence in the German

cause. This confidence is key to the subsequent evolution of German attitudes under escalating crisis conditions.

Chapter 4 examines popular responses to the July 20 plot against Hitler
and to the escalating Allied air war in 1944 as subsequent turning points in
how Germans experienced the war and related to the Nazi regime. Chapter 5 then illuminates popular reactions to total collapse in 1945. The conclusion reflects on what National Socialism meant to some of those who lived
and died during its violent dissolution. These chapters also feature rich and
imaginative gossip about some of the most powerful figures of the Nazi dictatorship, including Adolf Hitler, Hermann Göring, Joseph Goebbels, and
Heinrich Himmler, architects of many of the most brutal policies that defined the destructive, and self-destructive, end phase of the war. They examine the frustrations and trials of popular mobilization, the growing disappointments over the conditions of day-to-day life, and the creeping terror
of the possibility of defeat. They also suggest why these factors failed to oblit-
erate popular faith in the possibility of German victory for so long and why
many Germans proved surprisingly agile in their adjustment to defeat and
the post-Nazi world.

Chapter 1

STALINGRAD

The Right to Believe in Victory

January 30, 1943, marked the ten-year anniversary of Adolf Hitler's appointment as chancellor of Germany. Always an important date in the Nazi calendar, that Saturday would have seen all the pomp and circumstance the regime's propaganda apparatus could conjure to celebrate a decade since the Nazis' "seizure of power." But in the fourth year of the war, with the eastern campaign stalled yet again, the public mood was somber. The country anxiously awaited news from Stalingrad, where the Sixth Army was engaged in what a recent Wehrmacht communiqué had termed "defensive" battles. As hope for a "miracle at the Volga" dwindled, so did hope for a short war, and the Nazi propaganda ministry instructed that official festivities sound a calm and reassuring note. Party speakers were urged to emphasize that the German nation had faced countless challenges over the past ten years, many seemingly insurmountable until Hitler had found a way. He would do so again.[1]

For the first time since 1933, Hitler made no public appearance to mark the occasion. Instead, the main address that day was given by Reich Marshal

Hermann Göring, commander in chief of the Luftwaffe, who indicated in a speech broadcast live on all domestic and military radio stations that the Sixth Army had suffered defeat. Unable to deny or explain away a loss of such magnitude, he declared the men of the encircled army group dead and immortal. Göring did not acknowledge the one hundred thousand German troops about to surrender, some of whom famously listened in on the broadcast of their own "funeral oration" as he praised their ultimate sacrifice. Instead, he cast a mythical veil over a catastrophic loss.[2] Conjuring Leonidas and the three hundred Spartans who had died defending the pass at Thermopylae against invading "Persian hordes," he claimed that the German soldiers at Stalingrad, too, had chosen deliberate self-annihilation for the protection of their nation: "In the history of our own days it will be said: When you come to Germany, tell them that you have seen us fighting at Stalingrad, as the law, the law for the security of our people, commanded us." According to Göring, Hitler's leadership would ensure that their sacrifices were not in vain. A German victory, he claimed, was preordained:

> There is a certain logic in world history. Do you believe, my comrades, that destiny—I mean Providence, the Almighty—lets an unknown man rise up, a man without a name and without wealth, a simple fighter from the World War, then guides him through endless confusion, lets him become greater and greater, and, all of a sudden, all this should be senseless? That Providence sent the German Volk a man of such greatness in the Führer . . . and that he managed to fashion the strongest nation in the world out of the German Volk, which once was fragmented and impotent, then these are the guarantees which give us the right to believe in victory.[3]

Four days later, on February 3, 1943, German radio broadcasts officially confirmed the end of the battle at the Volga River and announced a three-day mourning period. A German victory had never seemed further out of reach, and morale monitors reported that news of the defeat caused grave distress and uncertainty "in the whole German community."[4] Thus began the Nazi campaign for total mobilization. At a crisis point in the war and with popular morale at an all-time low, Göring's speech had sounded the battle cry for the regime's proverbial "flight ahead" (*Flucht nach vorn*). And although not with blind determination, the German people followed. They did so at a time when the regime's successes dwindled and a string of military setbacks suggested that Germany had lost its momentum in this war, perhaps irretrievably. In the East, the Germans suffered a slow but sustained withdrawal and "front reduction" as the Red Army's counter-offensives drove them out of Rostov-on-Don, Kursk, Orel, Belgorod, Kharkov, Dnipropetrovsk, Kiev, and Kalinin by the following winter. In the South, Germany lost Tunisia as well as a quarter million soldiers, whom the Allies took as prisoners when the remaining Afrika Korps and Italian troops surrendered in late spring. The Allied invasion of Sicily and Italy over the course of the summer forced the Germans to mount a partial occupation on behalf of Benito Mussolini's regime, now unmasked as impotent. In the North and West, Germans anxiously awaited an Allied invasion that failed to materialize. But the war came from above, as enemy bombers wreaked destruction and caused mass displacement and massive civilian casualties in Berlin, Hamburg, Kassel, Kiel, Munich, Nuremberg, Vienna, the industrial centers of the Ruhr, and beyond.

A year marked by such tangible setbacks fundamentally transformed German experiences and perceptions of the war. As Allied successes mounted in the face of broader German mobilization, the war encroached on life at the home front in ways it had never done before, becoming a greater nuisance and menace at once. The events of 1943 also had a profound impact on people's relationship with the Nazi regime and, for the first time, even with Hitler, whose fallibility stood revealed after Stalingrad. Members of the military and civilian populations voiced anger over their ineffectual military and political leaders, whose obfuscations compounded the mounting burdens of war. As Germans struggled to make sense of the events of 1943, they frequently rejected official interpretations and forged their own accounts of the unfolding crisis, with important implications for the rest of the war. And yet, if the trying conditions of 1943 tested the bonds between people and leadership, they did not break them. Instead, many Germans emerged more disaffected with the Nazi regime and yet more determined than ever to fight its war. This chapter traces the origins of this new but enduring dynamic to the contentious aftermath of "the debacle in Russia."[5] It examines how members of the German civilian and military populations experienced news of the defeat and responded to official attempts to mythologize the fallen soldiers of Stalingrad. It also explores how the shock of defeat caused many Germans to reexamine some of the events of the preceding war years, and, most importantly, how the experience had a decisive and enduring impact on popular responses to mounting mobilization efforts and subsequent military setbacks.

Stalingrad had held a powerful grip on the German popular imagination throughout the summer and fall of 1942, when the rapid German advances in the East had been accompanied by a stream of celebratory propaganda and triumphant proclamations about the future course of the war. At the height of German military might, no promise seemed too fantastical and no goal out of reach. SD reports from the fall of 1942 repeatedly stated that large segments of the population believed a victorious end of the eastern campaign was imminent. Indeed, many Germans even hoped that a "final victory" and an end to the war were close.[6] Compounding military with propaganda miscalculations, Hitler himself repeatedly announced the impending fall of Stalingrad, a battle he had imbued with disproportionate significance. His public displays of unfettered optimism alarmed his propaganda minister, Joseph Goebbels, who worried about "illusionistic contemplations about the continued course of the war."[7] On October 2, 1942, when Hitler yet again promised the coming victory in a widely broadcast speech, Victor Klemperer took note in his diary. A German linguistics scholar of Jewish descent and an astute observer of the Nazi regime, Klemperer noted the gist of the "same old song, mercilessly exaggerated" that had accompanied the military campaigns of 1942: "The stupendous German successes, German morality, German certainty of victory—things are going ever better for us; we can hold out for many years yet."[8] Klemperer's quiet despair was drowned out by the many voices rejoicing at the prospect of a German victory in the East. Albert Neuhaus, a soldier at Stalingrad, wrote to his wife the following day that "the Leader's great speech has only strengthened our belief in [ultimate victory] by another 100%."[9]

For much of 1942, many German POWs in Western captivity shared the confidence that a German victory in the East was within reach. But as the year drew to a close, some worried about the implications of an unexpectedly protracted eastern campaign. Two German submariners discussed the situation in early December 1942, quibbling over when, not if, Germany would defeat Russia. One of them argued, "This war will go on for a good three years more. Say we finish off Russia next year—by that time they will have been bled white. Then the year after that we shall go for England—with lulls in the fighting and preparations that will certainly take two years." His cellmate cautioned, "Oh I don't know about that . . . I believe the Russian campaign alone will take another two years. Just think how long this Stalingrad business has been going on."[10] Late in the year, with no news of a German breakthrough in the East, some POWs began to feel equally apprehensive. On December 2, 1942, another group of sailors discussed how recent setbacks had begun to undermine morale among their peers:

> The mood at our base has changed dramatically. Before [the eastern campaign stalled], the strong conviction prevailed that everything will turn out alright, that we almost certainly would not lose the war, and that it was merely a matter of time [until victory]. But now the mood was completely different. Personally, I also think the situation is critical. First of all, things are going wrong in Russia; furthermore, I don't believe that the Italians will hold out much longer. And if the Americans are ready to land that many troops, tanks, airplanes, and stuff in North Africa, we'll probably get kicked out of North Africa.[11]

As fall turned to winter and the military situation in the East deteriorated, Goebbels finally tempered official Nazi rhetoric to bridge the gulf between people's expectations and the grim reality on the ground. With the Soviet encirclement at Stalingrad tightening, fewer and fewer letters from the battlefield reached the home front, and by December 1942, Goebbels purged any mentions of Stalingrad from all official reports. But the news blackout only transfixed people's attention on the outcome of a battle they believed indicative of the future course of the war. Some Germans turned to foreign propaganda and war reporting for information, though many distrusted foreign accounts as a source of deliberate misinformation. A submarine telegraphist, for instance, recalled, "We've sometimes heard news on the wireless—you heard a good, clear voice but it wasn't Germany, it was London. They told us all sorts of fairy tales about Russian counter-offensives and so on."[12] As late as December 1942, he still reflexively dismissed reports of Russian advances as "fairy tales."

In mid-January 1943, an official Wehrmacht report publicly referred to "defensive" fighting at Stalingrad for the first time. This stunning but oblique reference did not provide sufficient information about the actual turn of events at the Volga and thus merely stoked popular anxiety to new heights. Two weeks later, Göring's speech dissolved this state of suspended anima-

tion with its preposterous mythologizing of the defeat. As Klemperer reflected after the war, "Ammunition for future acts of heroism was to be
beaten out of defeat by claiming that many had loyally stuck it out until the
bitter end."[13] In return for the Sixth Army's alleged self-sacrifice, Göring had
demanded the nation's willingness to follow suit, as the foundation of the war
effort going forward. Like the soldiers at Stalingrad or the Spartans at Thermopylae before them, all Germans were expected to play their assigned role
in the unfolding epic struggle. By submitting themselves body and soul to
the cause of the German nation, they would achieve immortality, either in
victory or in defeat.[14]

Nazi morale monitors reported immediately that Göring's speech had
missed his mark. Only a small minority of regime loyalists, the most "mili-
tant characters" among the national comrades, understood "Stalingrad as an
obligation to the full use of all resources at the front and at home," as Göring
had intended.[15] SD informants lauded the intransigence of the steadfast few
who retained their faith in leadership and victory even in this darkest hour
of the war. As a morale report from late March 1943 put it, "A part of the
population refuses to be swayed by common concerns." The report continued, "In regard to the future, [this faction] trusts in the Führer, in the Wehrmacht, and in the resources of the nation and does not want to ponder the
details of the future course of the war." According to SD agents, loyalists rejected "discussions about this [matter] on the grounds that the individual
with his small horizon is incapable of comprehending all factors and arriving at a correct estimate of future prospects."[16] At the same time, the reports
acknowledged that the regime loyalists refused to be drawn into discussions
of "common concern," which meant that they made little impact on the
broader wartime discourse. Since loyalists considered the inevitability of a
German victory self-evident, they rejected debates over current events as
"pointless."[17]

The quietly entrenched stood in stark contrast to the vocal critics among
the German military and civilian populations who experienced the defeat at
Stalingrad as a personal and national calamity. Göring's heavy-handed attempt at mythologizing antagonized them and undermined his great popu-
larity. Still at the height of his power and widely deemed "the Führer's representative," Göring had long been admired by many Germans as a World
War I hero and as an honorable military man among the Nazi elite.[18] They
appreciated his outsized personality and brash conduct that provided fodder

for countless popular rumors about his escapades. An airman explained, for instance, that "Göring is popular in Germany, tremendously popular, first through his personality and secondly through his bearing."[19] Referencing Göring's famous proclivities for opulence and luxury, he asked rhetorically, "Why shouldn't he have his fun?"[20] Not surprisingly, such generosity of spirit vanished in the later war years when the Reich marshal's tastes and appetites made him an easy target of popular resentment.

As the burdens of war grew heavier, and Göring's Luftwaffe failed to protect German cities from Allied bombers, his personal and professional conduct came under popular scrutiny. For instance, in their cell two fighter pilots gossiped about the creeping debauchery of the Nazi elites, evidence of the "madness of the Caesars," of which their commander in chief, Göring, seemed emblematic: "I've heard that at teatime a court chamberlain carrying a staff enters first and announces him. Then [Göring] enters wearing a sort of Japanese tea robe as he receives his guests. . . . Then I've heard from officers who have attended conferences at the Berghof, with the Führer— they suggested that in terms of military matters, [Göring] has about as much knowledge as a first lieutenant. He sat down in a chair, acting like a boor in front of the Führer. . . . He's also supposed to be responsible for Stalingrad."[21]

Göring's failure to provide an air bridge at the Volga would give way to an endless string of calamitous failures of the Luftwaffe, both abroad and at the home front, eroding his standing in the Nazi hierarchy and in popular esteem. Indeed, the pilots' disdain for Göring as a military charlatan became a widely shared perception among Germans. Increasingly common, too, were popular anxieties that the conceit and incompetence among his henchmen sapped the Hitler's faculties with deleterious consequences for the war effort. As one of the airmen concluded bleakly, "The Führer believes every word that [Göring] says. That may be our downfall." In light of recent developments, his cellmate had also begun to question Hitler's efficacy: "One always said that the Führer is the 'man with clean hands' and even if [the other Nazi leaders] are scoundrels, he at least tries to preserve decorum. [He is] a respectable, clean-living man. But I'm beginning to doubt it."[22]

The German defeat at Stalingrad widely shook popular trust in Hitler and, for the first time, undermined his carefully cultivated image as an infallible military and political leader. His image never quite recovered from the debacle. Blindsided by the defeat, even some otherwise enthusiastic regime supporters experienced their first "struggle of faith," as the SD reported.[23] In his cell, a German corporal bitterly recalled Hitler's broken promises from the previous year: "Stalingrad will fall, Stalingrad will fall!" His cellmate interjected, "Sooner or later—and it did fall."[24] The shock of the defeat prompted some to search for other mistakes of the German military leadership. A captured SS man, for instance, argued, "It is certainly good that the Führer is so humane but if we had smashed England way back when, the war would have taken a different course." Still, by November 1943, his faith in Hitler was merely shaken, not broken: "I tell myself, we have held out for so long, I cannot believe that we suddenly would not hold out. . . . Up till now, Adolf has always delivered what he promised. He who has the last laugh . . ."[25]

Long after Stalingrad, Germans clung to the belief that under Hitler's leadership Germany would have "the last laugh" in this war. Many attributed the setbacks of those years to the faulty decisions of his political and military advisers. For instance, when two submariners in captivity discussed the "mess in Africa" in May 1943, they blamed Hitler's cabinet for all failures. A sailor by the name of Klotzsch observed, "Ribbentrop misinformed the Führer completely, telling him that the English wouldn't fight [in North Africa]. The Führer naturally wouldn't know about it, he doesn't know England. Then there was the completely false judgement of the Russians on Ribbentrop's part. With all the agents, spies and bribery money that Ribbentrop had at his disposal, couldn't he have found out how prepared the Russians were for war? Our poor Führer, he was very misinformed."[26]

Klotzsch's cellmate, a telegraphist named Masch, agreed with him that "Africa was a big defeat." He feared that "one more serious reversal and trouble will start for us everywhere." And yet, even as Masch contemplated the possibility of losing the war and "the Russians marching in[to] Germany . . . [o]ur poor womenfolk!," he did not blame Hitler but rather pitied him as a victim of circumstances beyond his control: "One must admire the Führer for still keeping up his courage after all these losses. He personally is in no way to blame [for] the war. With all due respect to the Führer, he is not a strategist. After all, he was only a corporal in the last war, how could he know all that?"[27]

In 1943, very few Germans questioned whether Hitler could ultimately salvage the situation in the East. Still, they frequently speculated about the causes of Hitler's recent missteps after a decade of seemingly unstoppable geopolitical and military triumphs. For instance, two airmen discussing the situation in April 1943 talked about how control of the war situation seemed to slip out of Hitler's hands. One recalled attending a Hitler speech in Berlin in the spring of 1940, before the beginning of the French campaign: "First of all [Hitler] spoke very seriously for half-an-hour, he reminded us of our duty and then he said: 'The war has assumed proportions which I never intended at first, it will probably even assume still greater proportions. We can do nothing to stop it and therefore our watchword must be: be determined, fight and win.'"[28]

In hindsight, the airman admitted being puzzled by Hitler's passive stance: "It strikes me as very strange that 'we can do nothing to stop it from assuming still greater proportions.'" He agreed with his cellmate that a "diplomatic fiasco" lay at the heart of Germany's current troubles: "Not to come to an agreement with England, that was our downfall." Still, he saw a surprising upside to a possible German defeat in the war: "If we were to lose the war, there would be one good thing about it. We should be rid of the Nazis."[29]

On February 21, 1943, two captured submariners were in agreement: "The Führer is no military leader. You can only be that if you have studied and worked at it all your life. He said: 'Stalingrad shall be taken, I promise you that!' Then the Russians simply concentrated all their strength in Stalingrad. That cost us 300,000 men, twenty-one divisions." By 1943, such resentments were widely shared by German civilians and combatants alike, and rumors about the ways in which members of the elites profited and profiteered while shirking their duties abounded. One of the submariners went on to speculate about who had borne the burden of their leaders' mistakes, railing against the corruption and cowardice of the elites: "And not one general was killed [at Stalingrad], although the Führer said: 'Generals and infantrymen alike will fight to the last round.' The generals weren't killed, but they drove their troops into [annihilation]. Now they are laughing up their sleeves."[30] Later, in a dark prognosis for Germany, he added that current events boded ill for the future, even in the case of a final victory: "When the war is over there won't be many left in Germany." His cellmate concurred: "I've thought that too. In my hometown there are tremendous numbers of killed and missing, although it's only a small place with 2,500 inhabitants. . . . [I]t's always the best men, the very ones who would belong to a sports club, who are killed. I just can't understand why we are doing so badly in Russia. If they were retreating slowly—but it's going so quickly and on such a wide front: Why has the Führer sacrificed such masses of men. What was the good of that?"[31]

Following the defeat at Stalingrad, similar conversations likely happened everywhere in German wartime society, but usually only after people carefully weighed each other's political leanings. This was true of German POWs as well. Germans in captivity remained hesitant to voice criticism of the highest echelons of German military and political leadership and did so only among those they trusted to harbor similar sentiments. In June 1943, shortly after their capture in Tunisia, three like-minded Wehrmacht colonels discussed their views of the situation in the East. According to the commander of an armored grenadier regiment, Hitler's catastrophic failures as a military leader now threatened to undermine Germany's rightful world hegemony. His was an unusually blunt and uncompromising view of Hitler's failures as military leader and their ramifications for the rest of the war. Still, after Stalingrad, he was not the only one to consider the possibility that the war in the East was unwinnable:

> Why did the ammunition shortage arise? Because the Russians had captured two Army dumps. That all happened and the Führer must take the blame for it. The Russians have robbed us of our aura of invincibility. In fact, against the Russians we have already lost. We have sacrificed the flower of our youth and lost our best divisions—eighty of our best General Staff officers were left in Stalingrad. Let us assume that the Russians would have attacked us; still, a war on two fronts should have been avoided *at all cost*, no matter what the cost might have been. . . . It had all gone so well. It was all so marvelous and so perfect, and then with that damned Russia it all went awry. There are two people who did not know that in Russia it is cold in the winter. One was Napoleon Bonaparte, and the other was the Führer, that dilettante general. But everyone else knew.[32]

Indeed, the Napoleon analogy was echoed frequently by German POWs in captivity, among all strata, and was likely deliberately stoked by their captors to elicit unguarded responses. In April 1943, an airman blurted out in his cell: "The Führer has a slight 'Caesar Complex'! One moment he thinks he's Caesar, the next Napoleon."[33] Even some of Hitler's generals shared this assessment. As early as December 1942, General Wilhelm Ritter von Thoma took a dim view of Hitler's chances in the East, and indeed for the whole war, with dire implications for the entire German nation:

> I recognize Hitler as a great historical character, but I maintain that he is the same as Napoleon was for France. If you read Michelet's history, for example—he was an authority on interpreting Napoleon—you'll see that he says, quite rightly in his conclusion: 'In a few years, Napoleon raised France to such a height that the nation may always be proud to remember him, but when making the final analysis of Napoleon, one must remember that he was a gambler and that we are still suffering in France from the blood which was shed then. And what is left?' The last word of a six-volume work is 'Nothing.' And it's just the same with Hitler. Hitler also went mad in the end, after a good start. He has the same mixture of genius and madness, but there's one way in which he differs from Napoleon. When people told [Napoleon] bluntly what they thought, he cursed them, then said, 'I will resign!' Whereas with us, nobody resigns.[34]

If von Thoma believed Hitler's successes through the early war years were the result of his genius, he took a much dimmer view of some of his henchmen, notably Göring: "Hermann the mighty, the mighty Nazi boaster. [The party bigwigs] all get country estates and big properties. I believe people in Germany are grumbling quite a bit."[35] The two submariners, too, agreed that popular enthusiasm for the war had waned precipitously now that early successes had given way to seemingly endless strings of military setbacks. As one of them bluntly stated, the reason for widespread popular dissatisfaction was that the war "had lasted so long."[36] Many soldiers in captivity were anxious that as the war dragged on and setbacks mounted, the home front would succumb to a general war fatigue. For instance, a German pilot relayed that throughout the war, his unit had "always received survey reports from the security service [SD] on the situation in Germany." According to him, the reports had been "quite frank" and "shattering" even earlier in the war: "After Stalingrad, people rapidly lost confidence and trust."[37]

Both Nazi and Allied morale monitors collected ample evidence that Germans in all segments of wartime society experienced Stalingrad as a grievous betrayal by their leadership. Thus, not only was the defeat a military and public relations debacle, but it also caused a serious and enduring rupture between the people and the regime at the very moment that the nation embarked on total mobilization. Göring's misguided attempts to shroud facts in myths illuminated this growing gulf. Going forward, many Germans no longer trusted official pronouncements and instead clamored for "raw" information and facts about the events at the Volga and beyond. Many desperately wanted to examine for themselves just what had happened, why it had happened, and what it meant for the future. On February 4, 1943, one day after the official confirmation of the defeat, an SD report summarized the new demands of the German people:

> First, people are asking for the *number of blood sacrifices*. Suspicions range between 60,000 and 300,000 men. People thus assume that the majority of fighters have fallen at Stalingrad. . . . Furthermore in all strata of the population there are discussions about the *inevitability of the developments at Stalingrad and the necessity of the awesome sacrifices*. Specifically, national comrades wonder whether the threat at Stalingrad was recognized in time. . . . The third point at the center of popular discussions is the *meaning of the battle of Stalingrad for the general course of the war*. In general, there exists the conviction that *Stalingrad constitutes a turning point* in the war.[38]

The regime's failure to adequately address these questions ensured that Stalingrad retained a powerful grip on the popular imagination for the duration of the war. It also irreversibly undermined the credibility of Nazi propaganda. As German military failures compounded, the regime struggled to convince its people of the veracity of its claims. Instead, rumors about official lies and obfuscations swirled in all parts of German wartime society, and Germans eagerly shared anecdotes in which they had uncovered official lies. For instance, an airman captured in North Africa in May 1943 recalled how he had been confronted with evidence of the regime's bold-faced lies earlier in the war: "I was sitting in the cinema with my wife, before I joined up. There was a soldier sitting next to me, and when the newsreel came on we were shown: 'The capture of a village in Russia and such.' It was horrible, the street fighting and everything they had photographed there. Then [the soldier] said: 'It is all faked; I was in it; we helped when they were filming it. It was done hundreds of miles behind the front lines.' He said it out loud and laughed."[39]

As popular doubts about the truthfulness of official reporting grew, many people tried to piece together their own versions of unfolding events from fragmented and often conflicting sources of information. The resulting pictures, though impressionistic and provisional, confronted many Germans with a number of facts they had been able to avoid or rationalize in the early war years when the German advances seemed unstoppable. The defeat at Stalingrad illustrated dramatically that the German military command was not infallible and that German armies were not invincible. Worse, it showcased the Russians as a formidable foe. In a conversation with fellow generals, one man who had been captured in the Middle East in November 1942 explained his grudging admiration of the might of the Russian enemy:

> In the Spring of last year there was a division of Siberian troops . . . in Leningrad, they came from the far east. There were magnificent specimens among them, active and cheery. One really must say of the Russians that, from a purely military point of view, one can learn a lesson from the way . . . they have organized things better in that huge land of theirs, with its dozens of races, which were still warring against one another up to a few years ago. Down to the part where we are fighting, the local people were still fighting against the Russians in 1936. Just consider how Stalin has drawn them all together—it's an incredible achievement.[40]

Whatever they understood about the reasons for the German defeat at Stalingrad, few people dismissed it as a fluke, the regime's loyalists notwithstanding. Instead, they were forced to reckon with the painful reality of the strategic and especially material superiority of the Russians. This is not to suggest that in January 1943 Germans confronted the specter of their own ruin at the hands of this powerful enemy. Far from it. But after that point, there were few among the German civilian and military populations who failed to understand that the future held in store costly and protracted confrontations with the Russians. Many, like Lieutenant Metzenthien, began to understand that even under the most favorable circumstances, they would likely not see butter or peace for many years.

Interestingly enough, when Germans imagined the Russian enemy after Stalingrad, they did not necessarily conjure the specter of "barbaric Asiatic hordes" that came to dominate the Nazi "atrocity propaganda" (*Gräuelpropaganda*) of the final war years. To be sure, many people assumed that the Eastern peoples were racially and culturally inferior, with an inherently brutal disposition. Occasionally, though, German troops' firsthand experiences in the East complicated this picture in surprising ways. In a conversation between three airmen in January 1944, for instance, one of the men fretted, "If we lose the war, it will be worse than in 1918. We've seen what Bolshevism has done." However, when his cellmate proposed that "the Russians are an inferior race," another cellmate objected: "You can't say that. Look at the health resorts in the Crimea or towns such as Kiev, Odessa, Sebastopol. They are first-rate."[41]

More commonly, though, Germans contemplated Russian prowess as measured in manpower, war materiel, and fighting ability, particularly in the winter months. Throughout 1943, they speculated anxiously about an enemy capable of producing seemingly unlimited numbers of tanks and weaponry. And even when the Wehrmacht made advances in the East that year, people nonetheless agreed that the Russians were "far from finished," as the SD reported: "To be able to offer such masses of people and materiel everywhere at the front suggested that the Soviet war machine still functioned very well."[42]

According to internal morale surveys from the home front, in the aftermath of Stalingrad, most people agreed that "finishing the Russians" once and for all was Germany's number one priority. This was true for German military personnel as well. However, in captivity, many POWs doubted that the German armed forces had the resources to match the Russian foe, with deleterious consequences for German morale. A captured airman told his cellmate that the interrogating officer "expressed the opinion that the German soldiers' morale is good until he sees that he isn't getting any more supplies, then he suddenly breaks down."[43] His cellmate eagerly confirmed, "Yes, that's right, it's happened like that," before launching into several tales of blown-up munitions depots and the devastating loss of materiel and supplies that German divisions suffered in various theaters of war.[44]

Circulating rumors and hearsay about German experiences at the eastern front going back to the first "battle winter in 1941" (*Kampfwinter*) confirmed these fears. A German lieutenant captured in October 1943 in Italy told his cellmate about what he had witnessed in Russia two years earlier: "[Our] men's boots were made of good stuff but the cold penetrated. First of all, they splashed in the mud for four weeks. Of course, they had wet clothes and boots, and they never dried. And then, all of a sudden, overnight, the terrible cold came." He described how the proper winter uniforms and attire never reached the front, and infantrymen continued to wear their summer coats and perhaps gloves, "but those quickly got torn." Some soldiers were forced to wear socks over their hands, and many took whatever gear they could from fallen Russians. In addition, armored divisions were hampered by catastrophic fuel and armaments shortages as supply transports got stuck in the mud. "Tanks and all kinds of things had to be blown up" to prevent their seizure by the enemy. His cellmate was particularly alarmed to learn that as early as 1941 there had been German deserters on the eastern front, men who "ran away to the rear, they wanted to go home":

> There are always some individual cases. People who had been in the fighting in Russia from the beginning and had marched most of the time in the swamps and forests and mud and everything, who had been through that dreadful autumn and then experienced the cold and then the Russian breakthrough, of course they became pessimistic and said: "It's all [over] now; now, our number is up." In order to get to the rear more quickly, several men threw away their rifles and so on, which is in itself not very serious, but they were condemned to death. They had to be because it just had to be made clear to them that a thing like that simply couldn't be done.[45]

Elsewhere, one captured airman also worried about the cohesion of the militarized national community under pressure, given the number of "deserters" and "shirkers" among the rank and file. Like Metzenthien, he was particularly disgusted with the opportunism and cowardice of the "young chaps" and the alleged party loyalists. Still, in late 1943 he could dismiss such concerns because of his enduring confidence in the führer. As he told his cellmate:

> I have had plenty of rows with people who sold the Infantry Assault Badge for cigarettes in the P/W camps. I have always said: "I am no Nazi, but all the same the Führer will see us through all right." The fellows who shouted the loudest for the Nazis went over to the other side at once. They were fine fellows apart from that, but they immediately turned Communists. Good comrades, but incurable Communists—what is one to do with them? I would shoot them in spite of everything. And once we have won the war, I should have them shot. What a lot have deserted.[46]

Indeed, he looked forward to the annihilation of the British enemy as well, anticipating an aerial campaign that "ought to begin on Christmas Eve, and so thoroughly that everyone is killed, women, children, and everyone, wiped out completely. These swine here don't know what is in store for them—but it will come."[47]

After Stalingrad, POWs from all branches of the armed services reexamined their own war experiences for clues of what the future might hold, often resulting in grave alarm about the shortcomings and failures they had observed in their own units. In these stories, they frequently cast themselves as victims of difficult and dysfunctional conditions in units that had stifled their own military prowess. They often bemoaned that lack of training and experience among the rank and file boded ill for Germany's chances after Stalingrad. For instance, a Wehrmacht interpreter told his cellmate:

> They sent us men to Africa who couldn't speak any German. The poor company and platoon commanders who set off with these men, could scarcely [communicate]. . . . That was the sort of rabble they sent us in Africa—the criminal division and so on. . . . Look at the 999th, they are all criminals. They have emptied out the prisons and reformatories in Germany. The concentration camps have been emptied and the people given the chance of fighting there, but they didn't fight. That was another big mistake. The people should have been made to work, but they shouldn't have been sent to the front, where they make trouble.[48]

An airman captured in Tunisia in May 1943 recalled his experiences in Russia between September and December 1942: "We had people with us who hadn't had more than ten to fourteen days' training, and sergeants who couldn't even steer properly to the right or left, and who had no idea of firing whatsoever. If only they had put people like that into the infantry and not into the [Luftwaffe]. Well, of course we had corresponding losses."[49] Elsewhere, another airman complained about faulty deployment: "People who have to have more than a year's training are being used as infantry, whereas an infantry man only needs three or four months' training. Panzer divisions were sent from Sicily without any tanks [and other equipment]. . . . That isn't only my own personal opinion, but it's been corroborated by commanders who were in Russia. If you try to start criticizing, you don't know whom to blame, since all the orders are given by the Führer personally."[50]

German POWs' disdain for the corrupt and incompetent upper ranks of their armed forces was common fodder for their war stories. For instance, one airman complained about his superior's rigidity in regard to the "damned business about leave." Indeed, stories about foreshortened, canceled, or denied home leave abounded and elicited near universal outrage among German military personnel and their families back home. As the airman recalled about his superior, "He was so petty. You couldn't do anything with him. He had absolutely no understanding in the matter at all. . . . Of course, it's quite a different matter in the East. They were advancing there, so, of course, every man counted. But in the [W]est. . . . He'd brought that idea with him from the East, from Stalingrad."[51]

German POWs rarely lauded their superiors' dedication and ability. But there were exceptions, as was the case of a platoon leader by the name of Geissler who told his cellmate about his long-standing dedication to the Nazi cause: "In 1932 I was almost thrown out of school because of National Socialist activities." Before his capture in Tunisia in May 1943, he had seen quite a few different theaters of war: "I joined the army in 1937. I was in Czechoslovakia in 1939. I also took part in the Polish campaign." But it was an episode in Africa that stuck with him: "I know of one member of the aristocracy who . . . commanded a unit. When things were coming to an end, he said, 'My family tradition does not allow me to give in. I shall fight to the end and ask the men whether they will fight with me.' But [his men] said, 'No thank you.' He actually went on firing from the hillslope there until his men killed him. They were such communists."[52] Geissler was clearly in awe of the commander's self-annihilation and disgusted by the sabotage that brought him down. Such tales of extreme military valor, though much in line with Göring's call for radical mobilization and self-sacrifice, were exceedingly rare, however.

The shortages of German supplies and manpower were as much a subject of speculation as their alleged abundance on the Russian side. German civilians and soldiers alike speculated endlessly about "what kinds of reserves of troops and weapons the Soviets had" and what these factors meant for the course and outcome of the war.[53] But many believed that even if Germany could somehow match Soviet resources, it would be unable to "focus all powers on one gigantic offensive in the East alone," as enemies closed in from all sides.[54] As 1943 wore on and the terrifying prospect of a "third battle winter in the East" became ever more likely, these tangible but unknown measures of military power assumed greater and greater urgency in the German popular imagination, both in the field and at the home front.[55] The Russians had already proved themselves to be superior winter fighters with seemingly inexhaustible reserves of manpower and materiel in the previous two winters. How could the German forces hope to persevere against them under ever more difficult circumstances?[56]

Morale monitors reported that many Germans at the home front voiced "a feeling of complete helplessness" after Stalingrad. People longed for the seemingly unimpeded advances and overwhelming victories that had marked the German invasion of the Soviet Union in the summer of 1941. Two years later, however, "there are no realistic indicators whether the Russian battle and armaments power has already been decisively weakened. . . . Thus, many comrades no longer dare to indulge in confident expectations in this regard."[57] Still, each successive battle in the East appeared as an opportunity to reestablish some semblance of balance between German and Soviet forces. In March 1943, SD agents noted, for instance, that people were "especially impressed by reports of the annihilation of some Russian troops including their commanders, as well as the numeric reports of enemy losses. The national comrades see here a partial equalizing for the German sacrifices in troops and army commanders at Stalingrad."[58]

Dread of a "second Stalingrad" became a common theme in SD reports from the home front at all important military junctures in the final war years. This was the case, for example, in April 1943 when the German hold on Tunisia slipped.[59] Observing the situation from captivity, the German pilot who had told of his access to German morale reporting from the home front explained that the experience of Stalingrad may have steeled the German public for subsequent setback: "In view of what happened at Stalingrad, people were much more prepared for Tunis—they didn't say much more about it than 'a scandal' and 'those poor fellows' etc. etc. At the time of Stalingrad, people still had confidence in Germany's strength, saying: 'A miracle is bound to happen.' After Stalingrad it was known that Tunis was inevitable in any case, so it was accepted."[60]

However, plenty of evidence suggests that the German public met subsequent failures with rising alarm, not acceptance. By June 1943, as the Italian ally faltered and German cities sustained heavy damages during air raids, morale monitors in the southwest of the country warned that "the national comrades are highly disinclined to consider Stalingrad, Tunisia, and the air war as flukes; rather, the opinion dominates that this is an accumulation of serious catastrophes."[61] Moreover, at each setback, people complained about the bold obfuscations of official reporting, though sometimes they found some humor in the obviously false reporting. That may have been what prompted a labored joke told by a bomber observer after his capture at Tunisia in May 1943: "The difference between a clock and Rommel is that a clock goes forward and says *tick-tock* and Rommel goes backwards and says *tactics*."[62] When he asked his cellmate, "What is morale like at home?," his answer was worrisome but not surprising in light of current circumstances.[63] The man replied: "I have been with a lot of people who are optimistically inclined. But there are many people, namely in the Rhineland for instance, in these Catholic villages, and it's quite dreadful there. [People there] agitate and stir up trouble. It torments me so much. . . . A comrade from my crew lives in Cologne and he told me terrifying tales. . . . There's nothing left standing there besides the Cathedral there, the entire downtown is gone." According to the comrade, people back home were only cheered up by a propaganda campaign promising retribution for Allied air strikes.[64]

And yet, fear predominated at the home front. When the Russian winter offensives began at the end of that difficult year, Germans widely feared the coming of a "second Stalingrad" at the Crimea.[65] To better gauge the situation, many tried to decode official propaganda by comparing the language of current news reports with the reports from the fall and winter of 1942. Each military setback caused people to return in their thoughts to January 1943 and reconsider the significance of that battle, the first in a long series of crises that seemed to lead into an increasingly hopeless future. According to the SD, the possibility that a third winter in Russia indicated that Germany had already lost the war became "an obsession with many national comrades."[66]

The increasingly vocal doubters among the German population frustrated the informants in their midst. In 1943, SD reports perpetually complained about the national comrades who scrutinized official reports for hidden meaning rather than trust the veracity of official propaganda. They noted that Germans compared different sources of information and deemed official pronouncements no longer trustworthy. Instead, they speculated about what they did not know and doubted what they were told. They started and perpetuated rumors about the course of the war and the failings of the German leadership. They pounced on any and all signs of trouble. They were fickle and volatile and seemingly impervious to most official attempts to reassure. These were the people who saw the specter of a "second Stalingrad" everywhere and became convinced that Germany's only hope lay in a successful summer offensive against Russia. They were paralyzed by fear of a third Russian winter and dreaded the prospect of a two-front war as the threat of an Anglo-US invasion seemed to grow day by day. By April

1943, SD reports captured images of a national community bewildered and overwhelmed by a war the German High Command no longer seemed to command:

> The population is currently again in *a state of anticipation*, as it *has become typical for this springtime*. A *comparison with the situation in the year before*, as conducted by many national comrades themselves at the moment, yields that a *larger part of the people than before is filled with worry and concern*. Everywhere there are the same trains of thoughts to express the attitude of national comrades about the situation. One may almost speak of public opinion when it comes to the idea that a third battle winter in the East under similar conditions as in the two years before cannot be borne. Out of this attitude springs the entire *hope* of a large part of the population for a *summer offensive* on the eastern front in which the Soviets have to be beaten decisively. But equally common opinion holds that it is absolutely not certain that we will finish with the Russians this year; after all it is still unclear what kinds of reserves in troops and weaponry the Soviets have. On the other hand, Germany cannot afford to focus all its resources on a gigantic offensive in the East alone, but instead has to prepare at the same time for the defense of a *threatening Anglo-American attack*, which may be directed against the Balkans, Italy, the western territories or Norway, or possibly even against several places of the continent simultaneously.[67]

These sentiments were also echoed by German POWs through the first half of 1943. As one airman put it succinctly, "One thing I'm sure of, that's if we still don't take the offensive this summer, Germany will have collapsed before the year is out."[68] His cellmate worried about the consequences of the plummeting morale he had witnessed all around him in the field and in captivity. He complained that the first group of fellow German POWs he had encountered "were a pack of swine. Terribly shattered morale; no wonder either, at home they only played about and earned a lot, then they were called up and had bad training and bad officers. These are the people who, if they are given a piece of white bread, immediately say, 'Oh, we are much better off here, and if we had known that, we should have come long ago; we aren't real Nazis at all.'"[69]

Back home, some members of this increasingly vocal majority had been skeptical about the value of official war reports from the beginning of the war. Despite prohibitions, they had habitually substituted them for alternative news sources to achieve a more detailed and ostensibly more truthful understanding of the international situation. Stalingrad only confirmed their low opinion of the value of official propaganda in the most dramatic fashion. But it had an important impact on them nonetheless, because it also changed their overall perception of the war. Official lies and misinformation were tolerable as long as the regime produced military triumph after triumph. But Stalingrad pushed the "final victory" further than ever out of German reach. Thus, the stakes became higher and people's risky scramble for information became ever more frantic.

For the growing legion of skeptics among the German population, there existed a clear hierarchy of information sources. People widely doubted the truthfulness of official Nazi pronouncements, which occupied the very bottom of the rung. By comparison, the war stories and reflections of German military personnel were deemed the most "authentic" and truthful and thus stood at the very top. By 1943, SD agents were well aware that the German people especially valued "oral or written eyewitness accounts" from soldiers in the East, whose observations they believed to be the most relevant and authentic. Across all strata of the German population, people scoured letters from the front (*Feldpostbriefe*) and cross-examined soldiers on home visits for information about a catalog of concerns, including the "effectiveness and course of the German retreat movement in the East; casualties and reserves of the troops; supply conditions; general battle morale of the troops; conditions among the Russian forces; position of the anticipated front; [and] the prospect for the coming winter."[70]

After 1943, field mail decisively informed the outlook of Germans at the home front. People scrutinized the letters of their sons, husbands, brothers, and fathers for the smallest details indicative of the broader course of the war. Then they shared and discussed their knowledge among friends and relatives. SD agents knew that a soldier's current war experiences and living conditions shaded the tone of his report and determined whether his letters had an encouraging or discouraging ripple effect back home. According to a report from November 1943, "The consensus [among SD agents] is that the troops who are still fighting mostly write and report optimistically while the troops from the rear areas often [have] great concerns about [the possibility of] a good end for this war and doubts about the possibility of finishing the Russians."[71]

In addition to letters, Germans also deemed popular rumors, speculation, and personal opinions more credible than official pronouncements. SD agents were dismayed to report that "for some national comrades," particularly for women and peasants, these private, subjective statements had become the exclusive source of information, a trend that soon encompassed all parts of the Reich and all segments of the population.[72] According to one representative SD report from August 1943, people got their information anywhere except through official channels:

> The population . . . is in a perpetual "state of *high tension.*" This manifests itself in the *depressed, insecure, and nervous discussions about the general war situation that take place everywhere in circles of family and acquaintances, in companies, in stores, in public transportation, in the streets etc. Accounts in newspapers and public broadcasts are hardly acknowledged anymore.* [Instead, military bulletins] and pure eyewitness accounts of military and political content are hotly anticipated and closely followed. People approach these reports with the hope that they bring no new terrible revelations. Beyond that there is no single consensus about the one basic question that dominates the day-to-day worries and joys, thoughts and emotions of the national comrades: "Can we still win the war?" They no longer expect an answer to that question from papers and broadcasts. They no longer deem the press and broadcast [media] competent to give an answer that can be trusted.[73]

But if Germans increasingly flaunted their disregard for official news channels, they had also learned to fear the absence of propaganda. For the rest of the war, many Germans would not forget that weeks of silence had preceded Göring's shocking revelation on January 30, 1943. From that point on, periods marked by few or no official pronouncements about the situation in any of the theaters of war caused popular anxieties to skyrocket. As long as the regime was making proclamations, many people believed that the situation was not entirely lost. Silence, on the other hand, was interpreted as the harbinger of doom. According to an SD report of August 1943,

> People desperately desire a *profound word from the highest echelons.* All discussions reflect the view that people want to win the war, that they will hang tough, but that [the authorities] need to "*speak up*" and need to "*speak the truth.*" The "Politics of Silence" from above is almost unbearable. People

don't understand why [the regime lets] the people wander in the dark. [They ask] *whether the propaganda, which for most people represents the leadership, was robbed of its speech*[.] Up to this point [the leadership] has been able "to put some positive spin on any situation." [They ask] *whether things are so bad that nothing can be said.*[74]

Were Germans ready to face the fact that they were fighting an unwinnable war in 1943? How to explain their obsession with "the truth" after Stalingrad? Why did they clamor for "accurate" and tangible proof of the war situation? What did they do with their information? What did they hope to achieve? Their ongoing struggle to procure and analyze information through various unofficial channels consumed tremendous amounts of time and energy. And it entailed significant risk at a time when the elastic charge of "defeatism" was cause for severe persecution. Also, the hard-won information often only confirmed the increasingly bleak outlook of many Germans. By the end of 1943, for example, Germans' hopes and expectations for the future had been whittled down to a modest common denominator. With the much dreaded "third battle winter" in the East now in full force, there was no talk of a decisive blow and final victory anywhere to be heard. People barely dared to hope that the German armed forces would make it through the coming months without "any further significant setbacks."[75]

At face value, the common quest for more credible information suggests that by 1943 the German people wanted to confront the reality of their war situation. That, however, was not the case. The same sources that capture people's scramble for "truth" also reflect their refusal to face it. Many Germans among the civilian and military populations spent much of 1943 in doubt, fear, and dread. They felt literally encircled by enemies bearing down on the Reich from all directions and from the skies. And yet, "defeatists"— people explicitly pronouncing doom—remained an exceptional occurrence worthy of special mention by SD agents. Part of the reason was of course an increasingly punitive and explicit policy of persecution that deterred people from crossing that line in public. But that does not explain why by December 1943, despite everything people had witnessed and learned over the past year, the SD reported that for most Germans "it remains the *unsolved and most difficult question*, how we can ever eliminate the Bolshevist threat with its seemingly inexhaustible reserves in people and materiel."[76]

Given the flagrant pessimism and fear that resounded in the 1943 SD reports, it does not seem to follow that Germans considered the outcome of their confrontation with the Russians an open question by the end of the year. And yet, this seeming contradiction remained part of Germans' mentality almost until the very end of the war. It serves as an important clue to the evolving dynamic between leadership and people that was marked by growing detachment, on the one hand, and a powerful connection, on the other.

Following Stalingrad, many Germans did not seek "the truth" to confront it. Rather, their scramble for unofficial "credible" information was an expression of dissatisfaction with a regime whose failings were painfully visible to all throughout 1943. The act of circumventing official news channels likely gave some of them a sense of agency and power in a war that had turned against them and that they otherwise felt impotent to control. It served as an early declaration of emancipation from a faltering regime without having to break with it fully. It afforded some Germans feelings of personal and intellectual maturity without having to bear the cost. And ridiculing the most outrageous propaganda provided a welcome relief from the worry and anxiety that marked people's day-to-day life during the war. SD agents were ever present to record the laments and grievances of a tired and stressed population, and their reports of 1943 captured a growing chorus of popular resentment and discontent with almost all aspects of Nazi leadership.

But if people claimed autonomy from the regime, their quest for self-determination only went so far. Theirs was a pursuit not of *the* truth but of *a* truth, specifically, of a *bearable* truth about the German chances to achieve a victory in a war of conquest that most deemed legitimate. To this end people had to deceive themselves even as they resented the regime's lies. They could not acknowledge that they used their hard-won information to produce their own versions of the truth that were designed to reassure rather than illuminate. Thus, while Stalingrad raised the specter of defeat, Germans did not engage with it fully in all its implications. Many refused to do so until after defeat finally came in 1945.

SD reports of 1943 showcase Germans' abortive attempts to truly contemplate the possibility of defeat. Whenever the German forces experienced another setback or stalemate, the home front obsessively pondered the implications—up to a point. These efforts at rational thought are noteworthy for both their frequency and their almost universal evasion of a conclusion. People did not envision encouraging or hopeful scenarios that would suggest wishful thinking or delusion. In 1943, the unthinkable was unspeakable. Throughout 1943, people from all social strata and all regions echoed the same refrain: "One simply cannot imagine how the war should come to an end"; "If one really thinks about it, it really is terrifying";[77] "One mustn't even think about what will become of this"; "One simply cannot imagine how this war against the Bolsheviks is supposed to end if we don't annihilate them this summer; but to believe in it is hard";[78] "A third battle winter in the East is unthinkable and therefore a decision must happen this summer";[79] "One simply cannot imagine how this war against the Bolsheviks should end."[80]

Despite their hunger for "truth," most people evaded the conclusion that Germany's military position was untenable in 1943. This is not surprising, considering what models or visions for defeat Germans had available to them. According to Nazi propaganda, defeat meant a fate worse than what had followed the armistice of 1918.[81] The sheer horror of personal and national evisceration made this outcome unthinkable, and Nazi propaganda deliberately and successfully raised the specter of 1918 to motivate an increasingly war-weary population. As one historian put it so succinctly, "One of the great triumphs of the Nazis was the standardization of the 'Stab-in-the-Back' legend."[82]

In explaining why 1918 had such a powerful grip on Germans after 1943, one cannot discount "the lingering effect of original traumatic experience" altogether.[83] True, Nazi propaganda imbued 1918 with a particular imagery and meaning intended to serve the regime's purpose. But the reason that these resonated so strongly with the German people lay in the fact that they identified as participants in post-1918 chaos long before Nazi propaganda told them to expect even worse. Among German POWs in the later years of World War II, 1918 and the possibility of a repeat of that experience were constant topics of conversation. For instance, in October 1943, a sergeant by the name of Hirschner calculated the likelihood of a successful spring offensive. He was optimistic: "If you think of it, the whole world is already against us and still they won't beat us." When his cellmate, Sergeant Molzner agreed, "Not this time," he replied, "They managed [to beat us] in the Great War only because of the revolution. That will never break out in Germany this time—I've still got complete faith in the Führer. He won't leave us in the lurch."[84]

Whether people had lived through its aftermath or had learned about it secondhand, the debilitating shame and despair connected with 1918 formed an integral part of their wartime discourse in World War II. Thus, whether lived or imagined, the specter of 1918 was an important landmark in the mental landscape of World War II. That's what made Nazi propaganda on the subject so effective, and it may also help explain why Germans gathered information almost compulsively after Stalingrad. To many German military and civilian observers, the events of 1943 signified a pivotal change in the war's momentum. They knew that something consequential had occurred, though the weight and long-term implications remained unclear. But in the coming months, as people searched for meaning amid the ebb and flow of the war, their thoughts would frequently return to the early months of 1943. They would wonder whether the destruction of the Sixth Army had marked merely a "low point in this war" or "the beginning of the end"?[85] Was this "*a* defeat," or was this "*the* defeat, the catastrophe"?[86] Was the clear and final victory that the regime kept promising even attainable, or was "the debacle in Russia . . . a real and decisive one," as Victor Klemperer speculated?[87] Only later did he realize that "ever since Stalingrad, since the beginning of '43 . . . I have been waiting for the end."[88]

In 1918, defeat had come as a shock, seemingly without warning. To Germans at war again merely two decades later, the only prospect more terrifying than defeat was another surprise defeat. In any case, Nazi propaganda about 1918 resonated with a population that remembered. In the same vein, Nazi propaganda's attempt to utilize a Greek tragedy to unleash popular heroism failed to resonate with people in 1943 because it had no relevance to their real or imagined identity. Germans had no experience or precedent for the act of taking a last stand for posterity, the act of self-destruction as an end in and of itself. Only over the course of the next two and a half years, when war and hardship actually invaded their existence, would people learn to think of themselves as participants in the life-or-death struggle of their nation. Only then would promises of heroic immortality win appeal for some.[89]

Chapter 2

Mobilizing the National Community

Do You Want Total War?

On February 18, 1943, Reich Propaganda Minister Joseph Goebbels staged a massive rally at the Berlin Sport Palace. Addressing an audience of carefully selected Nazi Party members, his agenda was ambitious and his strategy bold. He sought to arrest the alarming tailspin of popular morale after the "blow of fate at Stalingrad," channel it into support for total mobilization, and claim more control over total mobilization in the process. While Hitler remained ambivalent about full mobilization for fear of destabilizing the home front, Goebbels insisted that the new war situation called for radical measures. As he had explained to his fellow regional party administrators, "We are confronted in the east with a brutal opponent who can only be defeated by the most brutal methods. In order to achieve this, the total commitment of all our resources and reserves is necessary."[1]

The basic premises of Goebbels's speech that day would have rung familiar to the attendees as well as to the millions of Germans who listened to radio broadcasts of the event. He reiterated the war's origin as a preemptive strike against "Jewish-Bolshevist" aggression. He raised the dreaded specter of treason and defeat in 1918. And he extolled the virtue of fighting at all cost, proclaiming, "Stalingrad was and is fate's great alarm call to the German nation! . . . [T]he heroes of Stalingrad . . . put me and all of us under deep obligation."[2] Goebbels demanded that the German people repay the debt incurred at Stalingrad by becoming true warriors of the home front. Retreat into doubt and fear was not an option. In this war, the national community had to charge ahead as one:

> We are all children of our people, forged together in this most critical hour of our national history. We swear to you, we swear to the front, we swear to the Führer, that we will together mold the homeland into a force on which the Führer and his fighting soldiers can rely absolutely and blindly. We promise to do all in our life and work that is necessary for victory. . . . If ever we have loyally and unshakably believed in victory, it is in this hour of national reflection and contemplation. We see it before us; we need only reach for it. We must resolve to subordinate everything to it. That is the duty of the hour. Let the slogan be: People, rise up, and storm, break loose![3]

Like Göring before him, Goebbels tried to "beat ammunition for future acts of heroism out of defeat." He, too, sought to convince the German people that defeat would beget victory if the sacrifices of the few were answered by the sacrifices of all. And yet, where Göring had only exacerbated popular shock and alienation, Goebbels delivered what would become one of the most famous speeches of the Third Reich, a hallmark of the power of Nazi oratory.

Even at the time, Goebbels was exceedingly pleased with his performance. He later gloated that he could have ordered his audience to jump off a high building, and they would have obeyed.[4] Perhaps this claim was not entirely unfounded, because the spectators did agree to something that, in hindsight, appears equally self-destructive. During a frenzied climax, Goebbels posed ten rhetorical questions, inciting wild cheers and shouts of approval from his audience. "Do you want total war?" he famously demanded. "If necessary, do you want a war more radical than anything that we can even imagine today?"[5] And when thousands roared as one in the affirmative, they appeared to give voice to the collective will of the German people.

Did the German people want "total war"? Did they want "a war more radical" than anything they could imagine? Goebbels orchestrated a spectacular display of popular consent at the Sport Palace, and in hindsight it is tempting to cast that day in February 1943 as the moment when Germans surrendered to fanaticism and plunged headfirst into the wreckage of their next two and a half years. Much to Goebbels's disappointment, however, contemporaneous evidence suggests otherwise. This chapter treats the Sport Palace rally as a launching point into a new phase of German mobilization that grew out of the German defeat at Stalingrad and the Allied demand for "total" or "unconditional surrender" after the Casablanca Conference of January 1943. It posits that "total war" as presented by Goebbels entailed a pact symbolically forged between leadership and people at a crossroads. What did the pact entail, and what did it look like to those among the national community who entered it? What did they expect to contribute, and what did they expect to receive in return? The focus here is on "total war" as a political program rather than the yet unknown experience. What were the most prominent ideas about total mobilization at the very moment that Germans first embarked on this new chapter in the war? Which policies met with popular support and which aggravated long-standing tensions across the many fault lines in German wartime society? What do the heated discussions and conversations at the time about the efficacy and moral legitimacy of the regime's mobilization drive reveal about the state of the national community tasked to charge ahead as one?

Before Germans lived "a war more radical than anything" they could imagine, they imagined plenty about what was to come, and Goebbels's propaganda helped inform their expectation. Indeed, he contributed more than ideas. As Reich propaganda minister, he had been an early and vocal champion of total mobilization, agitating for the elimination of "bourgeois prissiness" and entrenched privilege from German society. His drive to radicalize the German war effort in order to create a true "warrior community" was energized with his promotion to Reich defense commissioner in November 1942, a position that bestowed him with executive power over the German civil service for the purposes of directing the home front. Goebbels believed total mobilization would not only harness the military and economic resources of the national community but unleash its spiritual potential as well. In total war and total mobilization, he hoped to achieve the full realization of the National Socialist revolution.[6]

Although Goebbels was thrilled with the immediate reactions to his Sport Palace rally, broader popular responses were conflicted. The now notorious question-answer segment, for instance, was roundly ridiculed across German society as transparently manufactured. Several weeks after the event, one German POW still raged in his cell: "'Heil, heil, heil.' The damn fools. 'Do you want total war?—Yes, we want total war.' . . . I know the game. I spoke to an SS man once. He was there: A microphone in every corner, which makes a terrific din."[7] Another POW believed that while many ordinary Germans rejected such empty theatrics, Goebbels would always find party cronies willing to do his bidding: "If he talks like this today or like that to-morrow, they will shout just the same, the damn fools. They only go to the speech so that they can shout. I know the trick: 'Heil, heil!'—ten men stand at the microphone."[8]

Part of the reason for popular criticism of the spectacle was Goebbels's tenuous standing among the German people, vividly captured in many CSDIC reports. As the Nazi regime's public face and main peddler of propaganda and manipulations, Goebbels bled credibility with each military setback. The submariner Klotzsch was one of many who thought of Goebbels as the "arch liar . . . with his evil tongue."[9] In captivity, many POWs described their efforts to circumvent Goebbels's propaganda apparatus in search of reliable sources of information about the war. A bomber gunner was among many to confess to having listened to foreign, and particularly English, broadcasts, for instance, because "the English always publish the exact figures of air-craft losses, not like Goebbels."[10] These men were not easily swayed by the spectacle at the Sport Palace.

Goebbels was a polarizing figure even in peacetime, and his reputation as an unscrupulous manipulator, hypocrite, and womanizer had long un-dermined his standing with the national community. To be sure, he was not the most detested Nazi leader of the later war years. That is a distinction frequently bestowed on boors like Julius Streicher, founder of the viru-lently antisemitic propaganda organ *Der Stürmer*, or Robert Ley, head of the Nazi Labor Front, whose drunken Jew-baiting and sexual degeneracy were the object of near universal loathing. Still, popular gossip about Goebbels, the "lecherous buck," was steeped in condescension and revul-sion.[11] Worse, many Germans saw Goebbels's dubious morality as em-blematic of a creeping degeneracy inherent to the Nazi Party infrastruc-ture that threatened to undermine traditional values in German wartime society. As crisis conditions arose and the regime's political and military successes dwindled, popular rumors about the many failings of Nazi lead-ers circulated widely.

Across all segments of wartime society, people gossiped freely about the debauchery and corruption that seemed rampant throughout the Nazi Party infrastructure, from the highest to the lowest echelons. Everyone in Germany, it seemed, had been wronged by blatant Nazi corruption. Lieutenant Metzenthien, for instance, had railed against the German administrators in Poland, the "chaps [who had come up] in the Party," had shirked their duty to fight, and instead had used the occupation as a chance for plunder and personal enrichment. In July 1943, a captured airman told a similar story about ordinary soldiers being mistreated by party functionaries in Poland. He bitterly recalled: "There was a bad mood among the rank and file, and they included many war heroes who were part of the invasion of Poland. [These soldiers said], 'I'd just like to know who it was that conquered Poland. Was it the pencil pushers, those few parasites who now sit around here or was it us soldiers?' I tell you it really seemed as if the civilian administration had conquered Poland. Man, what a pigsty."[12]

Similar complaints circulated everywhere. The airman's cellmate, for instance, told a story about a gauleiter (regional party administrator), condemning him as a "sensual swine" who had been dismissed from his post and yet secured himself "an administrative post in White Russia, and behaved like a swine there until [the Russians] shot him."[13] In another cell, an Austrian pilot relayed a story that illustrated the common belief that even decent and capable leaders and administrators caved to the overwhelming temptations:

> For instance, take Gauleiter [August] Eigruber of Linz. He was very thick with the Führer. He previously worked at the Steyr (?) Works. Not one of the leading lights, but in spite of that he might have made quite a good Gauleiter. In the beginning when he became Gauleiter, after the seizure of power, one saw pictures of him everywhere: Gauleiter Eigruber, with several children, in the family circle—I believe he has four or five children. All well and good. Now what's the position? Now his wife and family don't satisfy him any longer, he's already got another house and now wants to marry some hussy or other.[14]

Occasionally, popular criticism of the party elite even implicated Hitler. According to one airman, a song that had been widely sung in Vienna and elsewhere over the course of 1943 included lyrics that were both fatalistic and optimistic at once: "'Everything's going, soon all will be past. The

Führer goes first, and the Party goes last.' It has been sung all over the place for years now."[15]

According Klotzsch, elite degeneracy caused a larger societal ill. He believed that the National Socialist order had undermined the traditional nuclear family as the moral bedrock of German society. In a conversation with a fellow sailor, he explained his view that, under Nazism, state authority had usurped parental authority in pursuit of a dubious procreationist agenda:

> What is being destroyed in a child nowadays is, first of all, the respect for the father. The child says: "I must serve the state." That's one thing, you admit that! Secondly, a result of the propaganda concerning this mad outcry for the production of German children—a girl of very respectable parents and upbringing anticipated her father's horror, added that he could not punish her or throw her out because "producing children was in accordance with the Führer's will." Where's that going to lead? According to that, any woman could go with any man. If that were the will or unwritten order of a government, within a generation the whole of Germany would consist of prostitutes and pimps. I am convinced that the women who refused to play their part would have no means of livelihood.[16]

Klotzsch's cellmate, a submariner named Köhler, concurred: "In Germany today I should never marry a woman who is not a virgin." He then went on to speculate, "What you told me about that girl—I think there are thousands of cases like that. . . . I must say, especially now, that the problem of morals leaves much to be desired. I know enough about it myself."[17]

The veracity of such claims notwithstanding, many Germans shared the conviction that German society suffered an epidemic of moral corruption under Nazism. They believed that the "problem of morals in Germany" was "pure fact, pure political fact," as Klotzsch argued. He had clearly given the matter ample thought and believed he knew the source of the problem: Goebbels and other degenerate party cronies like him:

> That is not and *cannot* be the will of the Führer. It is the product of an incredibly low propaganda clamor of a so-called little man who wants to make himself important. It is the product of propaganda that the young girls, whose education has been on political lines, interpret it that way. The father cannot punish his child; if he turns her out of the house she will go to the Party, and

he will get it in the neck. The whole German people knows of the erotic degeneration of Robert Ley and Joseph Goebbels, and those are ministers, leaders of a nation, but the nation is not in a position to get rid of such artists of a debased culture.[18]

Incidentally, Klotzsch also had an exceptionally negative assessment of the führer. He was suspicious of the fact that Hitler was unmarried and childless, indicators, he said, that "Adolf hates humanity and is driving the whole German nation to ruin—he has no normal human feelings—he has a bestial hatred of mankind. We are bleeding to death in Russia—Tunisia has fallen."[19] However, such outspoken criticism of the führer's moral makeup was rare in 1943. Instead, many people trusted that he had forgone a traditional family life because of his all-consuming dedication to the German nation. Indeed, in Hitler's case and in his case alone, the absence of "normal" human ties and interactions tended to serve as proof of his impeccable morality.

Even in the wake of the shocking defeat at Stalingrad, Hitler's performance as a political and military leader was only occasionally a target of popular criticism. Instead, criticism of Hitler largely remained taboo, and derogatory comments by interrogating officers or by the English press often caused angry rebuttals among German POWs. For example, two captured airmen were united in their outrage at "the obstinate and narrow-minded English" who had captured them in Tunisia in May 1943. One of them raged that "the damned swine are to blame for our misfortune." According to him, not only did the English hinder Germany's critical war effort, but they also dared slander Hitler. As one of the cellmates argued, "If anyone ventures to pronounce judgment on National Socialism, he should be thrashed, and the same of anyone [who] ventures to discuss the Führer here. Anything so unbearably mean doesn't bear talking about. The Führer, who has lifted us out of the mire, who has never lied to us. [He is very different from] such agitators like this Churchill or other such dubious characters."[20]

Indeed, the airman also had a positive impression of Goebbels, at least in regard to the propaganda minister's professional performance. As he explained to his cellmate, "Goebbels told us in [his weekly newspaper] *Das Reich*: 'We must learn to hate.' He was right."[21] Given his hatred of the English and his faith in the führer, he might have agreed with the pronouncement of a submariner in another cell who blamed the war on "the Jews" and believed that Hitler would ultimately deliver the German nation: "We may thank God that we've got the Führer."[22]

By all accounts, Goebbels, too, was utterly devoted to Hitler. No one worked harder than Goebbels to publicize the image of a divinely appointed leader. For himself, he cultivated a somewhat more modest public image. Though he relished his own genius privately, in public he acted the role of tireless helpmate and facilitator of the will of a great man. And despite their misgivings, some Germans did appreciate some of his achievements, in particular in his role as gauleiter of Berlin. For instance, in late 1942, a submariner claimed, "[The] Gauleiter are all unpopular. The only one who is still popular is Goebbels. Goebbels is alright; he is a great man." He did not protest, however, when his cellmate, a sailor, countered, "But his reputation is such that he cannot live it down."[23] Months later, in the fall of 1943, a fighter pilot trying to convince his cellmate that "Goebbels is popular in Berlin" met with almost comic skepticism. "Do you seriously mean that he's popular? How is that?" the bomber observer demanded. But the pilot was adamant that "all of the inhabitants of Berlin swear by Goebbels. They stand by Goebbels."[24] The pilot's spirited defense of Goebbels notwithstanding, his cellmate's incredulity is perhaps the most telling indication of Goebbels's tenuous standing among the captured combatants.

The POWs' ambivalent responses to Goebbels and his Sport Palace rally mirrored those of many civilians at the home front. Not surprisingly, SD reports of the period documented few explicit personal attacks against Goebbels. SD agents may have been inclined to soften the blow by reporting fewer direct attacks against the propaganda minister. However, they reported frankly when Goebbels's speeches and other propaganda initiatives missed the mark. In regard to the Sport Palace rally, the reports claimed that both "national comrades" and party officials "in all circles" faulted the blatantly propagandistic design of the speech's climax. The manipulative character of the question-and-answer section struck many observers as transparent and obnoxious.[25]

And yet, all this is not to suggest that the rally should be dismissed as inconsequential. The German people paid close attention to it, and their rejection of the climax stood in marked contrast to their appreciation for the event as a whole. Many seized subsequent opportunities to listen to repeat broadcasts to fully absorb Goebbels's message. Others studied transcripts published in newspapers and pamphlets. SD agents reported that within a matter of days almost all segments of the population had been exposed to the speech and had discussed it with family and acquaintances.[26] And beyond near total saturation, Goebbels achieved wide-ranging approval for his message about impending total mobilization. At the eastern front, a paratrooper named Martin Pöppel recorded his and his fellow comrades' enthusiasm in his diary on February 19, 1943. He wrote, "I can't get the Goebbels speech calling for total war out of my mind. The speech was so tremendous and fantastic that I feel I have to write home with my own response. Everyone was carried away by his words; all of us were under his spell. He spoke to us from the heart."[27] According to the SD, many civilians at the home front responded similarly: "The effect of the message was unusually strong and overall quite positive. National comrades who had reached another low point in morale due to the recent developments at the eastern front, especially the alarming news of the evacuation of Kharkov, had been longing for a clear account of the situation. Despite its open depiction of the seriousness of the situation, Reich Minister Dr. Goebbels's speech had a soothing effect and has strengthened [popular] confidence and trust in the leadership."[28]

Indeed, popular approval grew exponentially after a five-minute segment of the event was shown in the newsreel of February 24, 1943. Moderated by Goebbels, it included the controversial climax and aired in all German movie theaters. Apparently, even many who had previously been dismissive of the empty spectacle could not resist its pull once they saw it with their own eyes. The SD reported that many in the remote audiences found their initial misgivings replaced by unbridled enthusiasm:

> It can be confirmed that the newsreel report significantly increased the propagandistic effect of the Sport Palace rally and subsequently heightened it even where until now skepticism was predominant. Even hesitant segments of the population could not resist the visual effects of the speech, or the perceptible echo of the rally's participants. It is commonly recognized that the camera visually translates the speaker's points and thereby transfers the characteristic "Sport Palace atmosphere" to the newsreel audience. It was said that there has rarely been a newsreel report that served as such an impressive and three-dimensional addition to newspaper and radio reports. "The pictures really sparked here. It makes a difference to see these things with one's own eyes because it is much more effective than the sound of the orator's voice alone reverberating from radio speakers." It was possible to see that the attendees were not mere "louts and yes men" but that they truly "rose up to meet the storm."[29]

Even if the Sport Palace rally did not single-handedly shape popular attitudes, it had an enduring impact. Goebbels's meticulous planning and wide dissemination of his message rendered it an important signpost on the German road to total mobilization. With Germans still reeling from the defeat at Stalingrad, his address managed to engage a dejected populace and reconnect it with its leadership. For the first time since the eastern campaign had stalled that winter, Germans were receptive to displays of martial enthusiasm and resolve from Berlin.[30]

It was an article of faith among many Nazi leaders that propaganda had the power to shape popular opinion at will, a sentiment also often echoed in early scholarship on the Nazi dictatorship. Initially, this resulted in a distorted portrayal of the German people as a mere receptacle of the party line, a brainwashed, homogenous object of total control. Since then it has become widely accepted, however, that propaganda's efficacy to shape consensus was limited and dependent on the leadership's willingness to adjust its message to values already prevalent among its audiences. In short, popular consent was malleable, subject to manipulations and deceit, but it could not be manufactured. This was true especially during the second half of the war, and widespread initial resistance to the more performative of Goebbels's rally is testament to this fact. Clumsy and ostentatious propaganda grated on people's nerves and insulted their intelligence.[31] Throughout 1943, Nazi morale monitors confirmed that the German people displayed a "skeptic predisposition toward political reports if there is a mere whiff of propaganda."[32]

SD reports suggest that one segment of Goebbels's speech met with near unanimous approval among German civilians: his discussion of the "measures to totalize" the war effort, which "captured the people's sentiments exactly." Some people expressed disappointment that Goebbels had not provided more detailed explanations of the new policies. Also, many observers expressed doubt that the new policies would be implemented justly. But beyond these lingering concerns, "the announcement of the most radical implementation of these measures [had] elicited the widest agreement everywhere."[33] According to these accounts the German people did want total war in 1943. And they wanted it fast. As relieved as many were about the announcement, some continued to bemoan the fact that the Nazi regime was implementing total war "quite late."[34] Indeed, as the German military crisis escalated over the final war years, Germans would habitually look back and lament that "total mobilization should have been ordered much earlier."[35]

Mere weeks after the German defeat at Stalingrad, many Germans were grateful for Goebbels's assurance that total mobilization would harness the powers of the national community. Moreover, like him, they imagined "totalization measures" as a great leveler of German society. As he put it in his address, "We now know what we have to do. The German people want a Spartan way of life for everybody. For high and low, for poor and rich." He drove the point home again during his tenth and final question: "Is it your wish that even in wartime, as the Party program requires, equal rights and equal duties shall prevail, that the home front shall give evidence of its solidarity and take the same heavy burdens of war upon its shoulders, and that the burdens be distributed equitably, whether a person be great or small, poor or rich?"[36]

Apparently, this last point was something most Germans with or without uniforms could agree on, as long as the "great" and the "rich," too, participated. Goebbels wanted to mobilize the home front by curbing domestic consumption and channel additional resources into the war effort. He promised the closing of most entertainment and luxury establishments. Restaurants and hair and beauty salons would be shuttered to no longer divert "light, heat, and workers" away the war effort. In his speech he demanded to know, "What good are beauty shops that encourage a cult of beauty and take enormous time and energy?" On the other hand, "theaters, movie houses, and musical halls" would continue operations to "give the working people the relaxation they need in these trying times. . . . We have no intention of inflicting a gray winter mood on our people."[37] Goebbels also promised streamlined bureaucracy and increased efficiency in the civil administration, as well as longer work hours for most. Most importantly, those who had hitherto been exempt from active participation in the war effort would now have to contribute their fair share. According to Goebbels, "The problem is freeing soldiers for the front, and freeing workers for the armaments industry. These are the primary goals, even at the cost of our living standards during the war."[38]

Unlikely as it seems, this motley array of ill-defined "totalizing measures" was the result of months of Goebbels's intense political scheming since the fall of 1942 to achieve control over domestic war policy. At the time, he had envisioned a fundamental reorganization of the German economy to channel all available resources into war production. Furthermore, he wanted to eliminate waste and duplication from the German bureaucracy. As the second winter crisis unfolded, he had repeatedly tried to secure Hitler's endorsements of broadly defined "totalizing measures." Indeed, the führer had gone as far as issuing a secret order "regarding the deployment of men and women in the defense tasks" on January 13, 1943.[39] But World War I cast a long shadow, and Hitler's fear of destabilizing the home front prevented him from fully committing to the implementation of measures that might prove unpopular. Instead, to the consternation of the economic and administrative planners around him, Hitler pitted several factions against each other in an open-ended battle of initiatives. He authorized the Committee of Three, consisting of some of his most reliable henchmen: the head of the Nazi Party Chancellery, Martin Bormann; the chief of the Reich Chancellery, Hans Lammers; and the chief of the Armed Forces High Command, Wilhelm Keitel. He did not grant Goebbels a formal role in this working group but allowed him to support its work in a consulting capacity. Despite his initial enthusiasm, Goebbels soon came to see the committee as an obstruction to the radical mobilization measures he envisioned. Lammers's refusal to agree to broad conscription of women and youths into the workforce irritated the former socialist Goebbels, who saw it as emblematic of bourgeois softness and idleness.[40]

The Committee of Three issued few specific directives. One of the first formal initiatives included an order for all men between the ages of sixteen and sixty-five and all women between the ages of seventeen and fifty to register for possible work deployment in ten-hour shifts. Government offices were ordered to transfer up to 30 percent of employees to the armaments industry. Fritz Sauckel, plenipotentiary for labor mobilization, publicized the new requirements on January 27, 1943. In other related issues, such as employment and tax laws, Goebbels continued to champion the most radical policies but achieved few concrete breakthroughs. His ambitions to streamline the German civil service and bureaucracy were undermined by Hitler's continued refusal to intervene.[41]

Early iterations of mobilization measures for the home front were proclaimed while the German people were still reeling from the defeat at Stalingrad. In substance, they were similar to those that would follow the Sport Palace rally. The SD reported on February 8, 1943, that the German people did not want to be roused. They wanted to be instructed: "Constant reminders that something needs to be done are unnecessary. The vast majority of the population is ready; [therefore] the only things of interest are practical

measures designed to allow [individuals] to help and engage."[42] In the absence
of clear policy directives, the German people were left to speculate what "total war" would mean for their lives. The vague concept inspired hope and
apprehension in equal measures:

> Even those national comrades who declare that they can no longer believe in
> victory, but especially the broad masses of positively inclined people, await
> with almost feverish anticipation the future course of totalizing measures as
> well as the deployment of their powers yearning to support the front service.
> In particular the working population is of the opinion that the time is less for
> writing about it than for acting quickly and with determination. The impres-
> sion that [mobilization] occurs bureaucratically has somewhat diminished
> the suddenly awoken will. The proclamation of the closing of certain stores,
> workshops, and luxury restaurants and others has caused general content-
> ment, especially since a date was issued and because this order was articu-
> lated more bluntly than the order for work registration. Especially the pop-
> ulation already engaged in work deployment continues to discuss the
> alleged attempts of "higher ladies" to withdraw from conscription in some
> way. They speak—not entirely without cause—of people attempting to get
> doctors' notices freeing them from conscription. Also, [there is talk] in
> many places that the labor departments and other offices . . . are overrun by
> women trying to quickly "score a pleasant office post" before they will be
> "thrown into a factory." Some women try to capitalize on their connections
> and relationships to secure a particularly pleasant position in an office or
> even just to pretend to work.[43]

Members of Germany's military population frequently reflected on the
mobilization of the home front. Many worried about what German women
would get up to in their absence. A captured SS man, for instance, was anxious how his marriage would fare in wartime. He told his cellmate, "I married in 1938, then I spent a year with my wife and since then I have been
away all the time. I have been married for six years and for nearly five years
I have been away from my wife."[44] A captured German airman told his
cellmate: "What worries me is the fact that we have got such crowds of [for-
eign POWs] in Germany. Whatever racial purity we may have been able to
preserve is going to the devil. With all the men at the front, the women
must have something to make love to."[45]

Indeed, many contemporaneous sources suggested that German men widely worried about the war's toll on female virtue. This was particularly apparent in POWs' discussions of women deployed in auxiliary services in western Europe, for instance. Perhaps their descriptions mirrored some of the debauchery Metzenthien had condemned in "our young chaps" there. However, descriptions of female corruption in wartime usually focused on their moral, not material, decay. Widely circulating salacious rumors suggested that many German men believed that female depravity thrived abroad under conditions of war. For instance, though his cellmate protested that "that's got nothing to do with National Socialism, those are only little things," Klotzsch was one of many Germans expressing disgust that "the morals of our German [female] auxiliary helpers in France are scandalous; in Nantes 70% of 900 of them are supposed to have [venereal diseases]."[46] Indeed, German POWs spoke about deployed women almost uniformly in disparaging terms, as an element not of societal mobilization but of societal degeneration. Not beholden to traditional social mores or to military codes of conduct, female auxiliaries deeply worried the men. This was in marked contrast to the gratitude they would express later in the war as women helped to staff the embattled home front.

Rumors of the allegedly rampant promiscuity of female auxiliaries, commonly termed Blitzmädel, or "Thunderbolt Girls," after their thunderbolt insignia, circulated in all segments of German wartime society. The gist of most could be summed up by a joke shared by two airmen in captivity in January 1944: "What is the difference between a Blitzmädel and the sun? None because they both sink in the West."[47] When three airmen discussed their experiences in France, an airman named Bikker recalled, "On Christmas Eve we made an intermediate landing at Villa Roche. We arrived there just in time to celebrate Christmas. The *Blitzmädels* celebrated Christmas there. That was *marvelous!*" But when his cellmate, a fellow airman named Schulze, asked, "What did they do, then?," Bikker became bashful: "I'm ashamed to describe it to you, it was really revolting." Their third cellmate agreed: "Yes, these *Blitzmädels*, that's a sad business. They are like that."[48] In another conversation shortly after his capture, Bikker had shared that "here were some frightful women running around at Bordeaux. They were representative of Germans abroad! But I'll tell you one thing: They always say that the women there are immoral, but just go to Germany nowadays. All the time in Schweine-münde I didn't meet one single decent girl."[49]

Besides upending societal mores, female wartime promiscuity threatened to undermine German racial purity. An SS officer by the name of Mayer, for instance, proclaimed that "German women are the wildest. The [Luft-waffe signals assistants] are the worst of all. There are few decent ones among them, but the number is growing smaller and smaller. We saw that at Rennes. In France even they even went with negroes. The German woman wants to try everything so that she can boast to her friends."[50] In another cell, a sub-mariner shared a similar story: "I was handed over in Paris. There is that huge prison at Davreux (?), which holds 2,000 people. There were 2,000 [Blitz Broads] there." When asked by his cellmate "What had they done?" he re-plied: "They had gone with negroes. Usually they were there on account of treason or spying. They may have given away information to some old French-man in the ecstasy of love. I looked out of my window at the back—usually it was forbidden. The whole front of the building—nothing but women, they undressed completely there—there were two women to each cell."[51]

Not surprisingly, German troops frequently cast themselves as victims, not willing participants, of female degeneracy. Tales of soldiers' sexual exploits were not cause for moral outrage, but they did raise questions of military ef-ficacy. In January 1944, two pilots discussed brothel "provisions" in France. The captain explained that in 1943 venereal diseases had run rampant among men stationed in the West:

> There are other ranks' brothels. Gonorrhea is a punishable offence. For quite a long time it wasn't punished. When I had the first case of gonorrhea in my [unit] I wanted to punish the fellow. They said: "No, no, that won't do, you can't do that." A fortnight before I took off on my last flight, the chief [med-ical officer] came and called the whole [unit] together and delivered a short talk saying that there were already about forty-five thousand men in France suffering from venereal disease. . . . As a result of that it is now punishable again, with imprisonment. It wasn't merely a military offence; it is because the man doesn't get treated for it.[52]

Occasionally, these stories also cautioned that promiscuous soldiers made themselves vulnerable to espionage and sabotage, thus threatening the Ger-man war effort. A submariner described clearing out a brothel in an undisclosed location: "There were foreign agents there, there usually are in those pubs. A girl working there would earn RM [reichsmark] 5 in ten minutes, but there aren't [usually] any seamen there because they [are not willing] to pay."[53] In a separate conversation, the same submariner talked about his experiences in "the Royal," a brothel in Paris: "There was a spy—an English girl. She was caught. The Germans didn't notice it, but the French girls did. She got into trouble with the French police. Some statements or others were false, and she was seized. She hadn't yet done any harm."[54]

In 1943, Germans with or without uniforms struggled to accept many of the consequences of "total mobilization." At the same time, they worried whether the burdens of war would be borne equitably by all segments of society. SD agents from all parts of the country reported again and again that many in the "working population" hoped that finally "those circles that have hitherto managed to shirk from work deployment" would finally be conscripted.[55] For many, especially of the middle and lower strata of society, a war more radical than anything they could even imagine was a war borne equally by all, one that was hampered neither by the privileges of the traditional elites in German society nor by the new elites of Nazi upstarts. Both CSDIC and SD reports frequently featured the exploits of "certain higher ladies" who whiled away their days in cafés as the masses toiled. The ubiquity of the trope suggests that traditional class resentments continued under National Socialism and had been exacerbated by the outbreak of the war. Many German civilians and soldiers routinely expressed bitter disappointment at the continuing social injustices that neither the Nazi revolution nor the demands of war had thus far eradicated. On the other hand, any blow to traditional privileges, real or perceived, was met with the kind of unbridled gloating (schadenfreude) that belies long-suppressed resentment. A sailor's anecdote of an unlikely encounter between a soldier on home leave and a "higher lady" illustrates the rage behind these sentiments shared widely among military and civilian populations. The sailor recounted,

A woman was sitting in a café in Munich. A wounded soldier came in, he was pretty badly wounded, and he sat down at the table. The woman looked at him for a while and then she asked the waiter to make the man at the table go away, she couldn't bear to look at him. This waiter was smart. He went to an infantry lieutenant and told him [about] this woman. . . . The lieutenant stood up, went up to the woman, drew his revolver and shot her in the middle of the café. He just said to her, "Are you the person who is supposed to have said such-and-such?," and she said quite imprudently, "Yes." Then he drew his revolver. Anyhow he was brought before a court martial but was acquitted.[56]

The shooter's alleged acquittal concluded this story to the satisfaction of the sailor's cellmate. "I should think so"[57] was his only response to this confounding tale in which class and gender clashed, as did norms of civilian and military conduct. It communicated a radical and brutal worldview, suggesting that under conditions of war, men could band together to free themselves from long-endured tyrannies. The woman was portrayed as an impervious parasite who used her social station to assert dominance over a soldier maimed in defense of the fatherland. Perhaps in peacetime, she would have been able to dictate whatever her upper-class sensibility could and could not tolerate. In wartime, however, the waiter and lieutenant worked together to punish her, rectify a social wrong, and pay the soldier his dues. The shooter's vindication by a court martial was an important conclusion. It served to emphasize that this was not an isolated incident but a harbinger of a new era in which masculinity could be proved, privilege was earned, and honor was restored. Wartime conditions had first exposed and then rectified longstanding social wrongs. To those who shared it, the story of the woman murdered in a Munich café was aspirational and a sign, perhaps, of a war more radical than anything people might have imagined.

While Germans frequently complained about the persistence of old privileges in Nazi Germany, they also detested new privileges. CSDIC reports illustrate soldiers' common contempt for members of the new elite of petty party bosses, usurpers who received their privileges neither by birth nor by merit. As a navy captain put it succinctly in December 1942, "After every revolution you have to get rid of the scum. That hasn't happened in Germany yet."[58] Instead, old and new privilege now often conspired together. A sailor relayed his stunted ambitions under National Socialism to his cellmate: "I joined the Hitler Youth in August 1932. They swindled me over the gold Party badge. I said goodbye to it all in 1937. Directors' sons came in and were made leaders and the likes of us were pushed [aside]."[59] Klotzsch, too, was among the many to lament the state of German society in which new inequalities had been heaped on top of old ones. He claimed, "All is not well in Germany. Everything went much too quickly; those who used to scream

'Heil Moscow,' those people are now in leading Party positions and can exercise their power over decent and honest craftsmen. It's a scandal! Germany is not yet politically mature—a nation that went downhill for twenty-five years cannot rise again so quickly."[60]

Some thought that the National Socialist revolution had already achieved many great societal improvements, such as "the abolition of unemployment by arming for the present war, the 'strength through joy' movement and all that."[61] Some believed, however, that the revolution would not be complete until the party ceded operations and the state could once again manage all affairs without duplications of effort and cost. As an Austrian pilot put it,

> The Party will have to be dissolved. . . . If there's only one Party, you can't call it a Party any longer. Everything might as well be put straight under state control. Then the state is the supporter of the whole idea. My god, one could start now, for instance, and . . . [merge] the regional administration with the district administration. Those are two different things with two parallel staffs. The money that costs! Local communities and municipalities should be amalgamated; a local community leader and a mayor are one and the same thing.[62]

Goebbels promised that total mobilization would rectify some of these wrongs. As he presented it, "total war" would mean the fulfillment of the National Socialist revolution. Perhaps it is not surprising that Goebbels, former disciple of the socialist branch of the Nazi movement, pounded the message that the implementation of "total war" would mean the shortest possible war and the most equitable war. In this role, he likely commanded some credibility and respect, because, whatever his many shortcomings, few Germans suspected him of material corruption. However, his efforts at spreading the burdens of the war more evenly were thwarted from above, not below. Göring, Reich marshal and commander in chief of the German air force, and Albert Speer, the new minister of armaments, successfully undermined Goebbels and the Committee of Three in their planning efforts. Goebbels's Sport Palace rally was directed as much at these competitors as at the German people. Indeed, it was also a display of strength directed at Hitler himself, who likely had sanctioned the event in advance but approved the specifics only afterward. Yet, regardless of what he thought of Goebbels's performance, Hitler continued to withhold decisive action and unanimous support from either faction for the rest of the year.

Lacking Hitler's support, the committee ran aground amid squabbles over petty policy changes by the fall of 1943. At the same time, Goebbels himself found many of his initiatives blocked by obstinate regional party administrators, represented by Bormann, and others who fought loss of control over production and consumption in their districts and factories. Goebbels would also find himself increasingly sidelined by Speer, who went on to reorganize his armaments ministry to effectively supervise all production. It was now up to him to battle obstinate political and economic factions, including Hitler. Allying himself with the SS, Speer was determined to achieve his goal of total economic mobilization even to the point of threatening uncooperative officials with incarceration in concentration camps. Addressing a group of party administrators at a war-planning conference in Posen in October 1943, Speer announced: "The manner in which some of the districts have hitherto obstructed the shutdown of consumer goods production will no longer be tolerated. I can assure you that I am prepared to apply the authority of the Reich Government at any cost. I have discussed this with the Reichsführer-SS Himmler, and from now on districts that do not carry out within two weeks the measures I request will be dealt with firmly."[63]

Speer's barely veiled threat was remarkable, particularly because it identified the higher echelons of the Nazi administration as the main obstacle to total mobilization of the home front. This was true even after the German defeat at Stalingrad, the surrender of the Afrika Korps, the Allied invasion of the Italian mainland, and the escalation of the Allied air war over the course of 1943. Goebbels shared his frustration. After witnessing Speer's Posen speech, he noted in his diary,

> The Führer has ordered [Speer] to transfer a million workers into armaments at once and, furthermore, to release sufficient young men from the armament industry to form about twenty divisions. This is a pretty significant project but there is no doubt that it can be implemented, and the Gauleiter will not be able to shirk from the difficult demands of this program. Of course, much of their flourishing and pristine [regional] industry will be liquidated. But in the current war situation we cannot avoid such sacrifice. When we consider what the enemy is producing today, we should be ashamed. . . . Basically, Speer's program implements total war, as I have already demanded it in my Sport Palace speech in February. Unfortunately, no concrete measures followed my speech.[64]

Before the so-called Speer revolution streamlined the German and pan-European industries in 1944, implementation of economic mobilization remained sluggish and haphazard. Throughout 1943, a number of decrees aimed to curtail not only conspicuous consumption but also the consumption of many basic necessities, causing growing consternation in wide segments of German society. A significant lowering of civilian meat rations in mid-May 1943 coincided with Germany's "second Stalingrad," the defeat at Tunis and the loss of some 250,000 men. In the interrogation cages, Klotzsch did not disagree with the new policies but believed they should have been implemented even before the beginning of the war. Deeming himself not "politically mature enough to be able to say exactly what the government of Germany should be like," he nevertheless believed that economic stability was the foundation for political stability and needed to be achieved before warfare. Dangerously destabilized by the Weimar period and the Great Depression, Germany had not fully recovered when war broke out in 1939. According to Klotzsch, "A people, which were so economically undermined, cannot possibly run a peace and war economy side-by-side."[65]

Nazi planners were not wrong to be weary of home-front backlash. Even the limited implementation of rations and restrictions exacerbated long-standing social tensions and resentments. A conversation between two submariners shortly after their capture in April 1943 drifted to the almost inevitable question, "What's morale like in Germany now?" Klotzsch, who had visited Weimar on his last home leave, recalled, "It's certainly not too good. The people's rations are insufficient, and the air raids give them no peace at night. . . . Those in the center of Germany . . . have no idea what it is like in the Ruhr. They have covered the Goethe-Schiller monument in Weimar with brickwork, against air raids, it's laughable. You can't get into the one theater as it's completely crowded with party bigwigs—there is no room for us frontline soldiers."[66]

Many household items and foodstuffs had been rationed since the beginning of the war in 1939. Consumer goods like clothing, furniture, or housewares were increasingly hard to come by, and their procurement required the investment of time, money, and enterprise. By 1943, black market trade bloomed as options for legal consumption shrank. As the SD reported, "The constant contractions of production for the civilian sector and the resulting growing need for replacement or acquisition of new consumer

goods of every kind have led consumers to pursue rare products through bar-
ter." Such trade often occurred in well-established circles between owners
and longtime customers. But it increasingly also involved the establishment
of more or less formal trade co-ops or trade between strangers facilitated by
newspaper ads. "Dutiful national comrades" who lacked the goods required
for this type of exchange were outraged when newspapers routinely printed
dozens of ads brazenly seeking and offering a wide variety of luxury goods,
including "dollhouses for poultry; radio speakers for rabbits; furniture for
fruit; furs for firewood; rabbits for women's boots or for a washing machine;
a golden wristwatch for a stroller."[67]

There were several categories of winners as the German economy reverted
to a more primitive form. These included members of the traditional elites,
the urban middle and upper classes with stores of expendable goods to trade.
But they also included farmers and other producers of foodstuffs. As one
sailor recalled of his visit home to Prussia mere weeks before his capture,
"Food may be short in the town, but when you get outside amongst the farmers, you don't realize there's a war on, and certainly not a war that's been
going on for four years."[68]

Members of the armed services with access to foreign goods were also
widely envied, even if some could see right through the bribery scheme. General von Thoma, for instance, told his cellmate in December 1942, "Now
the orders are that each soldier on the Eastern Front is to be given a parcel
to take home with him—that's nothing but a psychological measure to con-
sole them, so that when a man goes home to his wife, he can say, 'Look, I've
brought you something.'"[69] Von Thoma believed that ultimately such a
policy would backfire by destabilizing the home front:

> I would give the stuff to the people at home, because the soldier is actually
> twice as well fed as a man at home and if the home front collapses, anything
> the soldier achieves is useless. It's always been the wrong way around. I must
> work from the bottom upwards and in total warfare the bottom is the people
> and the top are the army. And if I treat only the army well and leave every-
> thing crumbling underneath, then the whole thing will collapse. . . . Morale
> is the lowest among the middle class because they receive the worst treatment,
> but you have no idea what things are like among the working class. I'll just
> give you some examples. In August, a building works manager made a big
> speech in a large factory in Munich which was nothing but boasting. A work-

man from the gallery shouted, [Y]*ou shut up and work with us and see how you'll like the food then.* Do you know what the result of that was? Several hundred people were sent to a concentration camp. That was the answer.[70]

Whatever they knew of the privations and hardships of the home front, German POWs routinely reminisced about the abundance they had enjoyed in western and southern Europe. An airman who had been captured in Tunisia in May 1943 remembered his life in France, for instance:

> It was really pleasant, except that money was short—everything was too expensive. The prices were absurd. There's a black market there. Well, I took quite a big part in this black-market business as far as it was possible and made money out of it and didn't need anything from home. And I managed very well. Because we were all over France, we had connections in all the larger towns, and owing to that network extended fairly far over France, right from the start, and so we had commercial connections . . . and we always got everything we needed.[71]

Indeed, for many military men serving in southern or western Europe, life there was often preferable to life back home. One pilot explained, "Of course, morale is good everywhere. In the first place, none of our soldiers are homesick. In the last war, everyone wanted to get home, but no one worries about that now. On the contrary, everyone who is at home is unhappy, because it's so rotten there."[72] Occasionally, soldiers reflected on the consequences of their plunder. For instance, two soldiers discussed the situation in Italy, where one of them had been stationed for several months. He explained that the "German troops in Italy behave like mercenaries of old," stoking tension and creating hostility in the local population, a "catastrophic mistake that the Germans make in all occupied territories":

> They are not in sympathy with us. The whole population breathed a sigh of relief when we left. I was in contact with the people, as an interpreter. They don't understand how to treat the civilian population. The population in Northern Italy was really well disposed toward us, they were friendly and forthcoming and everything. Before the armistice came, our people bargained for days and weeks; for every chair and every table there was bargaining and when the armistice came of course everyone went and said: *That belongs to*

me, bring it out, and they carried it off just like that. Then, of course, the people were indignant. The amount of stuff stolen. . . . And they snatched watches and rings off people in the street, like bandits. Our soldiers themselves told us how they carried on. They simply entered a village and if there was anything they didn't like, they just shot down a few people, just like that. . . . One man boasted of how they broke into a church and put on the priest's vestments and committed sacrilege in the church. They behaved like Bolsheviks there and then they were surprised when the people turned against them. . . . And then he told how a comrade of his had a whole stocking full of nothing but cold bracelets and watches, worth perhaps a million lire. He wanted to take it away with him but then he was killed. They simply broke into the houses and took what they liked and took things from the people in the street.[73]

Such critical self-reflection was rare. More commonly, soldiers fondly recalled the abundance they had experienced. In a conversation between two soldiers, a sergeant major by the name of Reinhardt asked his cellmate, an officer candidate named Wittenau, "Were you well fed in Italy?" Wittenau explained, "Yes. To a great extent we fed off the land. There were enormous numbers of sheep and pigs, and then of course we had whole herds of cows. In the winter every 'Batterie' had procured a herd of cows. Then when the withdrawal started—two days before—the herd of cows set off along the road." He clarified that there had been no regular food supply otherwise: "We had to supply ourselves, but we made a good job of it. It was very good because we had enough cattle. We were the first. The Americans who followed us didn't get so much, of course. We are burning down every village and every haystack for purposes of defense. Italy will be nothing but a heap of ruins." He acknowledged that such policies merely stoked "anti-Nazi" sentiments but did not appear too alarmed at the prospect: "The more hopeless the situation becomes, the more people will rail against the thing, and the more these types will come to the fore, and the less the others will dare to say anything against it."[74]

In captivity, many boasted about the goods they had been able to send to their families or had traded on home visits. An airman told his cellmate, "I sent my wife a whole box of clothes from France, including a fur coat that cost RM 600." The other man shared, "Yes, I sent home a lot of things from France too."[75] A German pilot who had been captured on January 1, 1944, told his cellmate about his last visit to Berlin the previous November: "They already had two terror raids. It was a damnable business . . .

[morale] was still alright, naturally. . . . [However,] in my opinion the people of Berlin won't stand up to it indefinitely." He went on to describe an encounter with a waiter working in the famous Regina Bar. The man "offered me RM 1,000 for a kilo of tea. I couldn't shake the fellow off. He wanted to give RM 1,000[—]I had a kilo of tea with me." His cellmate, a pilot who had been captured in Italy in December 1943, interjected, "He would have resold it later—at RM 20 per cup perhaps." The other man continued, "When I was with my uncle in November, we were eating butter that cost RM 80 a kilo. You can still get it! There was sausage there too. I reckoned that my breakfast cost me about RM 20."[76]

When it came to managing or circumventing the shortages and restrictions of wartime consumption, Nazi cronies were most brazen, stoking popular resentments against their ill-gotten gains. Both soldiers and civilians incessantly complained about the machinations and rampant corruption of petty party bosses. Many thrived and achieved levels of material comfort, even opulence, unheard of in peacetime. In captivity, an airman relayed the story of the regional administrator of Saxony, which captured many commonly voiced complaints: "[He] had his park laid out during the war and tennis courts laid down—which naturally gave rise to much talk. . . . Then—I'm not sure if it was at the same time—he had a rather unpleasant business in connection with coupons. Anyhow, there was quite a stir about it in February or March. He got more food—a considerable amount and then, too, he behaved rather extravagantly. That came to be known and there was a row about it. He got a reprimand from the Führer or something."[77]

The objection of the airman's cellmate, that "that's . . . everlasting gossip" and "hundreds of stories like that are being told," is as illuminating as the story itself.[78] Even if the charges of blatant corruption and cronyism among party officials were unfounded, "hundreds of stories like that" circulated in German society at the very time that the regime requested ever greater sacrifices for total mobilization. Ordinary soldiers and civilians alike heard, believed, repeated, and resented stories about the debauchery and squander perpetrated by party officials. These stories served as proof that the burdens of the war were not shared equitably and fairly. In addition, soldiers tended to paint party bosses as shirkers, cowards, and pretenders. Their transgressions were twofold: First, they had violated the old social norms and hierarchies that would normally have kept them in their place for life. Second, they had used their new positions in the Nazi hierarchy for personal enrichment.

The same double resentment was also reflected in the story relayed by an Austrian pilot about his experiences in Salzburg: "At Schloss Leopoldsk-ron where Gauleiter Dr. Reiner lives—what I saw there was more than enough for me." The property had once "belonged to the Jew Reinhardt of theater fame" but had been taken over by widely loathed party cronies: "People used to complain about the splendor of the bishops. But if they went today into the private houses of Party people like that and found the priceless old baroque furniture and of some prince bishop—to hell with them."[79] And worse, the party leaders' abuses of power robbed the com-mon people of one of the few enjoyments available to them in this war: "On the opposite side (of the lake) was a bathing place. 'Oh God,' the Gau-leiter's wife said, 'one can't bathe at all if that crowd of people is always bathing over there.' Not a soul had disturbed her, as it was far away on the other side. 'You must arrange at all cost for the bathing place to be closed!' Then the old boy had to arrange for the place—where the common people used to bathe—to be closed, in order that the Gauleiter's wife should not be disturbed."[80]

Even worse yet, the elite's corruption also victimized the one figure who should hold the place of highest honor in Germany society: the wounded sol-dier. The Austrian pilot continued:

> There is a large park right around the place. Two wounded soldiers were walking there during the festival plays. Then a [leader of the] B.D.M. [Bund Deutscher Mädel (League of German Girls)] ran out of the guests' quarters—she lived there too. "You have no right to be here, this is the private property of the Gauleiter!" "All right, all right," said the soldiers, "we're going. But he has got rich quickly!" It wasn't the private property of the Gauleiter at all, that was nonsense. "Heavens! How can one possibly manage with these few rooms?!" Whereas actually it was a small castle.[81]

His cellmate agreed that it was a sorry state of affairs in German society since "the idealists" were "all out there at the front."[82] The Austrian pilot con-curred, "The idealists have not reached those high positions."[83] The story illustrates the commonly held assumption that entitlement was rampant among the party elite, a symptom of a great social ill. The fact that the new elite often came from fairly low social origins only seemed to stoke the out-rage of many observers. According to the pilot, the party leaders in Salzburg had such an exaggerated sense of entitlement that they even complained about their new princely accommodations: "Those people used to be bank clerks with 300 schillings (a month) and a flat with two rooms. Now they can't manage with the few rooms in a castle."[84]

German POWs also discussed the many ways in which party corruption was creeping into military matters. One airman found that he had to agree with his interrogating officer that "there's certainly something rotten in our state": "[For example,] these exaggeratedly high ranks. If a man like Raeder—with such a very small navy—had been made Admiral, that would have been more than enough. And if he had had two vice-admirals, one for the Baltic and one for the North Sea, he still would have had enough. . . . But of course, he would have a Grossadmiral and a Generaladmiral and goodness knows what. And what a crowd of Generalfeldmarschälle, Reichsmarschäle." His cellmate agreed that the rampant rank inflation was "perfectly ridiculous": "After all, what is a Generalfeldmarschall today? He used to be a mere divisional commander." They agreed that "if they had captured a [marshal] in the Great War, that would have ended it. And here they are two a penny! . . . Every Tom, Dick, and Harry is today a [captain] who used to be a [sergeant]."[85] Both men bemoaned that the current system rewarded the young and the brash over the calm and mature, eroding military society from within and rendering ranks meaningless. It was a common complaint in the cages. Another airman ranted against the indignities and abuse he suffered at the hands of brash, young noncommissioned officers (NCOs), who, on the one hand, insisted on strict order in his unit but, on the other, routinely disrespected his men. When the airman protested this poor treatment, he was punished for insubordination: "Service life takes my gall. I had good reports wherever I went. I had done two years without any punishment or anything, and then I joined that awful crowd."[86]

While German forces plundered the continent, many German civilians lacked access to various necessities, let alone luxuries. They did not hide their bitterness over perceived waste and corruption. Excluded from the system's benefits, they focused on the hypocrisy that disadvantaged them despite the egalitarian social rhetoric. For instance, according to the SD, many people expressed anger at the moral inconsistencies: "[The press] preaches morals and conducts political and ideological propaganda on pages one, two, and three. Meanwhile, on the 'wanted page' in the back they give space to ads that reveal some dubious doings. . . . It is untenable that the commands of decency and steadfastness are constantly undermined."[87]

Germans at war kept a close score of the losses and gains of their alleged comrades in arms, whether at the front or on the home front. They never ceased to complain about the unequal burdens of the war and its unequal spoils. The trope of the "stuffed packages" that the deployed plunderers sent home to their families constantly appeared in German wartime stories in the later years, causing envy and consternation among those left out. For instance, Frau Maria Lakowsky had railed against the lazy soldiers in western Europe who had "spent three years lounging and luxuriating and resting in France, all the while sending heavy packages back home."[88] She likely was not a recipient of such packages.

Available evidence suggests that Germans from all walks of life engaged in various types of illicit economic exchanges. However, few of them caused the kind of moral outrage that met the activities of party members. For instance, in well-established circles of customers and proprietors there was a wide range of deals that violated anti-barter legislation. Yet, the regime's attempt to step up persecution in the later war years foundered on people's refusal to denounce most participants. An SD report from March 6, 1943, is particularly illustrative of the shadow worlds many ordinary Germans inhabited in the fourth year of the war. In explaining why few Germans reported illegal black market activities, it argued that "there are only a few national comrades who have not somehow reengaged themselves in bartering at some time or other." Consequently, they were not inclined to report on others engaging in such illegal activities. "It is common knowledge that those filing reports about bartering often do so out of base instincts, such as envy, spite, or malice. . . . In the face of labor and consumer-goods shortage[s] everyone is glad for whatever they can get and is therefore focused on maintaining [their] connections instead of disturbing them with official complaints."[89]

The detailed SD report reveals much about people's values and priorities as they navigated the consumer economy of the final war years. It illustrates that the experience of scarcity alone did not alienate people. Rather, resentment was stoked by the commonly held perception that the regime failed to curb corruption in its own ranks. Despite plenty of rhetoric about a unified national community at arms, many people believed they shouldered the burdens of war disproportionately. However, as long as the German people were not starving, the regime had little to fear.

Scholars have rightly paid attention to the Nazi regime's plunder of the European continent to buy the acquiescence of the German people.[90] Indeed, when compared with the occupied peoples and even the civilian populations of some of the Allied nations, the German people fared well, even under "total war." Though their diets had been significantly reduced in terms of volume and variety, most Germans did not suffer starvation until the immediate postwar period. Their monthly allowances included 9 kilos of bread, 600 grams of cereal, 1.85 kilos of meat, and 950 grams of fats.[91] However, supply was not always guaranteed, as it was increasingly disrupted by transportation bottlenecks, logistics mismanagement, corruption, and plain shortages. It did not help popular attitudes when the regime routinely made and then broke promises of extra rations as reward for outstanding work or heavy labor as part of total mobilization. In April 1943, some workers still waited for the extra bottle of wine promised them for Christmas the previous year, and excitement turned into bitter resentment. The SD reported the common attitude was that "many promises were made but none were kept."[92]

Germans did not compare their rations to the people in occupied Europe who had less or nothing at all. They compared their rations to their German peers who had more. Rampant corruption by proprietors of restaurants and stores outraged many clients, and SD reports featured their bitter complaints throughout 1943. Soldiers, too, were well informed of these conditions that bore heavy on the lives of their loved ones back home. One POW's detailed discussion of the size of fat and meat rations he had witnessed in Vienna in August 1943 was characteristic of this preoccupation. He also explained that although theaters were still open, "You can't get any tickets. You can't get anything else, either, no wine and no beer. You can drink two mugs at the most. You can't get anything to smoke, three cigarettes; it used to be five."[93] A sailor recounted, "You can't get anything at home now. I wanted to buy a new shirt to wear when I went on leave and I was told I must give up my old one as I was only allowed one. So, I tore it beforehand, so that I should get a new one."[94]

When soldiers shared their spoils and extra rations with their families and loved ones, they were met with enthusiasm and gratitude. For instance, a pilot told his cellmate, "When I went home on leave . . . I had a big rucksack of things, mainly wine. At home you can't get anything now, except, perhaps, a little weak beer."[95] But in 1943, beneficiaries rarely publicly discussed their good fortunes, and they certainly did not reflect on the consequences of their plunder. Instead, victims of real or perceived inequity and corruption were most vocal. For instance, a soldier reported how "high criminal officials" used to dine at the inn operated by his in-laws. "They handed in their coupons and then afterwards they went in the kitchen and took them back again."[96] An Austrian pilot relayed his experience with party privilege via a female Gauführerin in Salzburg: "I used to write to her, or telephone her and say, 'I'm in such-and-such place.' [She would say:] 'Oh that's nice, I'll come along.' Then the noble Gauführerin got into her car, with chauffeur, and visited me. It was a distance of 150–170 kilometers. The baker who wanted to deliver his bread, or the butcher, didn't get one liter of petrol in a month, but *she* can."[97]

It is hard to estimate the material impact of the exchange of goods between German civilians and soldiers. Combatants were assigned significantly larger rations and a wider variety of goods, like cigarettes and real coffee, long after these disappeared from German stores. But this hardly impressed the soldiers who compared their current living standard to peace times. An airman did the math: "A pound of margarine cost us 26 [pfennig] in peacetime and now it costs 1.10 [reichsmarks]. A pound of salt used to cost 6 [pfennig] and now costs 15 [pfennig]. The beer is hardly fit to drink; it contains only 2% alcohol. Sometimes the army gets it with 6%."[98]

Military authorities managed troop morale through material incentives. Much as civilian authorities encouraged Germans to supply themselves, their military counterparts encouraged soldiers to rob and shop their way across the continent, allowing soldiers to send parcels home as late as 1943 and 1944. The abundance of food and luxuries in some parts of Europe had clearly made an impression on many soldiers from all branches of the armed forces. In captivity they continued to marvel at these memories. Conversations about the good life they had lived or heard of particularly in France were a common and pleasant diversion in the POW camps. Few engaged in any critical reflection about the impact of their plunder on the native populations, and fewer yet asked openly what the legacy of their exploitation and destruction would be.

In February 1943, Goebbels declared "total war," a war so radical it was unimaginable. His radical pledge to eliminate privileges and divisions in German society to create a true "warrior community" never materialized. Instead, the early "totalizing measures" exacerbated inequities and stoked resentments that would grow alongside the burdens and sacrifices of the later war years. Members of the German civilian and military communities were perpetually disgruntled at the moral and material corruption they witnessed all around them, even as many reaped some of the benefits of Germany's Europe-wide plunder. The world at war was not a place for critical self-reflection. As the nation embarked on total mobilization, the fissures in Germany society were deepening and the gulf between people and leadership was widening.

Chapter 3

GENOCIDE AND MASS ATROCITIES

A Page Never to Be Written

In early October 1943, select members of the Nazi elite gathered in the Polish town of Posen (Poznan) for a wartime conference, rallies, and speeches. Heinrich Himmler, the Reichsführer-SS and newly appointed interior minister, took the podium twice to share his particular perspective on the many wars Germany was waging, none more ferociously than the war against European Jewry. On October 4, he addressed a group of SS leaders in the Golden Hall of Posen Castle. Speaking in his customary clear and dispassionate manner for about two hours, he finally arrived at a "truly difficult chapter," the "evacuation of the Jews." Though Himmler insisted on such innocuous wording even in internal reports, he continued more bluntly this time.[1] The real issue, he stated, was "the extermination of the Jewish people":

It is one of those things that is easily said. Every Party comrade states, "The Jewish people are being exterminated. Obviously, the elimination of the Jews is in our program. The extermination, we're doing it." And then there are some 80 million meek Germans, and every single one knows a "good

Jew." Of course, all the others are pigs but this one here, this one is a great Jew. But of all those who talk this way, none have witnessed it, none have endured it. [By contrast,] most of you here know what it means when 100 corpses or 500 or even 1,000 lie there. To have endured something like that and . . . to have remained steadfast and decent, that has made us tough. This is an unwritten and never to be written page of glory in our history.[2]

Two days later, Himmler assembled a group of party administrators in the same location. Their day had begun at around nine o'clock in the morning with Albert Speer's barely veiled threats of concentration-camp imprisonment should they obstruct his "totalizing" economic program. It concluded in the early evening with Himmler implicating them in mass murder. His speech had wound on for about an hour when he began talking about "the heaviest burden of my life," one he needed to share so that "the highest dignitaries of the party, of our political order" could know "how it was." Himmler told the attendees that their districts and provinces were now "free of Jews" (*judenfrei*) not because the Jews had simply been evacuated. Rather, the Jews, women and children included, had been made to physically "disappear from the earth," and by the end of the year he intended to conclude their annihilation in all of occupied Europe.[3] Having thus confronted this "most restricted circle" with the true nature of his answer to the Jewish Question, Himmler declared, "You are now informed, and you will keep your knowledge to yourselves. Later perhaps we can consider whether the German people should be told about this. But I think it is better that we—we together—carry for our people the responsibility . . . for an achievement, not just an idea . . . and then take the secret with us to our grave."[4]

By the time of Himmler's Posen address, most of the victims of the Holocaust had perished, although the extermination campaign continued until the war's bitter end. Today we know that the murderers of more than six million European Jews and other victims did not take their "secret" to the grave. And yet, the exculpatory fiction that neither most Nazi leaders nor most "ordinary" Germans knew about Nazi war crimes proved tenacious. For decades into the postwar era, members of the "wartime generation" reflexively denied all knowledge of atrocities and genocide, doggedly insisting "of *that* we knew nothing."[5]

Surviving evidence shows that rumors about atrocities circulated widely among German military and civilian populations just as they embarked on total mobilization to stave off the turning tide of war. Vivid descriptions of the sights, sounds, and smells of mass murder flowed from the military to the civilian populations, where they mingled with information gleaned from Nazi and Allied propaganda. The cumulative effect was that many Germans knew something. Or, as one historian has put it, at the very least, many "knew enough to know it was better not to know."[6] This chapter focuses on the dissemination and popular reception of information about mass atrocities and the Holocaust at its height. It examines eyewitness accounts, hearsay, and gossip that fed the ever-churning rumor mills of German wartime society to examine popular responses to evidence of German-perpetrated war crimes. It asks how Germans interpreted accounts of such atrocities against the backdrop of their own escalating national crisis. What did they understand about the scale and purpose of the German extermination campaign? Did people consider the wholesale murder of civilians a legitimate act of war? Or did they deem it part and parcel of a war "more radical than anything" they could imagine? Where did they assign agency and culpability? And finally, did such contemplations have an impact on how they related to the Nazi regime and to the war waged in their names?

Himmler, the Nazi "architect of genocide," never served as the public face of the regime the way that Göring or Goebbels did. Unlike his more illustrious peers, Himmler never commanded love, loyalty, or admiration among the general population. Devoid of charisma, the "bespectacled pedant" struck most contemporaries as deeply unlikable at best.[7] As one German POW confided in September 1943, "Göring, Hitler, etc. I hold in esteem; I won't abide anyone besmirching their image. . . . But that Himmler, I have to tell you honestly, I thought him unpleasant even in peacetime." And though his cellmate cautioned him to consider the subversive influence of British propaganda, he admitted that he too had thought "that guy" Himmler unlikable for the longest time.[8]

Himmler rarely spoke publicly, and never about his most important project, the destruction of European Jewry. However, even a cursory reading of SD and CSDIC reports suggests that, in 1943, many Germans had an acute sense that he had charted a radical, irreversible course. People commonly assigned a level of ruthlessness to Himmler that was matched only by his efficiency. His position at the helm of the SS gave him an air of menace and invincibility, shielding him from the casual popular ire that many of his peers drew in the later war years. Therefore, if the Reichsführer-SS inspired any popular emotion at all, it was dread, occasionally mixed with awe.

Himmler's promotion to Reich interior minister on August 24, 1943, had surprised some people, though the SD mostly registered the absence of a popular reaction.[9] Some believed that he had been assigned to crack down on internal instability and government inefficiency. A recently captured airman claimed that Himmler's appointment had been met with surprise among the general population: "But then it was ascribed to the presence of so many foreigners in Germany."[10] Elsewhere, people expected that Himmler's experience in handling the Jewish Question would have an immediate bearing on his conduct as minister. SD agents in Würzburg reported, for instance, that members of the local "intelligentsia" considered Himmler a most ruthless administrator because of his association "with all the measures taken against the Jews" and that "people believe he will stop at nothing [in this new role as interior minister]."[11] Whatever Germans knew or suspected of the Final Solution in 1943, the man in charge was widely believed to be devoid of moral scruples. Himmler's fierce ambition was a recurring theme in these conversations, as were the boundless, almost mythical powers ascribed to him. Contemplating the nature of the SS, for instance, two submariners revealed an uncommon admiration for the individual SS man, but they agreed that Himmler had turned the organization into a tool of abominable terror that held German society hostage while causing irreversible damage to its reputation. Declared one of them, "I mean, the SS is alright; the one drawback is the man at the head, he is the most dangerous—he has fashioned this immense instrument, and what he does with it is much more dangerous." Replied his cellmate, "Yes, as you say, [I have] no objection to the individual SS man, but to the idea and way the whole [SS] instrument is handled. The individual SS man is alright, there is no doubt about that. My only regret is that there is so much enthusiasm and so much good [human] material [in the SS], such highly qualified men from both the idealistic and physical points of view. [But the organizational] influences at work are bound to be unhealthy; I am sure the whole thing is going too far."[12]

In captivity, German POWs occasionally voiced such critical assessments more boldly than would have been wise in broader German wartime society. Beyond the clutches of Himmler's security apparatus, they complained about the fear and loathing that it inspired. Perhaps stoked by his captors, one airman vented, "We're a race of slaves, what with the Gestapo and so on, but I'm not allowed to admit it!"[13] Another submariner echoed several of these sentiments when he unburdened himself to his cellmate in March 1943. He carefully delineated his own military code of honor from whatever code guided the SS, a common feature of self-exculpatory accounts that would persist for decades into the postwar era. Of his own political integrity, he furthermore distinguished himself from "out and out Nazis" who could be found everywhere but "especially [among] the young people who were in the Hitler Youth." He went as far as criticizing Hitler, who had been "so farsighted" in many ways, for failing to reign in Himmler's unbridled ambitions:

> In other matters he has let Himmler have his own way, he has let him carry on and make a mess of things. One can really say that most of the discord, which has been sown [and which has caused] bitterness in our own country and abroad, came from [Himmler], from his side. Those are things with which a normal officer is not in agreement. Then there is his shortsightedness: anyone who is at all normal and intelligent realizes that it's sheer madness to have the army on one side and the Waffen-SS on the other. A thing like that is incredible.[14]

Often prompted when their Allied captors confronted them with evidence of German-perpetrated atrocities, captured German soldiers, airmen, and sailors frequently alluded to the "mad," "unhealthy," or "dangerous" goals pursued by Himmler and his SS. But just as frequently, POWs referred explicitly to their own experiences or to accounts from sources they deemed trustworthy. For instance, relaying rumors about SS-perpetrated mass shootings in the East, a Luftwaffe lieutenant explained to his cellmate, "Naturally I should never admit it to the English, but I'm quite certain that everything I've heard is true."[15] Also, in many conversations the exact nature of the crime remained unarticulated and obscured. POWs quite frequently referred to *something* having been taken too far. At the very least, the unexplained *something* alludes to a shared understanding of crimes better left unspoken in captivity.

By contrast, CSDIC agents recorded conversations that explicitly dissected the direction of Himmler's ambition and the nature of the force at his command. That was the case in a discussion between three German army colonels by the names of Egerschoff, Reimann, and Bordert in June 1943. In their prognoses for the postwar era, they were remarkably clear-eyed about the limits of England's industrial capacity and about the factors that positioned the United States as a future superpower. Their speculations about the postwar future of National Socialism were slightly more muddled, however. Ventured Colonel Egerschoff, "I don't believe, either, that even with luck, National Socialism will be able to continue in its present form after the war. Not as we know it, with everyone gagged and kept in subjugation." The SS loomed large in their imagination. Colonel Reimann declared that "the next in [line of] succession is definitely Himmler. He is already hovering in the background. . . . I have a feeling that he will take it all over some day." "Obviously," concurred Egerschoff. Bordert agreed as well, explaining that Himmler "has made himself exceedingly strong. He has his hands on the best of the young people." Reimann recoiled at the prospect of a Himmler-led Germany, entertaining instead the possibility that Himmler's instrument of power might turn against him:

> Yes, but all the same, I don't believe it—I hope to God, not. No, I don't think Himmler will live very long. I believe he will be done away by his own people. . . . They are all revolutionaries, just like the Praetorian guards in old Rome; always plotting assassinations and intrigue, etc. There are also a whole lot of one-time regular officers in the SS. We had one, a regular, a good officer—who for some reason or other joined the SS. . . . Yes, and he got an order from Himmler: "You have to execute so-and-so many men in Poland." He had to obey the order and did so for the sake of the service. And I could well imagine that it would have such an effect on the previously decent officer, that there wouldn't be a moment's peace for him. The business would prey on his mind every night; for he had to carry out the execution. In my opinion a man like that is done for. After the war, if by any chance the English would be at the helm, that they should be filled with rage . . . [inaudible] pronounce his own sentence; something like that will happen to Himmler.[16]

In concluding his dire prognosis for Himmler's future, Reimann stated, "It is a question of 'ill-gotten gains never thrive.' Nothing goes unavenged in this world."[17] Many POWs worried not only that Himmler's radical course in the war implicated his SS henchmen but also that the German national community at large now bore an indelible "blood guilt" (*Blutschuld*). Only a few were willing to explicitly blame Hitler for atrocities perpetrated under the cover of war. A notable exception was an airman who stated in April 1943, "The Führer has handed us a great deal abroad by his treatment of the Jewish Question." His cellmate agreed: "That showed a great lack of tact. You will see that when history comes to be written, the Führer will not get off without blame in spite of his achievements." The corporal conceded, "Yes, but that is inevitable; every individual makes mistakes."[18]

A fear of an impending reckoning for German-perpetrated atrocities permeated CSDIC camps. Frequently, inmates worried that Germany's enemies would extract a terrible revenge if given the chance. In the later war years, as Germans grappled with the specter of defeat, they anticipated post-defeat retribution that mirrored German war crimes in method and scope. A German victory was the only way to escape such punishment. As a colonel put it after his capture at Tunisia, "Germany's last chance is to win this war. If we don't win it, then there will be no more Adolf Hitler either. If the Allies are able to carry out their plans, then it will be all up with us. You can imagine how the Jews [!] will triumph then. Then we shall not simply be shot, we shall die in the most brutal way."[19] Elsewhere, a pilot stated, "I take a gloomy view of things if we lose the war and the Poles and Jews come to Germany."[20]

Often the cruelty that Germans ascribed to Russians and "Poles and Jews" mirrored precisely what they had inflicted on these victims groups. For instance, the colonel who believed that Hitler's treatment of the Jewish Question showed a lack of tact, explained, "I haven't seen it myself, but I've heard from other people how we treat the Russians . . . and the Russian civilian population too. Why do we do those things? It's not right."[21] Elsewhere, two airmen discussed "the most incredible things" that went on in eastern Europe, marveling at "the numbers of Jews that have been wiped out!" Responded a colonel, "[The Allies] have no idea that things like that are going on. I'm sure they haven't. Suppose one of these mass murders should somehow come to light after the war!" They both agreed that if Germany won the war, "then of course all will be well, but suppose things go wrong!" The sergeant concluded, "Then it will come to light anyhow; after all, they [the bodies] must be somewhere."[22] Elsewhere in captivity, a German airman had a pretty good idea of where the bodies were, telling his cellmate about bombing Warsaw in 1942: "Yes, the ghettos. 140,000 dead. Now they've found mass graves in Russia. In this regard you really have to be careful."[23]

In the German popular imagination of the later war years, Himmler and his SS occupied a unique position at the nexus of home-front terror, race policy, and field atrocities. When self-described "ordinary soldiers" in captivity discussed the SS, they usually agreed that worlds separated the regular armed forces from their SS counterparts. Admissions that the institutional borders were porous were rare but did occur occasionally, as was the case of the submariner who said, "I have spoken to a number of SS leaders, officers in the SS who aren't in the least in agreement with it. There are also many who are simply detailed into the SS from the army. I met some in Munich, who saluted us smartly. Some of them think things over quietly and in time form their own conclusion."[24] More commonly, when German POWs discussed the SS, they conveniently framed the organization as an entity apart, distinguished by its members' physical, ideological, and moral disposition. As one airman tried to explain: "The SS wields absolute power in Germany. Everything is SS . . . they are all powerful." His cellmate was skeptical: "SS be damned. They're in just the same position as ordinary soldiers who have no say in anything, those small SS men—they are soldiers just like any infantrymen." But his cellmate was adamant, insisting, "The SS officers as such have all the power in Germany. I am now exceedingly prejudiced against the SS because I have seen the whole damn crowd; they are, in fact, disastrous to our reputation. How they've infuriated me at times with these drastic measures they keep introducing. . . . The Waffen-SS are the SS leaders. They are the most powerful people in Germany."[25]

A month earlier the same airman had shared stories about events that may have colored his overall outlook. He had confided that he had taken part in SS-instigated atrocities against Jews and partisans in Poland: "[It] left rather an impression afterwards on me as an officer." When prompted he stated explicitly that he had fired his own gun. But for much of his account he assumed the passive voice, and his self-described role in the events vacillated between random observer and reluctant perpetrator. At the same time, there was nothing vague or conflicted about his description of SS men at the scene:

I once took part in it myself . . . that was when I came into contact with the war myself, during the Polish campaign, and I was making transport flights there. I was at Radom (?) once and had my midday meal with the Waffen-SS battalion who were stationed there. An SS captain or whatever he was said: "Would you like to come along for half an hour? Get your Tommy gun and let's go." So I went along. I had an hour to spare and we went to a kind of barracks and slaughtered 1,500 Jews. That was during the war. There were some twenty men there with Tommy guns. It only took a second, and nobody thought anything of it. They had been attacked at night by Jewish partisans and there was a lot of indignation about these damned Poles. I thought about it afterwards—it wasn't very pleasant. . . . Some of the people who were inside there said, "Here come the swine," and swore and threw stones and things at them. There were women and children too! . . . There were whole families, some were screaming terribly, and some were just stolid and apathetic.[26]

This account prompted his cellmate to relate a story he claimed to have heard about an SS man's brutal conduct at a Jewish labor camp near Papenburg. As suggested by his narrative, the SS had opened lawless spaces not only abroad but even on Reich territory. He explained how a brash young SS officer confronted a Jewish forced laborer, telling him: "'Listen, you see my pistol here. You've got two alternatives: either I put a bullet through your head now, or . . . you see those high ridges behind, that's firm ground.' There was a swamp in between. The Jew, of course, ran off and was swallowed by the bog. And that's the type of man who's a 'civilized being of the twentieth century' and belongs to the 'master race.'"[27]

The airman's admission that he had shot, albeit reluctantly, at women and children was exceptional. Much more common were accounts like his cellmates' that were phrased as hearsay or rumors. Still, surviving CSDIC transcripts illuminate the ubiquity and granular detail of stories of mass atrocities, particularly of mass shootings. A submariner, for instance, rendered a comprehensive description of what he claimed to have witnessed while serving for the Reich Labor Service (Reicharbeitsdienst or RAD) in Lithuania. Prompted by his curious cellmate, he explained that he had followed a procession of Jews to an execution site, where he observed German and Latvian auxiliaries collaborate in their slaughter:

They had to strip to their shirts and the women to their vests and knickers and then they were shot by the "Gestapo." All the Jews were executed [in their underwear] . . . so that they don't take anything into the grave with them. The things were collected up, cleaned and mended. . . . The German Gestapo were present, but nobody could prove that they were Germans, because they were wearing Latvian uniforms! If the Latvian "Gestapo" hadn't fired they would themselves have been shot. . . . Behind every two Latvians there was a German with a revolver in his hand. But they couldn't tell that those were Germans. . . . We knew alright that they were Germans, but they didn't. We were actually there when a pretty girl was shot. . . . They were all shot ruthlessly! She knew that she was going to be shot.[28]

The mention of the pretty Jewish girl elicited the cellmate's only sympathetic response—"What a pity!"—in a series of otherwise callous prompts for ever more shocking details. Asked why the shooter had not spared the woman by deliberately aiming wide, the submariner elaborated on the insidious killing system:

No one can do anything about it. . . . [The victims] arrived and the first ones had to line up and were shot. The fellows were standing there with their tommy guns and just sprayed quickly up and down the line, once to the right and once to the left with their tommy guns; there were six men there in a row. . . . They clipped on a magazine, first to the right and left and that was that. It didn't matter whether they were still alive or not; when they were hit they fell over backwards into the pit. Then the next group came up with ashes and chloride of lime and scattered it over those lying down there; then they lined up [the next group of victims] and so it went on.[29]

He explained that the purpose of the lime was "so that there should be no smell and all that." His cellmate then wanted to know "about the people who fell in there who were not properly dead yet." He laughed when he told, "That was bad luck for them; they died down there. . . . I tell you, you heard terrific screams and shrieking."[30]

The sensory experience of genocide—the chaos, the noise, and the stench of mass dying—figured frequently in these discussions as POWs formulated stories of what they had witnessed as others—SS men, Gestapo officers, or foreign collaborators—made the Jews "disappear from the earth." They often paid particular attention to the actions of the female victims and their expressions of terror and despair. A platoon sergeant, for instance, concluded his account of the roundup of Jews in Paris by stating, "There were fantastic scenes: Women jumping out of third floor windows into the street and so on."[31] Though expressions of sympathy or regret were exceedingly rare, some eyewitnesses did dwell on such scenes of female anguish. Tales of the mass killings of women and children, including tales that implied or explicitly referenced instances of sexual coercion and violence, betrayed a real understanding of the extraordinary nature of these events and of broader levels of complicity and responsibility. Even the submariner's callous cellmate made sure to verify, "Were the women shot at the same time?"[32] More than anything else, discussions of the herding and slaughter of women suggested POWs' widespread anxiety over their complicity in crimes that could never be righted.

Descriptions of women in the killing fields also frequently contained salacious undertones that point to their dual vulnerability as victims of sexual violence and murder. The submariner's account of the mass shooting in Lithuania, which so enthralled his cellmate, was largely driven by his description of the "pretty Jewess," a university-educated young woman from Landsberg an der Warthe. According to the cellmate's story, she had been forced to clean barracks in a camp run by the RAD in the East. He claimed that she was one of several "jew broads" (*Judenweiber*) there who were freely available for sexual exploitation. Posturing outrage, the submariner declared, "It was really a scandal, the way [the Germans at the camp] slept with those Jewish women." As he recalled, the woman did not fit into the wartime tableau of the East. He remembered her as smart and smartly dressed, even as she walked to her own execution: "She was certainly a marvelous girl." In fact, he said, "you couldn't tell that she was a Jewess. She was quite a nice type, too. It was just her bad luck that she had to die with the others. 75,000 Jews shot there."[33]

The sexual undercurrents of such conversations strongly suggest that many German military personnel in the field viewed Jewish women as prey. The submariner's cellmate was both excited and contemptuous to learn that such a beautiful woman had "allowed herself to be made a whore" in the RAD camp.[34] In another cell, an airman complained about "the damnable fact that the SS, in their uncontrolled sexual activities, didn't even stop at the Jews."[35] And elsewhere still, yet another airman revealed freely that he had seen "eight and a half thousand [Jews] being shot at Minsk": "I saw it personally. But those whom I saw were German Jews, what's more, and not Russian ones. The fellows spoke German" interjected a Luftwaffe officer, "As for the women, they are fine up to twenty-four years old." The corporal agreed: "With many of them you couldn't tell at all that they were Jewesses."[36]

In captivity, such stories likely served to release pent-up sexual tension. But the tone of many of these discussions suggests that the image of pretty Jewesses in the killing fields was a common trope, one both enticing and unsettling. When set in the seemingly lawless spaces in the East, female victims were rendered accessible and without protection, their imminent demise legitimizing other violations. But even without overt sexual components, such discussions were laden with meaning. Frequently, memories of "pretty Jewesses" belied Nazi propaganda's portrayals of the Jewish enemy. The contrast between German combatants' expectations and observations of Jews astounded many.

Not infrequently, descriptions of atrocities also served to release class resentment. The submariner's descriptions of the "pretty Jewess" not only focused on her pleasant looks and demeanor but also revealed details about her clothes and education—indicators of what once was an elevated social status, now rendered absurd in the world at war. Similar sentiments also permeated another airman's description of the conditions he witnessed in an Austrian labor camp for Jews, where formerly sophisticated Viennese Jews clashed with their eastern European counterparts as much as they did with the squalor of their new circumstances:

> I was in a punishment camp, which contained eight hundred Jews. . . . There were Jewish camp police with white armbands, perfectly dressed, with excellent cut breeches and riding boots. Jewish camp police—with heavy whips—they thrashed their own Jews. The actual camp commandant was a Viennese Jew. He told me he too was an officer, in the last war, and had already had charge of various camps to the satisfaction of the SS, and that was why he'd been given this camp. There were famous doctors in there, who were treating their patients in a dirty room. Tiny children were running about; men and women, all together in one hut which held about two hundred people—they were not in individual bunks, but all together. . . . They were all Viennese Jews. In all Jewish camps Viennese Jews are in control as camp police and camp commandants; I don't know why that has been done. They are big, good-looking fellows, with finely chiseled features and so on, not the dirty type of Jews.[37]

The lieutenant went on to illuminate the stark divisions that prevailed within the camp:

> I talked to the Jewish camp commandant and he said, "Look, those are Jews. They're scum, just look at this degenerate, criminal type—they are Eastern Jews. It's acknowledged that we Western Jews are better disciplined and more order-loving. That's why we're in charge." . . . The Jewish camp commandant is always accompanied by six camp police when he does his rounds. "Yes," he

said, "they all hope in their hearts that National Socialism won't win the day."
He was a dirty swine. "But we know it, don't we, sir?" he said to me. There
was nothing one could reply to the fellow. "Of course, these swine here hope
that things will go badly and then I should be the first to be bumped off."[38]

He then continued to describe the strange new world he had witnessed
at the camp: "It's only the people with a trade who have an advantage—the
electricians and so on; they were allowed (to live) with their families. I must
honestly say that there were some marvelous women there, wonderfully
dressed. They were naturally rather shabby, but one could see that they were
fine women, probably from the better classes. A former Czech minister is
knocking about there; unfortunately, I forgot his name."[39]

And finally, the lieutenant returned to the topic of well-dressed, beautiful Jewish women when he described what his father had told him of their
fate in eastern Europe. Though the specific details are rendered unclear in
the transcript, the gist of the story is clear: "When [the Jews] went to work
in the morning—we always had to pass the place on our way to the bombing ground—each morning they came along, old women and men, in separate parties. The women came along, all arm in arm; they were forced to
sing their Jewish songs. You couldn't help noticing some very well-dressed
women among them. They were some really attractive women there. You
could really have called them 'ladies.'"[40]

Perhaps the slaughter of children was the final taboo even among Nazi
Germany's brutal and brutalized combatants. At Posen, Himmler had portrayed today's Jewish children as tomorrow's avengers of the Jewish race. The
1943 CSDIC transcripts do not reveal whether many POWs made this connection. In one of the few accounts that details the mass murder of infants and
children at Lublin, the reporting airman portrayed two types of perpetrators
among the Germans and their collaborators: those who acted on orders but
suffered exquisite moral qualms and monsters who killed infants for sport.
His account, allegedly based on testimony by a fellow POW and unwilling
participant, employed most of the now familiar tropes and imagery: a small
but lethally efficient group of SS perpetrators with rifles rounding up unfathomable numbers of victims—eighty thousand in this case—to torment and
humiliate them. Clad in nothing but underwear, they were robbed of the last
of their property and dignity before surrendering their lives:

He said: "I had to block my ears out with cotton wool. I was half mad afterwards. All I did was to work on the machine gun, but I couldn't bear to watch it any longer. They couldn't kill the little children with machine guns, they weren't yet able to sit up. Then they took them by their legs and smashed them on the ground, so that their heads smashed to the ground etc. Many of them," he said, "were still alive. They fell into the grave. If anyone there took pity on them he took a pistol and shot them dead. The others were left lying there. The next day a few Jews were fetched to shovel them up." He said he was driven practically mad, that's why they released him. He couldn't stand it any longer. Nothing but shooting day after day for thirteen months on end. . . . He said: "I can't sleep even now. I run about this camp at night like a savage. I shall never know any peace till my dying day. They weren't human beings, they were bandits of the worst type."[41]

When Himmler revealed his "terrible secret" at Posen, he had registered emotions only once, namely, during his discussion of the management of Jewish property. In addressing the crowd of SS men, he had explained his strict orders that all Jewish property be handled correctly and that any thefts or other transgressions be punished harshly: "We had the moral right, indeed we had the moral obligation to our nation, to kill these people that wanted to kill us. But we did not have the right to enrich ourselves by taking even a single fur, a watch, a single mark or a cigarette or anything like that."[42] It was a particular point of pride for Himmler that the SS had not descended into material corruption despite ample opportunity.

German POWs were not convinced. The airman so fascinated with denigrated privilege and status in Jewish labor camps was among those who contemplated the fate of Jewish possessions in SS hands. He explained that much of his knowledge of SS conduct in the East had come from his father, who had supervised excavation work near Chełmno (Kulmhof). Initially, his father had also employed Jewish forced laborers there until the SS forced him to surrender them: "All those things I know from my father, how the SS carried out their house to house searches; from the doctors that were there they took away everything, all jewelry, they didn't even stop at wedding rings. [They'd shout,] 'Give it here, you don't need it.'"[43]

Some POWs made a point to portray SS men as both murderers and thieves. For instance, the soldier who had so vividly relayed the killing of eighty thousand Jews at Lublin also claimed that rampant corruption accompanied mass murder campaigns:

> They were just tormenting [the Jews]. The SS special disposal troops carried out all the shootings of the Poles. They marched from place to place and shot people everywhere. . . . As soon as the SS arrived, the Jews were fetched out, put in the marked place somewhere and then were shot in the presence of everyone. They tore all their clothing off them. Then they went to Lodz, what's it called now—Litzmannstadt—they shot 17,000 Jews there, including women and children. . . . First of all, they told the Jews that they were being moved somewhere else, to another camp and that they must take all their possessions with them etc. Then they filched them of all their things. They had seventy pounds of gold there and they had to hand that over. Diamond rings, gold rings, etc.—all that disappeared. The SS-Führer [kept] all that themselves.[44]

Indeed, the allegedly reluctant participant in these atrocities had stolen victims' property: "He said, 'The others have stolen, so I did too.' He said all this in a loud voice, and I was near him." Clearly fascinated with the other man's ill-gained riches, "a gold watch and a diamond ring for which someone had offered RM 6,000," the POW described in great detail what he had learned about the removal of this contraband. He explained that the man had hidden his plunder "in one of his boots," which had two layers of leather and "a little opening at the top so that he could push it in, a gold watch and chain."[45] The account resounds with envy and resentment. Notably, men who did not object to the murder of civilians on moral grounds took an ethical stand on property, if only to complain about their own missed opportunities for plunder.

In the later war years, POWs did not speak often about German-perpetrated atrocities, but when they did, they spoke freely and in great detail.[46] Their stories suggest that mass murder was just as acceptable a topic of conversation in captivity as it had been in the field. Frequently, POWs discussed atrocities in the abstract, suggesting that they assumed a shared store of knowledge so that specifics did not have to be spelled out. By contrast, they tended to describe the mass shootings of the eastern campaign in vivid detail. They also frequently mentioned victim groups from Germany or western Europe that had been transported to the eastern killing fields. And sometimes this included specific references to German Jews as well. As the secondhand chronicler of the SS murder campaign at Lublin explained, for instance, "Well, there were 50,000 Jews in the town who were shot first, and then foreign Jews were brought in, even from Germany etc., whether they were girls or children etc. made no difference."[47]

The murder of German Jews gave some soldiers pause. Ventured one airman, "We ought to leave the decent Jews in Germany. The racial question in Germany is utter nonsense. The whole thing has been carried out too drastically."[48] Elsewhere, another airman pondered the same issue, likely under the influence of British counterpropaganda. He proposed, "If a Jew in Germany has behaved badly, all right turn him out, just as you would anyone else. But one shouldn't go by what race a man belongs to, but by the way he behaves."[49] And elsewhere, another pilot also thought, "In principle, I think we adopted the wrong attitude on the whole of this racial question. It is utter nonsense to say the Jews have nothing but bad qualities."[50] Such conversations suggest that in some cases, their captors' influence undermined previously held antisemitic assumptions. They also suggest, however, that such notions had been held widely and unquestioningly before.

The question of German Jewry proved troublesome for many, perhaps because of the enduring interpersonal ties that Himmler had alluded to at Posen. One SS man, for instance, claimed, "[My family had] still bought things from [the Jews] even after the seizure of power—my parents bought things from them on the black market so to speak. It was all the same to me personally. I hadn't any hatred of the Jewish people." Considerably less credible was his other claim: "In our unit nobody had any hatred for the Jews. I never had anything to do with the execution of Jews or anything like that."[51] Elsewhere, the airman who had remarked that Jewish women "are fine up to twenty-four years old" explained how he had arrived at that conclusion. He confessed that he had dated a Jewish girl in high school, before the Nuremberg Laws of 1935 had stripped German Jews of their citizenship and had prohibited marital and sexual relations between "Jews" and "Germans." When his cellmate inquired whether he had known her to be Jewish, the officer explained, "Yes, I did know, but as a little girl she was in the same class as my sister, and we were together so often." He claimed to have last seen her during a home visit in 1941: "On the next day they had to buy the Star of David. She was at our home the day before that. I happened to be on leave. Then she said: 'Well, Gerd, we shan't see any more of each other now. I must wear the Star now.'"[52] The fact that he remembered his Jewish high-school sweetheart during a conversation about "eight and a half thousand [Jews] being shot at Minsk" suggests that he knew how she may have fared in the eastern killing fields.

At its height, the Holocaust, as told by German POWs in Western captivity, consisted of SS shock troops hunting, herding, taunting, and robbing Jews and other civilians from Germany and all over Europe before executing them in eastern killing fields. In part, this reflected the state of British knowledge. An airman, for instance, chewed over what he had learned during interrogation: "[The interrogating officer] said: 'Do you know how many Poles have been shot? Two million.' That may be true."[53] But the point is that most soldiers could not outright reject the validity of such information because it resonated with their own war experiences and the many tales they had heard.

The situation was different when British intelligence officers confronted soldiers with information about death camps. One airman raged against the English and "all these fairy tales about concentration camps!" His cellmate replied: "They are so stubborn here that they believe whatever a few people who've been in concentration camps tell them."[54] The cellmate's response entailed both a muddled admission that camps operated and denial that they served as killing centers. Indeed, if CSDIC transcripts are any indication, POWs captured in the southern and western theaters of the war rarely spoke of extermination camps, gas chambers, and crematoriums, the pillars of the industrial killing complex in the East that eventually dominated postwar understanding of the Holocaust. In fact, they had not featured in Himmler's exposé at Posen either. At the height of the campaign, information about industrial mass murder appears to have been significantly more restricted than knowledge of mass executions.

Captured SS men were most likely to share stories about extermination camps. For instance, in late December 1943 an SS officer told his cellmate about the "[Auschwitz] concentration camp in Poland." He repeatedly insisted that he really only knew it by hearsay: "I personally haven't seen any concentration camps, apart from [Auschwitz], which I saw from the train. It's not far from Krakow." Thus, securely buffered, he admitted, "It's a hutted camp, for Jews. I've heard say that there's a crematorium there, and that no one who enters the camp comes out alive." When his cellmate asked, "Were mainly Jews sent there?," he responded, "Yes. I should be interested to know what they have done with all the Jews in the Reich, and then the ones from Austria, since they started to get rid of the Jews. I wonder whether they've slaughtered them." His cellmate offered, "I heard from a fellow who was near Lemberg—he was overseer in one of those camps—that they work in quarries in Lemberg. A few hundred are put on at a time. A few collapse each day and they are always shot, and after a few weeks another lot arrives. Not many Jews will have survived."[55]

In another cell, an airman relayed what he had heard about "some concentration camp or other in Poland." He said, "At Lublin the fellows told me they were in a blue funk that the foreign powers would hit upon our communal graves, so they dug out the corpses with dredgers. Near Lublin there is another of those large burial grounds." When his cellmate inquired, "A German burial ground? . . . What did they do with the corpses, burn them?," he answered, "Yes. It reeked of human flesh for weeks. Once they had to fly over there in an aircraft and they actually smelt the smell of burning in the air."[56] Though this account certainly connected fields of corpses to "some concentration camp or other in Poland," the man could not or would not elaborate on the killing methods employed there.

Many POWs suspected something of industrial killing methods. Especially their more outlandish tales of murder in the East suggest that some suspected that *something* other than tommy guns was used to make the Jews "disappear from the earth." For instance, the Luftwaffe lieutenant with such detailed knowledge of Austrian labor camps for Jews explained to his cellmate what he had heard about the fate of some of the Jews transferred east: "The story went around that they were simply driven into a sort of reservoir. Then water was let in and ran out at the other end. By then there was nothing left of them at all." He then expressed as much sympathy for the perpetrators as he did for the victims, all the while securing his own alibi:

> The number of young SS fellows who had nervous breakdowns simply because they could carry on with it no longer! There were some real thugs amongst them too. One of them told my father he didn't know what he'd do when all the Jews were dead. He had got so used to it he could no longer exist without it. I couldn't do that either. I simply couldn't. I could kill fellows who had committed crimes, but women and children—and tiny children! The children scream and everything. The only good thing is that they took the SS and not the armed forces for that.[57]

The Luftwaffe sergeant who had witnessed the roundup of Jews in Paris also shared a story of their fate in the East. He claimed he had learned about it from "some garrison duty man who had worked in a Russian [POW] camp for a long time in the Generalgouvernement." With these buffers installed, he ventured to describe how the Parisian Jews were made to literally "disappear from the earth" in special delousing cells:

> "Yes," he said, "the transports arrived at our place. I was beyond Warsaw near Deblin, and they arrived there and were deloused and that was the end of it." I said, "[W]hy deloused? If a man comes from France he doesn't need to be de-loused." "Well," he said, "they are transit camps for soldiers coming from the eastern front, they are deloused there and then go on leave; and the Jews from the west go to these delousing camps too. There are large tanks there, only the Jews had a different delousing mixture in their bathing tanks. It takes perhaps half an hour to an hour, when there are about 200 men in it, and then you can't find anything but a few gold teeth, rings or something, everything else has been dissolved. That is drained off. . . ." That was the way they de-loused the Jews! They put them into baths, he said, and once they are all in, an electric current is passed through the whole then; that knocks them over and then the acids are added which dissolve the whole damned lot completely. Of course, it made my hair stand on end![58]

Whether framed as hard facts, eyewitness accounts, hearsay, or rumors, information about mass killings had traveled east to west, across branches and ranks among the German armed forces. In Sönke Neitzel and Harald Welzer's words, "Knowledge about what had been happening in Russia since 1941 and what had precedents in Poland was . . . common, far beyond the circle of perpetrators and observers. Transmission of rumors is a particularly fast and interesting medium when reports are outlandish, secrecy is desired, and the scope of information is limited."[59] This was also true when it came to the transmission of knowledge between military and civilian populations.

As seen before, in the aftermath of the German defeat at Stalingrad, members of the German military and civilian populations exchanged all information with urgency and purpose for a "truthful" reading of the war situation despite official prohibitions. The POW outraged over his country's enslavement at the hands of the SS continued: "When Germans asked us if it was true about atrocities in Poland, we had to say that it was only a rumor. I am convinced that it's all too true. It's a shameful blot on our history."[60]

Others were not so reticent about relaying what they had heard or seen in the killing fields in the East. Indeed, the fact that civilians were routinely inquiring about atrocities, thus circumventing military regulations and news blackouts. suggests they already knew or suspected something of *that*. Still, rumors and stories about mass atrocities often had a detrimental impact on home-front morale. A December 1942 report from SD Schwabach, for instance, stated plainly that "at the beginning of the month a depressed popular mood prevailed, caused largely by the tales of front-line soldiers." The report went on to explain, "Peasants and religious circles are very disturbed by news from Russia that speak of mass shootings and extermination of Jews."[61] By 1943, such information was traded widely, in Schwabach and beyond. This was also the estimation of SD analysts who concluded in a central digest in late July 1943: "It is a commonly voiced opinion that we have ruthlessly exterminated [*ausgemerzt*] our enemies in the East, particularly the Jews. In such estimations the reports from soldiers and other personnel stationed east play a crucial role."[62]

By 1943, Germans at the home front occasionally contemplated the state of the Jewish Question. As information about atrocity trickled in to German civilian society, people began to gather rumors and hearsay over the course of the year that eventually amounted to a quite accurate understanding of the fate of German and European Jewry. By the following year, the crumbling security apparatus captured some of the results. In November 1944, SD Stuttgart reported, for instance, that people openly discussed the situation: "We have slaughtered Jews by the thousands," and "Soldiers tell again and again that Jews in Poland had to shovel their own graves. And what did we do with the Jews who were in concentration camps in Alsace?"[63]

German combatants were not the only source of information on the Holocaust. Evidence had spilled out of Nazi-occupied Europe since 1939, and by late 1942 the Allied governments and media stopped turning a blind eye.[64] As part of the Anglo-American effort, British media published several reports about anti-Jewish and other atrocities against civilian populations at the time. On December 17, 1942, Anthony Eden, at the time Winston Churchill's trusted confidant in the British Foreign Office, publicly condemned such practices in an address to the British Parliament. The BBC and other national and international news outlets repeatedly echoed his declaration in the following months, eliciting worldwide protests against Nazi practices, though few understood the full extent of the murder campaign.[65] Referencing this coverage on Christmas Eve 1942, an imprisoned submariner told his cellmate, "It says in the newspaper that the Nazis intend to shoot all the Jews in Europe. That would be quite good, but we haven't got enough ammunition. What an outcry they are making here, just because a few Jews are shot."[66]

For Reich propaganda minister Goebbels, the Allies' public condemnations posed a serious policy problem. Though it is not clear how far into the Reich this information actually traveled, Nazi leadership seems to have shared the estimation of BBC monitors who believed that "black-listening is a very wide-spread habit" among German civilians and the military.[67] The fact that Goebbels felt obligated to engage suggests that he feared wide dissemination and negative repercussions not just from Germany's enemies but also from its own people.

Unable to refute the charges that German occupation regimes were committing mass crimes, Goebbels embarked on a two-pronged propaganda counteroffensive in late 1942. On the one hand, he instructed the German press to sensationalize all accounts of Allied atrocities, real and imagined.[68] On the other hand, after official silence on "the Jewish Question" had accompanied the anti-Jewish blitzkrieg of 1942, he launched a reinvigorated antisemitic propaganda campaign toward the end of the year.[69] Surprised by the aggressive tone, BBC monitors took note: "Apart from its functions as a diversion and as justification for Hitler's unaltered intention to eliminate all the Jews in Europe, this particular campaign may be meant as a counter-blast to the increasing publicity given by our broadcasts to the measure of the Jews in Poland; a reminder, as it were, of the desirability of carrying through the anti-Semitic campaign to the end, whatever the world says against the plan."[70]

In fact, Goebbels pursued another goal. While reminding the German people of the necessity of exterminating the Jews, he needed to impress on them that they were forever implicated in the mass murder committed in their name. Final victory was the only way to escape retribution. Thus, months before Himmler leveraged complicity among the Nazi elite at Posen, Goebbels had started the same process for all of German society, implicating the German nation in the ongoing genocide without revealing actual details. The effectiveness of this approach depended entirely on how much the German people already knew. In making his case for "total war" at the Sport Palace, for instance, Goebbels conjured an enemy force that was as frightening as it was fantastical. He explained that "the revolt of the steppes" threatened to flood into Germany and turn it into a Jewish-Bolshevist wasteland. Fighting such a fiend justified any and all means: "Jewry is a contagious infection. Enemy nations may raise hypocritical protests against our measures against Jewry and cry crocodile tears, but that will not stop us from doing that which is necessary. Germany, in any event, has no intention of bowing before this Jewish threat, but rather intends to act at the right moment, using if necessary the most total and radical measures to deal with Jewry."[71]

Victor Klemperer was among the few Germans who reacted to this threat. He relegated his summary of "totalizing measures" to parentheses, like an afterthought: "(Closure of luxury hotels and bars, ban on riding in the Tiergarten, universal labor service, heavier burdens placed on civil servants, no right to holiday)."[72] For him and his oppressed Jewish peers, "total war" raised the specter of escalated persecution: "The speech contains a threat to proceed against the Jews, who are guilty of everything, with the 'most draconian and radical measures' if the foreign powers do not stop threatening the Hitler government because of the Jews." In the aftermath of the Sport Palace rally that had so energized many other Germans, several of Klemperer's friends had become "very depressed," and Klemperer himself was inclined to take an alarmist acquaintance's "opinion and warning completely seriously."[73] The direction of German war policy as outlined by Goebbels boded ill for the dwindling number of Jews inside the Reich.

Like Klemperer, those Jews who remained inhabited a shadow world of poverty, isolation, and fear. Largely hidden from view, they received little attention from their "Aryan" counterparts. Occasionally, the SD recorded public expressions of compassion. For instance, on February 27, 1943, an SD agent in Höxter reported on the Jew Hartwig Israel Stein, who had not yet been "sent to the East" because of his marriage to an "Aryan woman." The wife's recent passing meant the end of the protection the unit had afforded Stein. The author urged that Stein quickly be "shipped to a ghetto east." An anonymous letter written on his behalf demonstrated that he "still commands certain sympathies among the Aryan population."[74]

Nazi morale monitors most commonly charged that "religious circles" harbored pro-Jewish sympathies. The SD office in Bielefeld, for instance, reported on February 24, 1943, that a "full Jewess" (Volljüdin) by the name of Elise Krebs had been baptized in the Paderborn cathedral. After several months of investigation, local authorities still did not know the identity of the responsible priest. According to the report, party members were rendered apoplectic by the incident. They believed "clerics intended it as a deliberate stab in the Führer's back against the National-Socialist worldview."[75] Occasionally, church leaders publicly condemned the Nazi regime's antisemitic persecution. SD Schwabach reported on March 3, 1943, that the local pastor Heller had proclaimed, "It is not true that Jesus was an Aryan; Jesus was of Jewish descent. It is therefore not right to persecute or exterminate, because it is the foundation of Catholicism."[76] At times morale monitors were exasperated to find "national comrades" even among the general population "who do not want to believe that the Jews had wanted this war and therefore bear the blame for it."[77] In Rothenburg, party representatives had to report in October 1943 that "the tale of the good Jew is currently circulating again."[78]

But for every expression of compassion, home-front morale monitors also recorded expressions of virulent antisemitism. At a time when the Nazi regime pushed to render towns "free of Jews," for instance, there were some who feared the subversive influence of the Jews who still remained. The Nazi Party district leadership (*Kreisleitung*) in Nördlingen, for instance, reported on May 10, 1943, that people "cannot understand that Jews still run around. . . . It is no wonder when rumors constantly swirl. Jews are bound to antagonize against Germany by deliberately spreading rumors."[79] Others wondered whether it had not been a mistake to "allow the Jews leave the Reich." The party office in Eichstätt reported in December 1943, "Here and there people voice the opinion that the Führer made his biggest mistake back in the day when he allowed the Jews to leave Germany. Today they act against us. There are still Jews in the occupied territories, and they are operating against us."[80]

Dread of Jewish vengeance reverberated in German wartime society just as it did in Allied POW camps. SD Schwabach, for instance, reported bluntly that soldiers' atrocity tales had depressed popular mood not because of compassion for the victims. They caused "great fear, worry, and anxiety" because "in the opinion of wide circles of the rural population, it is not certain yet that [Germany] will win the war and that the Jews will exact a terrible revenge when they return."[81] A local NSDAP cell near Rothenburg reported in October 1943, "One hears often that the Jews were treated too harshly at the hands of the party. This is coming to haunt us today."[82] In 1943, a member of the NSDAP office in Waigolshausen reported on a three-hour political discussion with a devout farmer, which "shows clearly the tendency prevalent in such circles": "Without Hitler no war—our battle against the Jews caused the current escalation of the war; Bolshevism isn't as bad as it is being portrayed—doubting victory—and if the regime interferes in religion there will be a riot."[83]

A curious tale circulating in southern Germany also suggests that popular knowledge of the Final Solution resulted from rumors, eyewitness accounts, and foreign and Nazi propaganda. According to a report by the Upper and Middle Franconian district administrator (*Regierungspräsident*) from January 8, 1943, people in Württemberg claimed that "Jews from the area work as commissars in the Bolshevist army in exile. They have helped German POWs escape. A former Jewish cattle trader from the area around Ellwangen and one from Crailsheim are said to have acted this way."[84] Similar rumors were still swirling in April, when the party district leadership in Nuremberg reported on Catholics in the Pretzfeld vicinity:

> A member of a Franconian troop contingent . . . escaped with a few comrades from Stalingrad. Retreating to join German troops, he passed through a village where someone called his name. The caller, a Jew, asked him whether he didn't recognize him. [The Jew] said his name was so and so and back home he used to sell him cattle. The Jew, a Bolshevist commissar, asked the soldier where he was trying to go . . . and then showed him and his comrade the right direction [to join other German troops] and let him go without any harm. People say that the Jew explained that there was no real animosity toward Bavaria, only against Prussia and especially against the SS.[85]

Reports from the southwestern regions suggest that people there commonly harbored hope that Jewish vengeance was aimed predominantly at the "Prussian" aggressors. The SD office in Friedberg reported on May 14, 1943, that people in Swabia believed Allied air raids to be the key indicators: "The enemy only wants to destroy Prussia. The objection that Bavarian towns too have had to stand bombings is countered by the assertion that too many Prussians are currently living there. The Augsburg synagogue alone guarantees that the enemy will spare Augsburg."[86] Whereas elsewhere people wished for Jews as human shields from Allied bombs, the Swabians expected the remaining Jewish institutions to serve in a similar capacity. Clearly, Goebbels's atrocity propaganda was deeply rooted in such assessments, though people appropriated it in surprising ways, depending on their needs.

The success of Goebbels's propaganda is most apparent in the seemingly widespread belief that Jews were escalating the air war to avenge their own destruction. Such responses betray the mixture of antisemitic indoctrination and guilt that made contemplations of the Jewish Question so compelling in 1943. As people dreaded the Jewish-Bolshevist "revolt of the steppes" of Nazi propaganda, they also feared the righteous vengeance of a brutalized people. When British bombers targeted dams in the Rhine region during Operation Chastise, for instance, German propaganda portrayed it as an "act of Jewish vengeance" (*Akt der Judenrache*).[87] In late May, SD Halle reported that people had followed such reports closely:

> The Jewish plan stimulates increased anti-Jewish sentiments. Proclamations from Delitz workers encapsulate this reaction: "All remaining Jews in Germany should be hanged in retribution." "Kill the Jews." On the other hand, others among the population registered the opposite reaction. People in Halle express opinions [that the] government and the NSDAP acted irresponsibly to deploy such [drastic] measures against the Jews. The coming Jewish vengeance will be awful and it is solely the government's fault. If the German side hadn't attacked the Jews, there would already be peace.[88]

Goebbels must have been despondent to find that his campaign to instill "strength through fear" was effective and counterproductive at once.[89] Though the notion of Jewish vengeance was shared widely, at least some Germans attributed it not to Jewish malice but to crimes perpetrated by the German government. As the party office in Rothenburg reported on October 22, 1943, "The first day of the Anglo-American terror attacks has depressed and frightened people.... National comrades commonly speculate that these terror attacks are a consequence of the measures taken against the Jews."[90]

One of the most commonly expressed opinions linked the Allied bombing campaign to the destruction Jews suffered during the Night of Broken Glass (Kristallnacht), the state-instigated pogrom on German soil in November 1938. After the bombing of Cologne, for instance, the SD central digest reported in July 1943: "There are also voices that connect the bombing of the cathedral of Cologne with the destruction of synagogues back in the day and the wrath of God."[91] The party office in Waigolshausen reported in August 1943: "What recently goes around in certain circles is the idea that fire rains on German towns and churches because [someone] had burned down the synagogues a few years ago."[92] And SD Würzburg reported on September 9, 1943, "In regard to the air war people say that it is in retribution for our conduct against the Jews in November 1938. People are also wondering whether the Jews would reclaim their apartments after we lose the war. In such talks, people refer to the fact that definite Jew cities [*ausgesprochene Judenstädte*] have been spared."[93] In October 1943, SD Schweinfurt reported that the ongoing bombing of German cities commanded the full attention of the rural population. Elderly Catholics, especially, believed the bombings were directly connected to the events of 1938. In the words of one local informant, "In the last few days the rumors circulated that Burgpreppach, Ermershausen, and Hassfurt will soon be bombed because Jews once had businesses there. According to a similar rumor, the Jew Eckmann, who used to live in Lendershausen near Hofheim, allegedly claimed before his deportation that the Jews will return by 1944. Apparently, people take this to mean that we are coming to an end and by 1944 it will be over with us."[94]

Kristallnacht had been a Nazi public relations debacle both abroad and domestically. Widespread popular criticism of the wanton destruction had been instrumental in shaping the regime's bureaucratic, semisecret approach to Jewish persecution. Even five years later, the memory ran deep in German society, however, perhaps in part because this most ostentatious display of antisemitic violence made it impossible to deny any knowledge of persecution. Faced with the destruction of their own homes in 1943, Germans recalled the destruction of Jewish property, the starkest indication that the Jews had likely suffered worse in the following years.

Some approached the matter from a decidedly more utilitarian perspective, particularly when it came to the question of Jewish property. The regime housed bombing victims in former Jewish apartments and houses. As seen before, people knew whose living space they occupied and feared they would be evicted if and when the Jews returned. Others were haunted by memories of things wantonly destroyed. SD Bad Brückenau reported, "Here and there one hears again that the measures taken against the Jews in 1938 were a mistake. The things that were destroyed then would be very useful today."[95]

Indeed, the fate of Jewish property seems to have captured people's imagination more than the fate of the Jews themselves. Reported SD Kitzingen in September 1943, about a civil servant who had complained:

"The rotten thing about our leaders is that after they exterminated the Jews, they started squatting in their houses and lay their Aryan asses in Jewish beds. Everyone knows how they plundered Jewish apartments for all the expensive rugs and furniture and silver in the dead of night."[96] One month earlier, the office of the Bamberg state courts had issued the following report:

> Given the large number of bombing victims, who have lost everything and often arrive with only the clothes on their backs, people are frequently discussing whether the property of those who have been spared will be seized to provide the homeless with basic necessities. Such discussions frequently raise the question [of] what happened to the furniture etc. of the many Jews that lived in Germany until a few years ago and that overwhelmingly belonged to the better classes. Their furniture would suffice to provide all bombing victims and therefore should be made available. It is an outrage that the people who seized this property for cheap and without any pressing need are allowed to keep their booty.[97]

And the police station in Sandberg reported in July 1943 that resettled bombing victims were spreading alarming tales even in areas of the Reich that had hitherto been spared, illuminating once again how information traveled in wartime Germany: "The local population is constantly preoccupied with the Anglo-American bombing campaign ever since bombed-out residents from Barmen-Wuppertal arrived here. People constantly want to know: Where did the enemy attack last night? How many people may have died? When bombing victims describe their experiences, they suggest that only the Jew can be responsible for such cruelty. The Jew does not like to see his property in Germany now in other people's hands."[98]

Germans habitually and casually expressed antisemitic ideas on a social, economic, and racial continuum, while rejecting the virulent propaganda that had planted at least some of the ideas in the first place. In other words, the available evidence suggests that by 1943 many people had been indoctrinated so deeply that they believed their ideas to be self-evident and logical, entirely unrelated to klutzy propaganda attempts. Reported the Party Chancellery on May 1943, "Overall people consider the propaganda too stiff and inflexible. . . . For instance, the anti-Semitic press campaign has begun so suddenly and is so exaggerated that it probably does not have an effect on the German people."[99] The report had been written in the aftermath of Operation Chastise, the British bombing attack on the Möhne and Edersee dams that caused catastrophic flooding in the Ruhr valley in May 1943. It explained that people were deeply disturbed by the failure of the Luftwaffe to prevent Allied advances into the Ruhr airspace, but they considered "dams, floodgates, etc." to be conventional and therefore justifiable targets in the escalating air war. Unlike the destruction of German cities, therefore, the Möhnetal catastrophe was no "Jewish-inspired abomination" but merely a manifestation of Allied air superiority.[100]

Elsewhere, Goebbels was more successful. His propaganda campaign had floundered until the discovery of mass graves at Katyn and the outbreak of the Warsaw ghetto uprising fell into his lap in April 1943. With Hitler's blessing, the Nazi media descended on the events to portray "Jewish-Bolshevist savagery" in vivid detail and remind the German people "it was high time to eliminate the remaining Jews from the General Government as quickly as possible."[101] The people took note. So did the BBC:

> During April, the promising beginnings of the Katyn Forest campaign led the Germans to give it pride of place even in their home service; the detailed descriptions of the corpses and the development of the situation in all its ramifications—antisemitism, anti-Bolshevism, Anglophobia, etc.—helped to take the people's minds off the air raids and the successive defeats of the Afrika Korps. Another use, in addition to its value as a grand diversion, made of this story was perhaps as the counterweight to our own increased propaganda about the extermination of the Jews. . . . A few attempts to repeat the success of the Katyn Forest story were made . . . but all of these attempts tailed off, and the propagandists returned to proving that Katyn and the RAF [Royal Air Force] air raids were manifestations of the same spirit of Jewish bestiality.

The BBC analyst then concluded:

> No reliable evidence of the German public's reaction to all this propaganda is available. From what is known of its attitude to Goebbels' propaganda in general, it seems probable that only the stupidest members of the public will have attached great importance to the details provided so copiously. But letters written by Germans, and the testimony of many neutral observers, make it clear that, however overdone they may be, anti-Bolshevism and antisemitism will strike a responsive chord in the heart of most Germans. Next to the horror at German losses, horror at the nature of Russians—their alleged cruelty, backwardness, brutishness—and fear of Russian victory are the chief features of the German attitudes.[102]

Katyn did capture the popular imagination for many reasons summarized by the BBC monitor. Nazi morale monitors agreed that Germans were sincerely shocked and disturbed by what they learned. According to an SD central digest from April 4, 1943,

> The sensational news of the discovery of mass graves in the Katyn forest preoccupied large numbers of national comrades. Numerous morale reports testify to this fact and all agree on the following:
>
> 1. A not insignificant number of national comrades who had recently come under the influence of mottos like "The Soviets aren't as bad as they are being portrayed," and whose feelings of hatred and fear of Bolshevism had been weakened, have had those feelings revived. The fate of the 12,000 Poles is understood as an example of what large segments of the German population would suffer in case of a Russian victory.
> 2. Relatives of soldiers at the eastern front, especially among relatives of officers missing since Stalingrad, are extremely anxious that the Soviets will do the same to them as they did to the Polish officers.[103]

According to the office of the Swabian district president, the news inspired some farmers to "treat their Polish and Russian farmhands better even than their own compatriots."[104] However, the campaign had an unintended consequence. According to the Swabian report, the Katyn propaganda campaign also led people to discuss the treatment of the Jews in Germany and in the eastern territories."[105] Indeed, according to the central digest, a large number of people of "intellectual or devout persuasion" felt that it was "'strange' or even 'hypocritical' that the German propaganda now has 'a heart for Poles.' . . . '[W]e have no right to make a fuss about Soviet measures, because Germany has eliminated a much larger number of Jews and Poles.'" According to the author, this was a proclamation representative of this type of thinking: "If I did not know that all means are justified in the fight for the nation's existence, I would not be able to stand this hypocritical display of empathy for the Polish officers."[106] SD Brückenau reported that there are voices among the rural population that say, "We haven't done it any different with the Jews, when we too eliminated a dangerous enemy."[107] And later the same office reported, "Large segments of the population understand the extermination of Polish officers as a radical extermination of a dangerous enemy, which is unavoidable in war. This is similar to the Anglo-American bombing of German cities and even to our own war of extermination against Jewry."[108]

In 1943, the first year of German total mobilization, the world at war was a setting for German-perpetrated atrocities as well as a setting for their emerging popular representations, myths, and alibis, many of which reverberated for decades in German postwar society. Today, we understand that "information is different from knowledge."[109] The available evidence suggests that, by 1943, rumors about mass murder and atrocities circulated widely among German civilian and military populations, even those with no first-hand experience of the eastern front. If information on industrial killing methods was scarce, mass shootings were a not uncommon topic of conversation. In their discussions against the backdrop of an increasingly exacting war with an ever more tenuous outcome, German perpetrators and bystanders occasionally framed mass shootings of Jewish and other civilian populations as legitimate acts of war. More frequently, they matter-of-factly acknowledged that mass killings occurred under the cover of war, perpetrated by the SS or others. Such alibis first forged under the crisis conditions of the final war years endured for decades. At the same time, the often-agonizing tales of women and sometimes children in the killing fields also betrayed a real understanding of the extraordinary nature of these events.

The same is true of the outlandish rumors about industrial killing methods: Germans knew enough of what was happening in the East to entertain notions of even the most bizarre means of mass murder. They knew to know that in their world at war, anything could, and indeed did, happen. Enough information circulated to support the common dread that the German nation had assumed an indelible "blood guilt" for which it would be made to pay in case of defeat and for which it could never atone. However, just as Germans in all strata of wartime society grappled in whatever limited forms with their own culpability for the events of this extraordinary war, they also reimagined themselves as future victims and reimagined their victims as future perpetrators. Interestingly enough, then, as the tide of war turned in 1943, and as the conflict became ever more lethal and destructive for the German nation, many considered the continuation of the war ever more urgent. The world at war was no longer merely the setting for German-perpetrated atrocities. It also became the only setting that could provide any meaningful protection from the consequences of such crimes, including counter-atrocities and other acts of vengeance that Germans imagined would be pursued by their victims and their descendants after a German defeat.

Figure 1. German soldiers enjoying exercise and games at the beach in northern France, fortifications of the Atlantic Wall in the background; summer of 1943; BA-BA photo no. 101I-M1015-331.

Figure 2. Civilians sit in a mine shaft serving as a shelter during an Allied air raid in the Ruhr region; ca. 1943; BA-BA photo no. 183-R71086.

Figure 3. Civilians reinforcing a public air-raid shelter in Berlin; August 2, 1944;
BA-MA photo no. 183-J30283.

Figure 4. A procession of German soldiers captured with the fall of Aachen; fall 1944;
NARA photo no. 260-MGG-1061-1.

Figure 5. British soldiers in a liberated Belgian village. Retreating German forces painted this message on a building: "We shall never capitulate"; November 1944; USHMM Photo Archives no. 97474.

Figure 6. A refugee wagon column near Dresden; spring 1945; BA-MA photo no. 183-W0425-015.

Figure 7. German soldiers retreating from the Soviet advance; March 1945;
BA-MA photo no. 183-J28759.

Figure 8. The damaged Brandenburg Gate on the left, the ruins of the Reichstag building
on the right; Berlin 1945; BA-MA photo no. 183-M1015-331.

Chapter 4

Enemies Within and Without

A Sign of Providence

Sometime between 12:40 and 12:50 p.m. on July 20, 1944, an explosion ripped through a briefing room at Wolf's Lair (Wolfsschanze), Hitler's field headquarters near Rastenburg in eastern Prussia. Among those in attendance was Wilhelm Keitel, chief of the Supreme High Command of the Armed Forces. Disoriented and lightly injured, Keitel nonetheless focused his attention immediately, reportedly crying out, "Where is the Führer?" Hitler had suffered a contusion, several abrasions, and two pierced eardrums. He was confused and agitated, and yet, according to several witnesses, he also appeared relieved, muttering that "he had always known that there were traitors around him, and now there was a possibility of rooting out the whole conspiracy."[1]

Over the next twelve hours, chaos ensued in Germany as the Nazi regime stifled a coup attempt carried out by a group of army officers and civilians around Colonel Claus von Stauffenberg, chief of staff of the Reserve Army, and Major General Henning von Tresckow. Most of the conspirators came from the conservative nationalist circles that had initially supported Hitler's revisionist foreign policy and expansionism but had become disillusioned with the disastrous war effort. Stauffenberg had concluded after Stalingrad that removing Hitler, although high treason, was a moral imperative to protect the German nation from impending disaster, and he had planted the bomb at Wolf's Lair before rushing back to Berlin. As rumors of Hitler's survival spread, the plotters' attempts to occupy government buildings and seize key Nazi institutions and radio stations and telephone offices in the capital and beyond unraveled quickly. Stauffenberg was arrested the same evening alongside his adjutant and several other coconspirators.[2] Shortly after midnight, the condemned men were executed by a firing squad in the courtyard of the army headquarters at Bendlerstrasse in Berlin. Tresckow committed suicide the following day.[3]

Rumors and speculations about the unfolding events swirled for hours before the first official announcement reached the German public at 6:30 p.m. via a brief radio address.[4] Finally, at 1:00 a.m. the following morning, Hitler himself addressed the German people over the radio so that, he said, "(1) you may hear my voice and know that I am not injured and am healthy and (2) that you may learn more about a crime that is without precedent in all of German history." His speech was halting and disjointed as he explained how a "small clique of ambitious, unscrupulous . . . and criminally stupid officers" had plotted to kill him and overthrow the Nazi government. Their failure, he claimed, was yet again a sign of divine intervention and evidence that under his leadership the German nation would prevail on its chartered course:

> I am completely free of injury except for a number of small abrasions, contusions and burns. I understand this as a confirmation of Providence, to continue the pursuit of my life goal, as I have done until now. . . . At a time when the German armies are struggling hard . . . there came together a small band that believed it could carry out a stab in the back as in 1918. But this time they were very wrong! . . . I am certain that with the elimination of this tiny clique of traitors and conspirators we will create in the home front—as the backbone of the fighters at the front—the kind of atmosphere that they need. Because it is unthinkable that hundreds of thousands and millions of brave men give their all while at home a tiny clique of ambitious and pathetic creatures constantly try to undermine their stance. . . . Only few people may perhaps fathom what fate would have befallen Germany if today's assassination attempt had succeeded. I myself thank Providence and my creator not for sav-

ing me—my life is nothing but worry and my work is for my people—but I thank him for allowing me to keep carrying this burden and to continue with my work so that I may answer before my conscience with a clear conscience.[5]

Isolated and cut off from the rest of German wartime society, Victor Klemperer did not hear the actual radio broadcast. But later that day, an air raid on Dresden sent him to the "Jews' cellar," where conversation was dominated by rumors of the "sensation," the "attempt on Hitler's life." The following day, he tried to analyze a transcript of Hitler's address. Searching for clues about the impact of the unfolding events, he noted the inherent contradiction in Hitler's claim that the "small clique" of perpetrators had already been squashed and warning of active subversive elements. It gave him hope that perhaps "the liquidated and the hunted down must still hold something they usurped." He speculated that for the Nazi regime, the aborted insurrection might count as "a worse defeat than the loss of a battle or even of a province." To be sure, he noted that "even now it is still not possible to say whether this is really the beginning of the end—how many such beginnings have there been, which then got no further than the beginning!" Later that evening, Klemperer dejectedly concluded, "July 20 will remain an incidental date."[6]

Klemperer misjudged the import of the failed coup. Although it was soon overshadowed by the many other disasters that marked the final war year, the events of July 1944 were not incidental. Instead, they set the stage for the war's brutal end phase. This chapter focuses on voices from the front and the home front during Germany's transition into the battlefield for the Nazi regime's final stand. It examines popular responses to the July plot and to the regime's violent suppression of dissent that followed in its aftermath and that went hand in hand with a structural reorganization of German wartime society and armed forces. It asks how Germans experienced the internal radicalization and mobilization that occurred against the context of visible dissolution. And it explores how these factors converged with the external radicalization of the war that resulted from the dramatic escalation of the Allied air war and its combined impact on the national community as it entered the final year of the war.

Since they began their withdrawals in the South and East in 1943, German forces had given up vast swaths of territory, looting and murdering in retreat and leaving "scorched earth" and ruins in their wake. Nonetheless, by the spring of 1944, the Third Reich still controlled most of Europe, from France in the West to the Black Sea in the East, from Norway in the North to Rome in the South. Over the next few months, however, the situation changed dramatically and undeniably as Allied armies pushed onto Reich territory from all directions. By mid-1944, German morale was at an all-time low, and even Hitler's credibility suffered under the combined impact of unimpeded arial bombings, a successful Soviet summer offensive on the eastern front, and the long-dreaded Allied landing in western Europe.

By early fall, many Germans reckoned with the fact that untold sacrifices and casualties notwithstanding, German armies controlled roughly the same territory as they had shortly after the beginning of the war five years earlier. In response to the setbacks and failures of 1944, Hitler withdrew from public engagements, leaving a vacuum that people filled with anxious speculations about the future course of the war. But if most people resented the regime's crude and transparent wartime propaganda, they had learned to fear the regime's news blackouts even more. Hitler's disappearance boded ill at this low point in the war, and many experienced his silence as deafening.

News of the attempted coup against their elusive führer shattered this anxious state and thoroughly shocked the German nation. But the regime's deft exploitation of the events for propaganda purposes caused a surge of popular goodwill for the führer that muted widespread discontent among military and civilian populations alike.[7] Many who believed themselves encircled by enemies without and infiltrated by enemies within found renewed purpose in the aftermath of the July plot. As Frau Schaaf wrote to Corporal Schaaf in September 1944,

> It is such a shame that Germany is alone in its fight against three major powers, and now, on top of everything, we're being sold and betrayed by our friends. First Italy, then our own bastards, and now the bastards in Rumania. I think the longer this [war] goes on, the more traitors we will discover in places we don't even know yet. That's the same type of betrayal as in [World War I] when Germany was betrayed by Austria in the end. And can we really believe that our armies are free of traitors? They caught many and hanged them, but who can vouch that they got everyone? Let's hope this war ends soon so that all this betrayal comes to an end.[8]

Many Germans experienced the assassination attempt against Hitler as a personal betrayal and an attempted "stab in the back" of the entire nation. In early August 1944, Corporal Habich wrote from the East to Frau Edith Gehm, residing in Vogelbach at Hitler Street No. 1: "All of us here are beside ourselves. We can't believe that they wanted to eliminate the very man who gave us everything. We would not have retreated as far as we did if we had more support. All of [our recent setbacks] are connected to the assassination attempt against our beloved Führer. We are entering a heavy battle now, as it befits a German soldier, a battle till the death."[9] A couple of weeks later, Colonel Heinrich Schmidt reflected in a letter home, "This latest example of July 20 has shown again that God protects the Führer of the Reich for his people. And this is precisely why I have great faith that there can be only one winner emerging from this final stretch."[10] And, joining the chorus of Germans who found their faith in führer and victory reaffirmed after the failed coup attempt, Frau Wagler wrote from Dresden to her deployed husband in September 1944,

> Today, six years ago, there were the first battles in Poland. Those lasted six weeks. After six weeks we achieved the first victory and now, six years later, we're back to the same point. Of course, meanwhile, the German soldiers have defeated many enemies in battle, but the final victory is not in sight yet. But that is not the soldiers' fault but the fault of those who have tried to betray us. Those people have caused so much damage. Until now we have achieved so much, so I believe we will manage the last steep climb. Let's hope for the best. Our Führer has managed all situations up until this point, and that is how it will be going forward. We are anxious because there are reversals everywhere. But the Führer will draw the right conclusions and will discover the right moment for us. I keep wishing [for] when all our enemies get clobbered. I hope that day comes soon.[11]

Throughout 1944, German POWs, too, found reason to reaffirm their faith in a coming German victory. Two airmen discussed the "general morale" in their respective units before capture, with one of them insisting that 100 percent of the men "reckon a German victory." His cellmate tried to make a more reasonable counteroffer, perhaps in preparation for their interrogation: "Well, let's not say 100% but certainly 90%. . . . Of course we shall win, one doesn't worry about it much. One knows that the situation is difficult but one is still confident that it will all come out right in the end. Certainly the outlook is by no means rosy now, that's obvious, but it's actually a question who can hold out longest."[12] But as the year dragged on and German setbacks mounted, some Germans began to wonder how long they would be able to hold out against an overwhelming enemy coalition.

The July plot proved an unexpected gift for the Nazi regime. It provided a welcome distraction, and its perpetrators, the "clique" of treacherous aristocrats, became a perfect foil on which to shift blame for recent reversals. Many Germans gladly accepted this new explanation for the dismal war situation. Throughout the fall of 1944, for instance, German civilians and combatants commonly attributed "the collapse of the western front . . . to the betrayal of July 20," as a Wehrmacht mail censor put it.[13] Sergeant Lembeck shared rumors that Germany's western troops had been widely infiltrated by conspirators and saboteurs. He wrote that as Allied armies advanced on Germany's western borders, "[German troops] did not merely flee in a panic there. No, a not insignificant number of troops defected to the enemy. Frequently even officers. We owe all that to the saboteurs of July 20, many of their supporters were likely stationed in the West."[14] And, echoing many of the commonly expressed sentiments, Fräulein Haas wrote, "There is a lot behind the betrayal of July 20. . . . The betrayal really affected the situation in the West more than the East. Our Wehrmacht has failed in many places because the leadership failed. They drank and carried on. [In the West] our army has been without leadership. Generally, the ones that failed were those who spent all those years lounging around and living the good life."[15]

If Germans eagerly blamed the "July traitors" for recent military setbacks, they also attributed new military successes to the fact that the conspiracy had been rooted out successfully. For instance, Frau Titze reflected on reports about German counteroffensives against Russian armies: "It is really noticeable now that the saboteurs have been eliminated. Only now can you begin to measure the extent of the betrayal at the front. At home, there is a great purging."[16] And Corporal Karl Loose reported from the East to his family: "We just barely escaped the red hell, but now things have settled down and supplies are coming in again. Ever since the Führer wiped out the dirty lot that tried to take his life. We would have never gotten to see our loved ones again if those lords had succeeded in their enterprise. Because of that dirty lot, thousands of brave soldiers have lost their lives. Let's hope that our dear Führer now cleans house so that something like that never happens again."[17]

Not all Germans welcomed the unfolding purge. From the safety of Allied confinement, some German POWs protested against the "Grand Inquisition" happening back home, and their outrage reverberated into 1945. For instance, a General Rothkirch proclaimed on January 3, 1945, three days after his capture at Bitburg: "Just imagine those good people in Germany who were detained for examination! The Generals! I've spoken to them myself."[18] However, German POWs were far more likely than their peers back home to voice criticism of the Nazi regime and even of Hitler himself, both before and after the thwarted July plot.

While the regime exhorted ever greater sacrifices from its civilians and military populations, some POWs began to wonder whether the führer really had charted the self-destructive course first announced after Stalingrad. While many had vowed to carry on "until the bitter end," German military directives took on an ever more radical, self-destructive tone. For instance, on September 16, 1944, Hitler ordered that the German forces in the West fight until the last man: "Every bunker, every block of houses in a German town, every German village, must become a fortification in which the enemy bleeds to death or the occupiers are entombed in man-to-man fighting."[19] In captivity, Lieutenant Goltz discussed the "much disputed order of the Führer's that he expected of every German that he would let himself be buried in the ruins of his house, and on in that strain, or even more so. . . . Even the fanatical Party men were horrified at that order, it was so severe and so grossly worded."[20] At home, too, many soldiers recoiled as the idea of "fighting until the bitter end" ceased to be an abstraction and became the actual lived experience of German troops and civilians. Corporal Karl Hofbeck, for instance, wrote to his parents: "No one feels up to [fighting] anymore. The rank-and-file soldier is being corralled into holding the front. The [new] laws are so extreme, one feels like a slave."[21]

An exchange between an army general by the name of Eberbach and an SS commander named Meyer illuminates common popular anxieties about Hitler's unstable mind and its impact on the course of the war. Both men had been captured in the late summer of 1944, and sharing a cell several months later they contemplated the odds of a brokered peace in the West, much like what many of the July plotters had hoped to achieve after Hitler's removal. Both agreed that they knew of no German military commander powerful and courageous enough to take such steps against Hitler's will. Moreover, they believed that the führer continued to command loyalties among all ranks of the armed forces. Eberbach explained, "Their allegiance to the Führer, of whose failure they are ignorant, is so strong that if you were to present them today with those ideas they'd only say: 'There is something the matter with him, he has been infected with British propaganda.'" Meyer agreed: "In my opinion the Führer hasn't been quite himself since the winter of 1941 and 1942, as a result of all the happenings. He gets some sort of attacks of hysteria. Despite all that I must say, that he has achieved an incredible amount after Germany collapsed and even if the whole Reich collapses once more, he is responsible for a tremendous awakening in the German people; he gave them back their self-confidence." Eberbach concluded:

> It won't survive this collapse. There is so much false pathos and fundamental wrongness in what he taught the German people. Despite all that I'll admit that much of National Socialism—not in the form and shape in which Hitler's program presents it—but in its fundamental ideas, has passed beyond the frontiers of Germany and is alive in Europe and the world. Perhaps that was the mission decreed by Providence. . . . But with us, as is unfortunately always the way with Germans, it was carried to extremes, as in everything, and it ran itself to death.[22]

There were very few among the active German forces or at the home front who dared speak critically of Hitler. Corporal Josef Tobisch was an extreme outlier when he wrote of his wish that the July plot had succeeded so that the war could end: "If only it had worked with Hitler, everything would be over already. . . . You can't call this life anymore. There is no vacation, so you lose all motivation. And anyway, no one is interested in this deceitful business anymore. Those [Nazi] liars and crooks really made idiots out of us stupid Sudeten Germans in 1938. I'm just glad I'm not in the party because when things go bad, those party bosses can brace themselves for a reckoning."[23]

By contrast, many Germans in the field and at the home front truly believed in Hitler as a divinely appointed and protected leader who would lead them to victory. Letters between front and home front abounded with abject gratitude for his survival. As Sergeant Walter Gläser wrote in a letter from September 1944, "Providence has put its protective hand over our dear Führer. [The conspirators] have achieved the exact opposite [of their goal] because now we will smash our enemies even more violently. The entire nation is rising up in order to fight for victory. Nothing will stand in our way, we can only win!"[24]

People's faith remained intact even as evidence of imminent collapse mounted. As Frau Schumacher wrote in a letter to her deployed husband in September 1944, "It doesn't look rosy in the West but the English and Americans will have their comeuppance because our Führer knows what he is doing. He will not allow our ruin. Don't you think so, too . . . ? So let us not lose our hope and faith in victory."[25] Elfriede Götz echoed this common refrain when she wrote, "Nevertheless, everything must and will turn out all right. I am absolutely certain that it will. I have to tell you, the more critical the situation, the stronger is my confidence in our victory because I tell myself that the Führer knows what he wants."[26]

If Hitler's survival in July 1944 restored many Germans' faith in "Führer and final victory,"[27] they also welcomed the violent crackdown on its aftermath, which amounted to the largest purge of the German political and military apparatus since the Nazi "seizure of power." Indeed, the events invigorated the home front. Official explanations for the repression drew on long-standing class resentments and widespread anxieties about "another stab in the back." Organized by Himmler and fueled by extreme paranoia, this massive sweep of the military and civil establishments of German wartime society ultimately led to the arrest of several thousand people. Among those incarcerated were a large number of family members and friends of the men implicated in the July plot as the Nazi terror apparatus escalated its enforcement of "clan liability" (*Sippenhaft*) in the final war year. Importantly, observers reacted to Nazi terror not with fear but with relief. As Fräulein Kinne wrote from Gross-Schierstedt in September 1944,

> The war in the West has assumed shapes that no one would have believed before. The enemy is near the border. And if we are unable to stop them, they will roll through German territory as if it was ordained. It is all the traitors' fault. Sometimes you lose faith in the honesty of people because it is hard and bitter to be so let down. What I don't understand is that the powers that be did everything to prevent a mutiny among the little people, but no one cared to look at the elites. So far all the traitors were members of the [upper classes], and nothing has changed. Why does no one inspect and control those [elites] but only ever [does so of] the little people? . . . I hope they have learned to keep an eye on those who have power.[28]

The Nazi regime not only instigated a massive terror campaign to root out alleged saboteurs and defeatists in the national community; it also reorganized its own ranks into what Joseph Goebbels called an "internal war dictatorship" after Hitler finally agreed to many of the radical mobilization measures his propaganda minister had long agitated for. Much of the power for this new phase in the war effort was vested in a ruthless and ambitious "quadrumvirate," consisting of Martin Bormann, head of the Nazi Party Chancellery, now imbued with immense power over the regional defense of the Reich; Heinrich Himmler, now in control of all instruments of home-front military forces and instruments of terror; Goebbels as the new plenipotentiary for total war in charge of home-front mobilization; and Albert Speer, the minister of armaments charged with keeping the German war economy from collapsing.[29] Together, they escalated the regime's political, economic, and social control over all aspects of German life and death in war. In the military sphere, this meant that the armed forces and Waffen-SS were structurally fused. On the home front, party administrators were empowered to mercilessly corral the people into service and root out shirkers. Both penal and military law were drastically reshaped to punish alleged defeatists and saboteurs. The regime also stepped up its indoctrination and propaganda campaigns abroad and at home to impress all members of the German militarized community to fight until the bitter end.[30]

Available evidence suggests that many people initially welcomed these new "totalizing measures," hoping they would be enforced equitably for the full mobilization of all national resources. A Wehrmacht censorship digest of September 1, 1944, claimed, "The orders for the execution of total war meet with excited consent. At the same time there is the question [of] why these measures to utilize all reserves for war and labor have not long been implemented. There has been talk of 'total war' since Stalingrad, but nothing has been done."[31]

The prospect of "total war" restored popular hopes for a German victory among civilians and combatants alike in late 1944. Many at the home front vowed to do everything in their power to support the newly invigorated war effort. Frau Schmidt wrote in mid-September 1944, "You know I have volunteered for war service for five years now and am doing my duty for my home. Now I am here and support the great challenge for the construction of the [eastern border fortifications]. Every day I go to work, shovel over my shoulder, despite my arm and everything else. I am proud that I get to help and make things a little easier for our soldiers out there."[32] Similarly, Frau

Kammsee vowed her unwavering support for the war effort and the culmination of the National Socialist revolution:

> The home front is holding strong until the end. You hear some unreasonable idiots say we don't need to do all this. But thank goodness there are men here who are teaching these cowards a lesson, sometimes even with harsh methods as it seems. In Germany's hardest hour we will come out all right because there are men here like your father who at 63 years old never waivers and steadfastly maintains his faith in the nation and Führer and gladly fulfills his duties. Thank God there are many [like him] and that the [National Socialist] education of the past . . . years was not for naught.[33]

As the summary of German wartime mail from the fall of 1944 suggests, popular hopes for an equal distribution of the burdens of war soon clashed with a disappointing reality. While many civilians proudly reported on their own tireless contributions to home-front mobilization, others buckled under the relentless, exhausting drudgery. As Colonel Gerhard Bischof replied in a letter back home in September 1944, "As I can see from your letter, there is much to do at home. It seems you only have work and more work but why and for what?"[34] Most people believed that members of the upper classes did not contribute their share. In July 1944, Corporal Herbert Wolf responded angrily to the news that "now even women up to the age of 50 have to register with the labor service" and remarked that "things just keep getting crazier, they keep squeezing the last reserve from the people." What upset him most was his suspicion that "officers' wives and those of the higher civil servants" likely would find ways to evade the new directives: "Total war is only for the working class, because Frau Dr. Weidner continues to sit around at home and if she has to she gets a sick certificate. . . . My dearest little woman, you can imagine how these and other injustices are eating me up. Many others feel the same and only hope that this wretched war will soon come to an end for us. Perhaps then we can punish those that have shirked their duty to their Fatherland. If only the Führer should know how much injustice happens on the lower levels."[35]

In response to these perceived inequities, some of the deployed soldiers advised "their women to refuse total labor deployment," as a Wehrmacht Field Post censor lamented in the fall of 1944.[36] However, many could not escape the clutches of civil mobilization, and even those who entered willingly into their "duties" experienced the burdens of home-front mobilization as crushing. And popular anger and resentment over the burdens of the war grew as evidence of their uneven and ineffectual distribution mounted. Frau Liedke vented her frustration with the privileges of the home army in a letter from Berlin- Niederschöneweide to her deployed husband. Furious that her letters were not being delivered and that she was no longer allowed to send him packages to the front, even as those safely ensconced at military barracks [at home] were allowed to receive packages of up to twelve pounds, she raged,

> The injustice screams to high heavens. They've been deploying 16- to 60-year-olds for a while now, and they are supposed to achieve our victory! And millions of other [capable men] are sitting pretty in their military barracks and have never seen a battlefield. . . . And those are the ones that wish the war would last until 1975. And they are the ones that get promoted. . . . You know, like that Artur Galen[,] who is constantly traveling between barracks on business trips. Because he is stationed near Cottbus, he was promoted to sergeant. Our clockmaker is home all the time [too]. It is quite a comfortable war for millions, and they get promoted! Meanwhile the workhorse pulling its weight does not get fed.[37]

The idea that members of the old and new elites enjoyed a "comfortable" or "cozy" war (*gemütlicher Krieg*) as late as 1944 rankled those who toiled at the home front and the battlefield, and this common complaint was one of a growing list of popular grievances about the indignities and injustices of the war. Thus, rather than unwavering and unified, the militarized national community became more fractured and polarized than ever before in the final war period. Everyone, it seemed, had a story about the brazen shirkers and profiteers in their midst. They tirelessly complained about the petty party bosses, able-bodied men who had finagled exemptions from military service, deriding "those customers who just have big mouths" while others carried their loads.[38] Fräulein Louis reported in a long letter from Cologne about the latest injustice she witnessed when Herr Volk, her sixty-five-year-old neighbor who suffered from "terrible asthma," was called to build entrenchments in Aachen alongside twelve thousand other conscripts despite the fact that the city had already been evacuated. Her letter expressed common outrage at the blatant corruption and the breakdown of civic norms and orders that marked the chaotic home-front defense in the final war year. It also serves as one of many examples in which Germans told and retold others' wartime stories with the same fervor and investment as they did their own:

> When [the conscripts] got [to Aachen], the party lords gave a big lecture.... They were housed in groups in large factory halls. They did not receive a single crumb in provisions. In the evening, the American artillery attacks started, and half of the "lords" ran off home. The next day some of them returned in bad condition. But as soon as the artillery attack started, the lords faded away and were never seen again. So the [conscripts] made their way back home without leadership and without train tickets. In Aachen and surrounding areas, some handed out food to the [conscript] columns, but many of the people also just plundered the stores because money and food stamps were useless. According to Herr Volk, many made off with shoes, clothes, hats and more that they had robbed. [He told me,] "From all this you can see what a great time this is for us, how there is winning on all fronts, but not by us." Our stores are no longer being stocked well and wherever you go, "evacuation" is what people are talking about.[39]

Throughout the war, home leave had been one of the most coveted commodities for German troops and their families. The fact that the deployed were able to periodically return to their loved ones had significantly shored up civilian and military morale. In the final war year, when regular leave was largely suspended, troops could still apply for home visits to help their families after Allied aerial attacks. However, authorities frequently denied "bombing leave" (*Bombenurlaub*) or "clearance leave" (*Räumungsurlaub*), particularly in the final war year when the Allied air war reached its culmination, creating a perfect recipe for popular resentment and tension. Frau Fischer from Kreuzingen vented her frustration to her deployed husband, who had been denied leave after their home was destroyed: "Apparently the powers that be do not have enough empathy for how a person might feel when they have lost everything. I would like to see what those lords would do if it happened to them, whether they would forgo leave. How strange that Pohl already has 10 days' leave, and he suffered no damage."[40] Frau Kulemann from Düren echoed the same lament that rose wherever Allied bombers wrought destruction: "There are many soldiers here on 'rubble-clearing leave' so that they can help their loved ones, but not you! I guess you have to [stay in the field] so that you can somehow support the easy life of the lords."[41]

And finally, Frau Polzer poured out her anger and exhaustion after fighting a long war at the home front while her husband fought in the field:

> Adolf Beier is already back home again on a ten-day vacation. He was already back here at the beginning of June, and now again! It's infuriating because for you it has been over a year [since your last leave], and you are not allowed to come home[,] while others get to come home and help their women. And I am all alone and have to work and take care of everything by myself. . . . Why is there so much injustice in the world. It has been four years since you left, and that I've been alone with such small children. And I have to tell you I've worked myself to a nub. And you get no leave. If I did not have to mind you and the kids I would have already done myself in because I am tired of living.[42]

The Allied bombing campaign against German cities and industrial centers between March 1943 and March 1944 wreaked havoc and destruction all over the country but failed to "break the will" of the German national community; quite the opposite happened. In the late summer of 1944, the Allies resumed their campaign in earnest, this time with larger payloads that could be deployed with greater accuracy by growing enemy bomber fleets deployed from airfields in liberated western Europe. Of the entire tonnage of Allied bombs dropped on Germany during the war, more than half was unleashed during the aerial attacks of the war's final eight months. The results were devastating. During this period, more than 223,000 German civilians died as their towns and cities were reduced to rubble and firestorms raged through the ruins of the Reich.[43]

The escalating air war had a devastating impact on the morale of the German military and civilian populations. A Wehrmacht censorship digest of September 1944 explained, for instance, that in letters to and from the front, "people wonder in general how things will turn out if the Reich becomes [an] actual battle territory and the continuous Anglo-American air raids don't come to an end. The final and only hope is rooted in expectations for new weapons and people hope they will bring a swift end to the war. . . . It cannot be denied that there is a general hopelessness permeating the home front."[44]

In 1944, Nazi morale and censorship reports abounded with popular resentments against the Nazi Party, deemed corrupt and ineffectual in its management of the escalating refugee and homeless crisis. The popular consensus overwhelmingly disparaged the network of party members and their kin and cronies. It was the commonly agreed-on weak link in the national community at total war. Meanwhile, the party responded with a propaganda push in 1944, portraying itself as the backbone of a society under duress. It was, perhaps, official propaganda's most blatant divergence from people's war experience yet. In July 1944, for instance, a likely little-read magazine article made a case for the much-maligned Nazi Party's role in responding to the Allied air war. Propagandist Hans Uhle explained that as "the degenerate war of Anglo-American terror rages over the cities and villages of Germany, hoping to force the homeland, the backbone and source of strength of the fighting front, into a shameful capitulation like that of November 1918[,] [t]he homeland itself has become the front in the hardest sense of the word." In Germany's hour of need, he argued,

> the party stands in the front lines of resistance in this battle against terror. This is its greatest and hardest test, and never has it been clear[er] and more evident that it is a popular movement in the truest sense of this important word. No one today doubts any longer that this war of terror against the civilian population, against women and children, the old and the ill, would be impossible without the party. During the brief years of peace, some saw the party's efforts merely as "organization." Today, it has proved itself a well-organized, beneficial community of fighting men and women who, in addition to full days at their jobs, are willing to sacrifice all their strength for the good of the community, proving it countless times through their actions.[45]

The author's portrayal stood in almost comical contrast to popular perceptions of the Nazi Party's failings in the final war years when crisis conditions compounded deep-seated grievances and resentments. At a time when the Nazi regime demanded more and more tangible sacrifices from its citizens, its party embodied an amalgam of new and old privileges. This was true especially after 1944 in the context of the suffering wrought by the escalating air war and of the party's ineffectual management of the resulting destruction and displacement all over the Reich.

In the final war year, very few Germans remained unaffected by these bombings. Everybody knew somebody among their family, friends, and acquaintances who had lost their home and possessions. The numbers of those left homeless and displaced were staggering. In captivity, German POWs ruminated endlessly about the fate of their loved ones back home. Those who had experienced air raids firsthand during home visits, like Lieutenant Metzenthien, were haunted by the memories of some of the most "hellish things" they had seen during the entire war. Moreover, their captors apprised them in great detail of the latest developments of the bombing campaign, perpetually stoking fear and anxiety. For instance, in February 1945, a captured sailor from Essen lamented about the latest raid on his hometown: "Two-hundred-and-seventy-five-thousand people were made homeless at Essen after the raids."[46] Elsewhere, a Lieutenant von der Heydte told his cellmate, "Münster has been razed to the ground. It was like this—I lived in Münster for six months, but I lost my way, you can't even recognize the town! You can't tell there was ever a station at Giessen, not a house is intact there."[47] The fact that Germany had become unrecognizable was a refrain heard over and over again among the captured troops. A Sergeant Schnös bemoaned that Allied bombers "[have] destroyed absolutely everything at Schweinfurt. There's not a house left standing, quite literally, everything has gone." He explained, "The last raid on Schweinfurt disgusted me. It wasn't really a proper air raid. They dropped two mines and those two mines wiped out two whole streets. No air raid warning—it was a single aircraft." Replied his cellmate, Sergeant Schnuch, "It's exactly the same at Kassel. In Kassel itself there are no industrial plants, only outside . . . the Henschel Werke, and then the tank factories near Wilhelmshöhe. In the last six air raids they've mostly dropped their bombs amongst the rubble."[48] A Lieutenant Kogler inquired, "Do you know that Memmingen has been completely destroyed; they had nothing but 500 kg bombs there, a few hundreds of them. Three carpets on one day and two carpets some time before that. . . . There is only part of the guardroom left standing. And the station headquarters. Everything else is in ruins."[49] Elsewhere in captivity, a sailor by the name of Limbach recalled, "I've never seen anything like it. I went through many heavy raids on Cologne when I was still at home, I was in the Fire Service, but I've never seen anything to compare with Königsberg! The population was at their wits end there! I've rarely seen anything like it. I recently drove over the Rhine bridge near Cologne. The Deutz Engine Works have hardly been damaged at all. All the factories are still standing there; everything is still standing there, and all the damage is just across the Rhine, that's to say in the residential district."[50]

If despair over the wanton destruction and loss was common, solidarity with victims was not a given. For instance, Metzenthien reflected at length about the abject despair he witnessed among German bombing victims on his last visit home. Still, when he recalled arriving at his house "in a side street off Hammerlandstrasse," he was irritated to find "two [homeless] families living" in his home: "Of course I couldn't do anything about that."[51] This was a common response to the misery of others. Germans who had been spared direct bombing and had to take in refugees from the East and the bombed-out homeless frequently expressed resentment over overcrowding and strained nerves. In a letter from September 1944, a displaced woman by the name of Gerda Müller complained to a Sergeant Werner Scheel about the poor treatment she experienced at the hands of her reluctant benefactors,

> The people in the suburbs of Kiel have not truly grasped the seriousness of the situation and make life for the evacuees even harder. One is constantly treated like a foreigner and one feels barely tolerated. Furthermore, we get to hear the complaints of those who provide our quarters, that they don't have furniture, that we are staying in their best room and much more. I can tell you, dear Werner, sometimes one wants to despair. This is compounded by the endless workdays. I get up at 3:45 a.m., take the train at 4:30, and return home at 8:35 p.m. You can see that these are not bearable conditions for the long run.[52]

Clearly, the national community did not rush to share the burdens of war equitably. In the later war years, while there were some "haves," the ranks of the "have-nots" swelled precipitously. Occasionally, people noted instances of kindness and solidarity in a period of national crisis. For instance, a letter from Ursula M. in Mecklenburg to Liseselotte G. in Westphalia from March 26, 1945, describes a rare instance of shared misery and sacrifice: "We have refugees. A woman, an old grandpa, and two boys. The family is from Stettin. They are simple, pretty nice people. Before that there was a family from Bromberg here. And we had a whole group of ten soldiers that stayed with us for 14 days. One wants to do whatever one can; if only this misery would end soon."[53] Other times, stories about the events of the final war period contained clearly fictional elements that belied the extreme stress and chaos many Germans experienced during this time. Rumors about Hitler's positive interventions in the war effort abounded, for instance. In their stories, Germans imbued the führer with mythical powers and infinite righteousness that stood in stark contrast to the cowardice and corruption commonly attributed to party and even military authorities. As Willy Laubscher from Neidenfels relayed to his deployed son about the German reversals in the West:

> Traffic on the roads has let up a lot. There are still military vehicles going in every direction, but not in the same volume as last week. The only refugees you see these days are the farmers with their horse-drawn carriages. We've already had several refugees spend the night at our farm. The ones that came yesterday told us that in Kaiserslautern the Führer himself inspected the vehicles. There must have been quite a lot of crooked dealings at the west front. The "lords" escaped from the front with their vehicles packed full [of plundered goods] and simply abandoned the rank and file. You hear about this everywhere, especially from the refugees. It's a good thing that the Führer himself took charge of the situation, otherwise we might already have had to flee.[54]

Refugees caused strains on limited space, resources, and goodwill. Moreover, they brought with them information, sometimes unwelcome, and rumors about events unfolding elsewhere in the Reich. Herr Hansgen reported in a letter from Hastenrath in September 1944, for instance, "The English will be here tomorrow" according to "[the new] lodgers, two Bavarians who came today from Hasselt."[55] Most commonly, refugees carried with them tales of despair that depressed the outlook even in regions spared direct fighting. In April 1944, SD Bad Brückenau reported that "the very pessimistic mood and increasingly fatalistic indifference are strongly influenced by the arrival of a large number of bombing victims from Frankfurt and Schweinfurt.[56] One month later, on May 8, 1944, the Bad Brückenau office reported that people doubted that Germany could recover from the level of destruction suffered by German industrial and armaments installations: "According to many national comrades, [a German] retribution offensive is not currently possible after so many of our industrial cities have been radically destroyed. People use the destruction of Schweinfurt's armaments industry as proof of this assertion. And it looks in most industrial areas in Germany as it does in Schweinfurt."[57]

Letters from bombed-out areas carried tales of destruction into the remotest corners of the Reich. On March 26, 1945, a woman described the state of her Berlin neighborhood to her sister in Westphalia: "We now have had five weeks of alarm day and night. There were heavy, heavy attacks from above. But with God's help we have escaped without damage thus far. But it looks really bad here. You will hardly recognize the town, even residents can hardly recognize their own streets. Last week real heavy stuff came down really close to us."[58] She asked, "Do you still have your home?," a common question in correspondence in the final war period as Germans shared tales of lost homes and possessions.[59] For instance, in September 1944, Lilli Schlösser wrote to her deployed husband, Hans, "You probably won't get your home back as we have to leave here. It can happen any minute now. You can imagine everything. I am crying my eyes out. We pinched pennies so carefully to pay for everything and now we have to simply give everything up, even the cattle. It is an outrage, it is simply terrible for us. And also we are under alarm every day. The planes fly really low and shoot constantly."[60]

What heightened the terror of the Allied air war was the fact that many Germans could not understand it from a strategic standpoint. This was true for civilians as well as members of the armed forces. Thus, in wartime correspondence and conversations, the enemy's method in choosing targets was a topic of endless speculation and debate. A Corporal Reifenscheid offered the following story as explanation for why Dresden had escaped major bombing as late as mid-December 1944: "Prague is said to have been completely undermined by us and is to be blown up if we have to surrender it. That is known in Czech circles, and [former President of Czechoslovakia Edvard Beneš] is to put in a claim for Dresden as capital. Dresden is the future capital of greater Czechoslovakia."[61] Conversely, a gunner by the name of Rademacher warned his cellmate, "At all cost avoid telling the IOs [interrogation officers] that there are anti-Nazis anywhere, else that place will immediately be bombed. It was the same at Cologne, because England knew that there was a strong anti-national socialist feeling in Cologne, for that very reason they bombed Cologne. That is really a false conclusion on the part of the Allies. They have in fact lost the sympathies, which they formerly had in Cologne, through their senseless bombing."[62]

Not surprisingly, as their situation discernibly deteriorated over the course of 1944, Germans continued to speculate that the air war was an act of Jewish retribution. In an undated report from 1944, SD Schweinfurt stated, for instance, "Many bombed-out national comrades are of the opinion that we would not have to suffer so terribly now if we hadn't treated the Jews so poorly."[63] Clearly, however, Germans could also tolerate only so much of Goebbels's propaganda portraying the air war as Jewish terror. SD Schwerin reported on March 7, 1944, "Some people critiqued the coverage of the

Mecklenburg press regarding the air attacks of February 20. . . . They find the following smells of propaganda: 'We won't bow to the infamous terror instigated by the Jews.' The people of Rostock have a too serious view of the military impact of the attack to want to see it used for propaganda games."[64]

While civilians largely blamed Nazi authorities for the "poor treatment" that Jews had suffered, German soldiers occasionally contemplated their own culpability in the bombing war. That was most likely to happen under the immediate influence of British news and propaganda material in Western captivity. But even there such moments of critical self-reflection were rare. For instance, Sergeant Wuttge pondered in his cell, "In air raids on London in 1943 we fired on women and children! They mustn't know that here. The things we did!"[65] Elsewhere, a captured German airman by the name of Hartigs expressed similar sentiments when he told his cellmate, "I flew to Southern England. In 1943 we flew over hourly in flock formation, and we were ordered to fire at everything except military targets. We killed children and women with prams." When his cellmate, fellow airman Synowzik, countered that "the English were already machine-gunning women in 1943," Hartigs protested, "No, no, we introduced them to the methods that they employ today."[66]

More than anything, the Allied air war also exacerbated soldiers' anxieties about the stability of the home front and raised the specter of the collapse of 1918. In captivity, they vividly described the scenes of mayhem and destruction they had witnessed in German cities. In these descriptions from 1944 and onward, bombs obliterated whatever distinction between front and home front had remained. The belief that home-front morale was a crucial indicator of the wider war situation was apparent in Metzenthien's conversation with one of his cellmates, a Second Lieutenant Keser, who confessed that he was feeling "pretty pessimistic" about Germany's chances in this war. He said, "I don't know if you've seen Berlin. The best houses are all down. Near the Kurfürstendamm there isn't a single cinema left, and the church is destroyed. The heaviest bombs fell there." Even Metzenthien was forced to agree: "Yes, God knows how things are going to be. It's terrible to think of all these who have been killed."[67]

In 1944, the German war became truly total. Under the impact of aerial bombing and the systematic German-on-German terror campaign that followed the July plot, most Germans lived and fought total war. Civilian and military populations exchanged information during a period when the German war effort underwent internal and external radicalization. As the military situation worsened and Nazi propaganda raised the specter of a catastrophe worse than 1918, Germans believed that they had to hold out against an overwhelming enemy force in an infinite war of attrition. Members of the German military population became preoccupied with the condition and morale of the home front as a way to measure the likelihood of "another" stab in the back and to gauge the odds of victory or defeat. Meanwhile, civilians depended on soldiers' letters and personal reports to compare their impressions of the war situation against the regime's official propaganda. In fact, in wartime Germany civilians considered the Wehrmacht in general and soldiers in particular as one of the most reliable sources of information available to them.[68] Critically, both sides believed the other possessed knowledge and resources critical for victory. Their constant contemplation of the other's position and the frequent exchange of information between them blurred some of the identity boundaries between soldiers and civilians. It forged common perceptions and attitudes that informed their respective interpretations of war experiences. And it created shared expectations about the future of the war and the Nazi regime.

Chapter 5

DISSOLUTION

History Is the Arbiter

In the spring of 1945, the Nazi regime orchestrated the epic of its own destruction. The continuation of a war already lost also amounted to an act of national self-annihilation virtually without precedent. Traveling between Hamburg and Berlin in April and May 1945, an OSS operative by the name of Henning Jessen-Schmidt witnessed near-apocalyptic scenes. He reported, "It is safest to drive at night on account of the strafing planes, which have a terrible effect during the day. One sees burning cars everywhere, heaps of dead horses and naturally there are also dead people from time to time.... The confusion in the German lines was beyond description. Corpses, dying civilians, and the stench of dead horses, burning cars were liberally strewn along the highway. We were under constant bombardment by Allied planes."[1]

Hitler presided over this final chapter from the seclusion of his führer bunker. Beneath the streets of Berlin, he suffered bouts of depression punctuated by apoplectic fits, while directing phantom armies against the Allies' inexorable march on the capital. Remarkably, he still commanded loyalty among many members of his beleaguered national community, the civilians and soldiers staffing the battlefields of the home front, and the legions of POWs who observed the final war months from captivity. Among them was a twenty-two-year-old second lieutenant named Reisiger, a university student from Berlin who had been captured in northern Italy in January 1945. Reisiger struck his captors as "not too bright and a typical product of the Nazi education system."[2] Under interrogation, he professed "firm loyalty to Nazi principles." Despondent over Germany's dismal military situation, he believed, "Everyone is to blame for these misfortunes that have befallen us," everyone but Hitler. In conversation with a fellow German POW, Reisiger pondered, "If we really lost the war . . . [b]ut that's impossible. Hitler can't possibly be such a fool as to continue to fight if the situation really is hopeless. . . . It would be the greatest crime he had ever committed if he did. And I've still got enough faith left to believe that he wouldn't."[3]

But rumors about Hitler's declining mental faculties swirled widely and stoked anxieties about Germany's prospects. In captivity, one POW claimed, "I heard the Führer has gone mad and has been throwing telephones about and gnawing rugs. . . . But that's not too hard to understand: to be betrayed on so many sides would drive any man crazy!"[4] And one of his generals reflected wryly that the führer had acted "like a man possessed": "He believed in his astrologers and soothsayers, who had told him he would live only to the age of 56 and he wanted, therefore, to get everything done before 20 April 1945, when he reached that age."[5] Indeed, by mid-April, US forces crossed the Elbe, while the Red Army obliterated the last German defense line to the east. On Hitler's fifty-sixth birthday, the Soviets began shelling Berlin. The following day, Russian tanks arrived at the outskirts of town, and Hitler readied for his final act. As chancellor and supreme commander of the armed forces, he had spent more than twelve years "wedded to the German people," a union he unceremoniously dissolved in the early morning hours of April 29, 1945, when he married his longtime companion Eva Braun under the ruins of the Reich capital. With the civil ceremony under way, Hitler's secretary transcribed his last will and political testament. His final message to the German nation amounted to thirteen pages, in three copies. He signed the document at 4:00 a.m. The following day, around 3:30 p.m., Hitler took his own life ahead of the Allied capture of the Reichstag building. As he abandoned the German nation to the wreckage wrought by twelve years of Nazi rule and nearly six years of war, he tiredly proclaimed,

I die with a happy heart, aware of the immeasurable deeds and achievements of our soldiers at the front, our women at home, the achievements of our farmers and the work, unique in history, of our youth who bear my name. That from the bottom of my heart I express my thanks to you all is just as self-evident as my wish that you should, because of that, on no account give up the struggle but rather continue it against the enemies of the Fatherland. . . . From the sacrifice of our soldiers and from my own unity with them unto death, will in any case spring up in the history of Germany, the seed of a radiant renaissance of the National-Socialist movement and thus of the realization of a true community of nations.[6]

In his last will and testament, Hitler had appointed Grand Admiral Karl Dönitz president of the German Reich, the new head of state. He had named no successor as führer, and some of his most important henchmen dispersed before the fall of Berlin. In a last-minute purge of his inner circle, Hitler had disowned both Hermann Göring and Heinrich Himmler as traitors and stripped them of their titles and offices. Himmler attempted to go into hiding but was detained on May 21, 1945. British intelligence soon discovered his true identity, and the former Reichsführer-SS killed himself by poisoning on May 23. Göring fled west and was arrested on May 6 by US forces. He became the second-highest-ranking Nazi official to be tried at Nuremberg, where he was sentenced to death by hanging for crimes of conspiracy, crimes against peace, war crimes, and crimes against humanity. Göring killed himself by poisoning mere hours before his execution on October 15, 1946. By contrast, Joseph Goebbels, newly appointed Reich chancellor, followed his führer into death. He and his wife, Magda, murdered their six young children and then killed themselves at the Reich Chancellery in Berlin on May 1, 1945. Thousands of lower-level party functionaries followed suit, taking their own lives and the lives of their families rather than face the coming reckoning. Their deaths are a dramatic testament of Nazism's self-destructive power that prevailed until the bitter end.[7]

The Berlin garrison surrendered on May 2, 1945, and while pockets of resistance remained, the country's total and unconditional surrender went into effect on May 8. Millions of Germans were finally faced with the incontrovertible fact that Hitler had not conjured a miracle to wrest the nation from the brink of defeat. Instead, their total mobilization had culminated in total defeat. This chapter examines popular responses to the violent dissolution of the Third Reich in the spring of 1945. Specifically, it asks whether the stubborn popular faith in "führer and victory" endured as Germans took their final stand. How did they confront the specter of defeat that had loomed in the far-off distance since 1943? Did they go down fighting as Göring had demanded after Stalingrad and as many had vowed that they would in the intervening years? And for those who took their final stand, what were they fighting for and against? Did they hold out "until the bitter end" in hopes that their self-sacrifice would ensure a "radiant renaissance of the National-Socialist movement" in the far-off future? Or could they envision a future for themselves and the German nation in a world beyond Hitler, Nazism, and war?

Throughout the fall and winter of 1944, Germans at war had vowed, "On our own soil we won't yield a single step," as Lieutenant Metzenthien had put it.[8] And yet, yield they did. Moreover, the Nazi regime did not hide the evidence of the devastation it wrought as it "deliberately orchestrated Armageddon" within Germany's own borders.[9] The last German counteroffensive on the western front had collapsed in December 1944. By January 1945, Soviet and Polish forces pushed into eastern Prussian territory and advanced into Silesia and Pomerania by the following month, while the Western Allies crossed the Rhine north and south of the Ruhr industrial area. By March, the Russians had repulsed Germany's last major offensive against the Red Army near Lake Balaton in Hungary and were advancing on Vienna. They captured Königsberg (now Kaliningrad) in April, ending one of the final stands of the German East Prussian Offensive. At the same time, the Western Allies broke the stalemate in Italy and occupied most of the northern and western territories of the country, while closing in on Berlin. These dramatic ground fights unfolded against the ongoing aerial war, with Allied bombers dropping nearly four hundred thousand tons of bombs on German territory during the first four months of the year. Visual, visceral evidence of the nation's imminent collapse was inescapable.

As their country transformed into a battlefield, many Germans finally had to grapple with the inherent nihilism of Hitler's command that they fight "until the bitter end." Some, it seems, only now contemplated the fact that in fulfilling this alleged duty to the nation, they were ensuring its destruction. Frau Weichardt puzzled over the question in a letter she wrote in September 1944:

We have decided we will stay. After all, we have to reckon that we will not surrender. As our beloved Führer says and Dr. Goebbels constantly demands in his published appeals for full mobilization . . . : "We will fight until the last woman, no even until the last child!" But I do have to wonder who is supposed to be left in the end to celebrate victory when even women and children will be sacrificed to the enemy. Maybe the [German] POWs will be the only ones left. But I keep hoping that somehow there is a ray of light, perhaps at the very last moment. The prospect of the final victory cheers me up but the question remains, who will survive until then.[10]

Allied forces met with pockets of stubborn German defiance wherever they went, and as late as March 1945, some German soldiers still vowed: "There is no capitulating with us, we'd rather croak."[11] At the same time, some contemplated the implications of Germany's devastating losses in the second global conflagration in a generation: "Think of how many families there are, where the father was killed in 1917 and the son in 1942."[12] On Christmas Eve 1944, Colonel Piringer, a thirty-two-year-old economist from Vienna, reflected: "How many young men have been lost in this war, men in the full bloom of life!" The devastating impact, he speculated, would reverberate for decades to come: "Perhaps it's not so very noticeable at the moment. But when it's all over, and everyone goes home, then for the first time it will be possible to really reckon [how] much of this generation has been sacrificed. You'll notice most of all in the small villages when the sons of the villagers fail to return. . . . And the full tragedy of it will only reveal itself after the war. And who will there be left to rebuild Germany? Greybeards and children!"[13]

Just as there had been no single German experience of the war, there was no single German experience of defeat. Many Germans' perceptions of the collapse were undoubtedly colored by their experiences and perceptions of the conflagration leading up to this point, but few left behind reliable indicators of their observations and aspirations in the chaotic final period of the war. The few surviving letters and diaries from the final war period reflect widespread fear, anxiety, and exhaustion commensurate with a nation facing a bitter end after more than five and a half years of war. Some records document an enduring resolve to keep fighting, but few point toward a broader suicidal national consensus among the militarized national community. The many German towns and villages that submitted to Western Allied occupation well in advance of the official surrender are testament to a popular desire for self-preservation. Moreover, millions of German soldiers surrendered to Allied captivity rather than go down fighting. While the Nazi fanatics in their midst tried to galvanize a German "resistance until the end" by force and persuasion, most people simply wanted to survive. For instance, Frau Scharrenbach recounted in a letter a recent radio address by a functionary who had claimed, "Once the enemy breaches the border, he will have to walk over the dead bodies of [German] soldiers and we are all soldiers then." She angrily dismissed the appeal, stating that "we have had it up to here with the stuff he was saying." Her letter was marked for "defeatism" (*Miesmacherei*).[14]

Popular anger mounted against Nazi officials as hope for a victory dwindled. As Louise Wolters wrote in a letter from Niederrhein as early as September 1944, "It's bad here in the countryside, everyone is turning on everyone. They all believe we will lose the war, and that's why everyone is picking on the Nazis. I'm really worried about father."[15] In many places, the long-simmering resentments against the corrupt party apparatus now erupted with full force. Frau Jansen for instance, vented her anger at the party bosses' heavy-handedness during evacuations from Iversheim:

> It's total chaos here, and everyone wants to share the latest news, and you hear the most terrible tales but also some very sad factual accounts. I can tell you that the behavior of the party bigwigs is appalling. Jean Neuburg wants to use violence to force the people to evacuate, and he is mean and nasty to anyone who wants to stay. I think I understand what's going on. On the last wagon of every refugee column that passes by here there is always a party bigwig all decked out in his uniform as if to signal, "Look at me, I'm the very last to leave after everyone else has been brought to safety." But one can still remember well enough the [sorry] fate of the refugees out on the road during our last war against France. . . . Meanwhile, the [Nazi] district administrator has safely evacuated all his belongings alongside his family. And he wears civilian clothes and sits pretty in his office.[16]

As the Allied armies advanced through German territory, fewer and fewer Germans maintained their belief in a "final victory" and instead began confronting the notion that the war would end in a German defeat. Letters from the home front, now the last battleground, document an enduring desire to prevail after defeat and to be reunited with scattered family and loved ones. Frau Scharrenbach wrote to her deployed husband, "I constantly worry whether we will see each other again," a refrain that echoed through the missives from the final war period.[17] Frau Baumgärtner in Düsseldorf wrote to her husband of her war exhaustion and enduring hope to be reunited after the end of the war: "There is no more joy because the alarm sounds every day from morning to evening, and there is no quiet at night. It's terrible and frightening. Dear God, when will this finally end, it's unbearable. . . . As long as I live I shall always think of you and kiss your dear eyes. I trust that God will protect us and bring us back together."[18] And in mid-January 1945, Frau U. from Angelsdorf, in Westphalia, told her deployed husband of the evidence of impending defeat that mounted alongside her desire to be reunited after the war: "Today one can hear the front again. Some days it is quiet and then it is noticeable again. They are still standing at the Ruhr. No one attacks there. When the house doesn't shake, we don't even hear the shooting anymore. Thus one can get used to anything. The planes on the other hand cause quite some fear. Let us hope that the Almighty will continue to protect us and that we will all see each other again soon healthy and well. That is our sole wish."[19]

Perhaps more than any other factor, geography had an impact on how Germans experienced the final war months. People in the country's eastern regions encountered a very different conqueror than those in the West did. The German suicide wave that swept those territories ahead of the Russian occupation had no equivalent in the country's western territories. For those who remained, the final war months were filled with dread over the arrival of the Red Army. As Frau Radhofer wrote in a letter from Vienna to her deployed husband in the East,

I started to despair when I read your letter. I can't help it and feel powerless over what comes next. So often I wake up at night terrified: the Russian. Maybe he'll knock on our doors today. He is advancing so quickly. And then I keep asking myself why don't we stop the enemy, and will everything be reduced to rubble? If only we had already deployed the [miracle] weapons to fortify ourselves. People here are talking mindlessly about what the future will bring. It's a nauseating prospect. I've always believed in our victory, and I've always had faith that the Führer would pull this off. But now there are only reversals and there is a lot of [uncertainty among] those who used to believe so firmly. It's really sapping my confidence.[20]

The continued fighting led to brutal confrontations, especially between German and Soviet forces. In a letter home in mid-November 1944, Corporal Erwin S., proclaimed the common resolve to defend German soil from the Soviet invasion at all cost. He inquired: "How is the weather at home? It is really cold here ... and when it gets to be real winter temperatures are supposed to reach minus 30 degrees, and we only receive coals at minus 20 degrees. But this winter too shall end, and this will be war's final winter. We will beat back the Russian if he somehow attacks again."[21] In captivity, Lieutenant Hofmann echoed this grandstanding sentiment, claiming, "There's one thing I'm sure of—my father will never fall into the hand of the Russians while he is alive, and neither will my mother. They'd sooner kill themselves first." Responded his exasperated cellmate, "Oh man, for Heaven's sake, stop prattling like this. Your parents aren't any more heroic than anybody else's parents."[22]

By all accounts, the dreaded specter of Russians raping and pillaging and eviscerating the German homeland held a powerful sway over the German public imagination. It was one of the most effective weapons in the arsenal of Nazi atrocity propaganda that Goebbels unleashed in full force against the national community in retreat, and it helped fuel a futile yet destructive German resistance until the bitter end. On January 4, 1945, Victor Klemperer reflected on how the government carried out the war with "tremendous tenacity and repeated ingenuity" and people "indeed [did] have a right to talk about a 'German miracle.'" Almost exactly four months before the German surrender, this astute observer of the Nazi order pondered, "I am truly no longer so certain of [a German] defeat; at the very least they will continue resisting for too long. [The Nazis] do not keep the mass of people in line by tyranny alone." Instead, Klemperer observed that after years of indoctrination, most Germans had internalized a pervasive terror of the Russian enemy that galvanized the ongoing German fight. Most people seemed to believe the official message: "Our enemies, and in particular the Bolshevists, want to annihilate you, literally kill you." Hence, he concluded that the Nazis "owe everything to the bogeyman of Bolshevism, even though they themselves are the most Bolshevik of all."[23]

OSS operative Jessen-Schmidt also observed firsthand the popular fear of the Russians that was rampant among the embattled population of Berlin. He reported about the chaotic situation he had witnessed in the capital, Germany's final battleground, on April 1, 1945: "Spandau [Berlin] badly damaged. Many dead bodies burnt with flamethrowers. Coffins can only be obtained on ration card and even then only with difficulty. [The People's Militia is] training with poor equipment." Several weeks later, as the battle of Berlin began on April 16, he reported that the people of the city had "bought flowers for [the arrival of] the Americans," whom they regarded "as the lesser evil." He noted that although there were communists among the lower German classes, "most circles do not desire Communism (that system is too much like the one they have had for so long)—everything that I write is the opinion of the people." Based on his conversations and observations in the besieged city, he predicted that "the upper class, [the intelligentsia], merchants etc. and some officials will greet the Anglo-American troops as liberators but are panic-stricken about the Russians."[24]

While Jessen-Schmidt tried to gauge opinions among German civilians in the Reich capital, other OSS operatives were tasked with assessing the German military population in the later stages of the war. An OSS mole by the name of Gerhard Levine, for example, went undercover among German POWs, albeit not in a CSDIC facility. A thirty-six-year-old private in the US Army, he was of "Jewish extraction" and had been born in Berlin. A trained economist who had left Germany in 1936, Levine now applied his critical faculties to gauge the opinions and attitudes prevalent among German soldiers in captivity. His report suggested that the POWs shared the same preoccupation with the Russians that Jessen-Schmidt had observed in Berlin. In an attempt to explain their ferocious fighting even late in the war, he emphasized that the Nazi regime had successfully indoctrinated its armed forces. He stated that more than anything, Nazi propaganda had "succeeded in planting into the mind of the German soldier" that this war could only end in one of two ways, victory or Siberia (*Sieg oder Sibirien*). He explained, "It is a good slogan, even better and more catching in German because of its alliterative rhyme. It is a success because only a very few don't believe this to be the alternative." Based on his observations among German POWs, Levine concluded, "The fear of Bolshevism has been instilled early and systematically into the German mind. After all that has happened they don't have to strain their imagination to realize and fear the prospect of forced labor in Russia. With the same feelings they look upon a Russian occupation of their territory. . . . Those from South and West Germany consider themselves as lucky aristocrats and often ask interrogators to confirm the rumors that their parts will be occupied by the Americans and British."[25]

Levine was right that especially combatants with experience of German occupation practices on the eastern front would not have had to "strain their imagination" about the revenge that Russians might extract. Indeed, by 1945, widespread German fears of the Russian enemy were based not only on Nazi propaganda but also on eyewitness accounts. A steady stream of refugees carried into the western regions of the country stories of German suffering and misery at the hands of the Red Army. For instance, Corporal Paul-Diedrich N. wrote to his friend Fritz in November 1944, "I had already expected the evacuation of your parents. And now it has indeed happened. It can't be easy for your dear parents to abandon home and yard. And especially since they must assume that they are going to find everything laid to waste. This war demands terrible sacrifices from everyone."[26] Several months later, in March 1945, Corporal Ernst M. wrote from Gotenhafen (Gdynia), in West Prussia, to his brother about his encounters with German refugee columns in the East: "I can tell you I have experienced some outrageous days and nights. Yes, I can say that I have seen scenes of wretchedness that were absolutely extraordinary to me. . . . It is a shame for the columns though that could not be rescued. One has to assume that Ivan does not know mercy even when it comes to women, children, and the elderly."[27]

Vast swaths of German territory were occupied by the Red Army. Once the frightening figment of Nazi propaganda, its brutal occupation practices now helped legitimize the Nazi regime in its final throes. Jessen-Schmidt reported, for instance, that Russian forces had entered "Berlin as conquerors [and] did not bring food with them but relied on supplies they could find en route," so that "everything that was edible in Berlin was taken over by them." He continued, "During all this period I observed the Russians going berserk in the city, raping, looting and drinking."[28] As Germans suffered under the Russian occupation, they believed the most frightening specter of Nazi propaganda realized. Never mind that much of the Russian conduct mirrored the ruthless brutality with which German forces had advanced into eastern Europe and then retreated. On May 3, 1945, Jessen-Schmidt spent the afternoon at the Russian headquarters where he spoke at length to a political commissar, discussing "politics and Russian motives for what they were actually doing in the capital." According to his report, "Part of the civilian population was fed by the Russian military authorities, but there was a complete absence of bread for civilians. Everyone in uniform was arrested from partymember to streetcar conductor. Everyone who was relatively well dressed was arrested. The commissar told me that Stalin himself had issued orders that women were not to be raped and that the soldiers were not to pillage and loot the city, but he asked me frankly whether I didn't think what his soldiers were doing was not the right thing."[29]

It is exceedingly unlikely that Germans spent the final war period reflecting on the six years of suffering their war had inflicted on others. Instead, they bemoaned German suffering inflicted by the Allies in ground fighting and aerial attacks. A letter from Frau Orlowski from Labiau, in East Prussia, is indicative. She wrote, "I cannot describe how things look here. Downtown there are only ruins. The sight of it churns your stomach." Reeling at her town's destruction in a war unleashed by Germany, she lamented, "[Is it possible] none of the [Allied] criminals will be held responsible for this? No, that's impossible. That would mean there is no more justice in the world. There must be a reckoning for such crimes. And that's why we have to endure and carry on even if it is hard, so that we can win this war and pay these dogs back for their crimes."[30]

As Germans insisted on the legitimacy of their cause and focused on the gravity of their misery, they formulated the tenacious narratives of their German victimhood that would persist for decades in the postwar era. Indeed, in their suffering at the hands of "these dogs," many Germans also reaffirmed notions of their inherent superiority. As one mole reported, "The Nazis have succeeded in making the Germans believe one thing, first of all, namely that they are better than all other people." Among German POWs, he observed that "the great masses of German soldiers still believe that they are the best soldiers in the world . . . and if there were not this lack of raw materials, they would be invincible. . . . The excuse of the raw material must be given the lie as well as the myth of the invincibility of the German soldier. Or are those terms to be allowed to build up a new [stab-in-the-back] legend like that after the war of 1914/18?"[31]

According to their monitors, German POWs postured as conquerors even as their ill-gotten empire crumbled. As one OSS mole put it in early 1945, infiltrating a POW camp "somewhere in England" meant entering "another world": German POWs, he observed, "still speak the 'conqueror's' language and live according to their own mentality of a German soldier and a German subject. They have brought with them a piece of Germany, Hitler's Germany."[32] Other intelligence officers corroborate the mole's observations that many German soldiers continued to rely on the "old slogans of former days" to frame their private conversations during the final war months.[33] Based on his observations of German POWs in a US-run camp in late 1944, one OSS mole wrote a scathing indictment of the mental and moral faculties of the German prisoners after more than ten years of National Socialism and five years of war. According to him, the period had fundamentally transformed Germans, rendering them "mercenary creatures without a will of their own." He wrote,

> The Nazis have succeeded in infecting the broad masses with their criminal instincts and this is the main reason for Hitler's war crimes being supported by the whole nation. . . . The Nazis have succeeded in destroying all progressive tendencies and to silence all progressive circles. The Nazis have succeeded in suppressing completely, or making uniform, every attempt at thinking individually with nearly the whole population. The Nazis have succeeded in drumming into the brains of the broad masses their "master race" ideas and to develop, to the highest degree, the arrogance and conceit of every individual. The Nazis have succeeded in making the broad masses believe in only two alternatives, namely victory or destruction, and to suppress every normal consciousness of guilt. The Nazis have succeeded in planting their deeply rooted antisemitism in its most brutal form into the people's minds, as an unavoidable necessity.[34]

Taken at face value, the operative's assertions suggest that mere months before Germany's unconditional surrender, the fanatical militarized national community of Nazi lore thrived even in captivity. According to him, German soldiers had completely internalized extreme nationalism, collectivism, antisemitism, and racial determinism, all key components of Nazi ideology that now framed their discussions and outlook in the face of imminent defeat. Other Allied intelligence materials corroborate at least some of his pronouncements about the remarkable breadth and width of ideological conversation among Germans at war. They suggest that some of the mole's key observations, although hyperbolic and devoid of nuance, were perhaps not entirely unfounded. CSDIC analysts, for instance, frequently complained about their prisoners' perceived lack of common sense and reason. As one analyst put it in a heavily annotated transcript titled "Nazi Philosophers, 1945": "However bravely the German may still fight in the field, it seems that his thought processes no longer include any concept which can help him form a logical appreciation of the world as it is to-day."[35]

Jessen-Schmidt drew similar conclusions about the population of Berlin under siege, as he struggled to "explain the workings of the minds of the civilian population prior to the Russians occupying the city." He recalled that the "ever increasing crescendo of Russian artillery" had forced the people of Berlin permanently underground. It was "fatally dangerous, particularly for women and children, to leave the shelters even for a moment. After April 25 the food shortage became so acute that people who stayed in the shelters ran out of food completely." Down below, the "stench of decaying bodies" permeated every shelter. But amid the sights, sounds, and smells of defeat, hope for a final victory lived. He reported that it "was quite current to hear Germans speaking about the impossibility of the Russians breaking through to the [Brandenburg Gate] without the Führer producing a last minute secret weapon which would put an end to their suffering. The Germans could not comprehend that everything they had been told was merely a pack of lies." He continued, "It is interesting to have observed that even during the last few days when we were surrounded by the Allies and could hear their broadcasts in German, that the Germans in the air raid shelter, even those who were not staunch Nazis, refused to listen to anything beyond straight news broadcasts, everything else being considered pure Allied propaganda."[36] If true, this was a stunning reversal of the trend that had unfolded after Stalingrad, when Germans had learned to shun transparent Nazi propaganda. Instead, Jessen-Schmidt observed that with insurmountable evidence of total defeat all around them, remnants of the embattled national community continued to put stock in their führer's promises, waiting for the vaunted miracle and victory.

If fear fed popular hopes at the home front, Allied observers also encountered zealotry and fanaticism among German combatants late in the war. To be sure, they tended to be more pronounced among the young and among those who had only recently been drafted. Few of the older soldiers and those who had fought for the past five or six years would have been capable of the war enthusiasm of Corporal Paul-Diedrich N., for instance. In a letter from November 1944, he reminded his friend Fritz, "Next Saturday, on 11/25, we both have our one-year anniversary as soldiers. Unbelievable, no? I already feel like an old [fighter]. If we were still together we would celebrate, of course. Well, we'll do that later sometime."[37] OSS operative Levine also observed a tenacious commitment to the German cause among many of the POWs he encountered. He summarized, "There was confirmed the known tendency among older age groups to be less pro-Nazi than the younger ones. The same applies to Catholics and those from the South or West of Germany."[38] Jessen-Schmidt, too, had made similar observations about the "German troops in Denmark," whom he described as "domineering, boasting . . . particularly among the young officers." "There are still people amongst the youth who believe blindly in [Hitler], they don't know anything else and have no other ideas."[39] He was equally worried about the feral and damaged children he had encountered at the German home front. As he relayed in one telling anecdote: "A small 12-year-old boy who was carrying a very large pistol was asked what he was going to do with it. He replied 'I am a Wehrwolf and I am going to fight to the last.' The young people are completely wild, but if suffering is remedied effectively, so that parents and schools regain their influence, a great deal can most certainly be saved. But they must be taken away immediately and completely neutralized, otherwise no propaganda will help."[40]

To be sure, the reports of Allied observers like Levine and Jessen-Schmidt are neither comprehensive nor conclusive. They were not based on any representative samples of German society or the military at large. And yet, their observations cannot be dismissed entirely. After all, these operatives tried to report their insights into prevailing popular mentalities as carefully and comprehensively as possible after listening in on hundreds of German civilians and prisoners of a wide range of ages, social backgrounds, and military ranks and branches. Intelligence operatives dealing with German POWs reported consistently until the very end that "Nazi influence could be proved with all prisoners, with some of them more, with others less."[41] Levine confessed that "living together with [German POWs] for a while in order to know more about their state of mind" was an extremely challenging task. However, he believed that "the unpleasantness of this task was more than compensated by its instructiveness." While he was clear to state that his report was "not the dictum of somebody pretending to know all the relevant facts of the discussed subject," he did feel confident that his interactions with interned Germans allowed him to point out "trends" of thought in the POW camps.[42]

The available evidence suggests that many Germans continued to view Hitler as their nation's savior as he drove them into defeat. Even as his charismatic influence waned precipitously by 1945, he continued to loom disproportionately large in the popular imagination. As Wehrmacht censors were frequently relieved to report, "[Popular] trust in the Führer prevails . . . [even]

when there is disparagement of the [Nazi] Party."[43] In one theme on a common topic, a POW by the name of Elger, for instance, explained, "I have trusted the Führer all this time because I know he is a soldier." His cellmate Krause agreed: "He has an iron will. That is why everything has always clicked. If it were as bad as it looks, the Führer would have asked for peace terms long ago. That's why he's got something up his sleeve. And it's a good idea not to use it until everything is ready."[44] Still, many Germans had experienced Hitler's withdrawal from public engagements as a painful abandonment that gave rise to ample speculation. For instance, in Berlin in November 1944, mere months before the end, Nazi morale monitors reported that "many rumors still swirled around the person of the Führer" and that "[people] often emphasized that lately there has been no footage of the Führer in the [the daily news cast]"; many people assumed that "the Führer was seriously ill as a consequence of the assassination [attempt] of July 20, and that he even may have lost his mind and have been detained."[45] An article by Goebbels addressed widespread rumors about Hitler's declining health on December 31, 1944, claiming that Hitler's "enemies spread rumors that he was ill." Victor Klemperer summarized this official denial on January 1, 1945: "Twice it says he walks with a slight stoop, which is due to his study of maps; once, his hair has turned gray; once, at the same age Frederick the Great was already known as 'Old Fritz.' [But most importantly,] he was healthy, his eyes still gleamed youthfully and he would break his silence, when it suited him, and not when it suited his enemies." Klemperer drew one conclusion from Goebbels's vehement denial: "After this article I thought it certain that Hitler was ill."[46]

German POWs in Western Allied captivity had plenty of time for similar speculation. For instance, one German POW pondered, "There might be something in all the rumors one hears that Hitler is dead. If it is really true, then something is going to happen in Germany. No one will take the oath to Himmler. They'd have to bring out the whole of the SS with machine-guns first." His cellmate responded, "If it becomes known that Hitler is dead, that will be the end."[47] Elsewhere in captivity, Lieutenant Strobel speculated, "There must be something wrong with the Führer. . . . Yes, the Führer has been ill, I was told so by several officers back from convalescing." Responded his cellmate, a Lieutenant Münch, "I'm sure it won't be long before the Führer dies. He's ill anyway."[48]

While many Germans observed Hitler's decline with growing alarm, some welcomed it, anticipating his death as the end to Germany's self-destruction. Since 1934, members of the German civil service and of the armed forces had sworn an oath of personal allegiance to Hitler, and evidence suggests that many never questioned the legitimacy of the bond that had been forged through the Führer Oath until the very end. Colonel Piringer, for instance, claimed, "The only thing that makes the officers go on fighting nowadays is the feeling that they are bound by their oath. But if Hitler were dead, they wouldn't feel themselves under any further obligation. There would be no question of a further oath being taken." His cellmate Sergeant Dobberstein replied, "What a disaster Adolf Hitler has brought on us! Nazism is the invention of the devil."[49] Indeed, it was not only their allegiance to Hitler that bound the German forces to continue the fight to the point of self-destruction. Peer pressure and a pervasive sense of military duty and honor did the rest. As one mole observed, German officers, in particular, were bound by "manly and military virtue" to continue fighting. He reported that this was true "even for those that see that Germany's cause is lost and a prolongation of the war is to her disadvantage. . . . To them, the decent thing is to die fighting."[50]

In captivity and under the influence of their British captors, some POWs also came to see that the wages of the war's destruction were untenable. A German corporal reflected that Hitler had coldly and deliberately instigated this war from the very beginning of his reign. He said,

> No, no, there was only one reason for the war and that was there from the very beginning: Greed for personal power. Everyone was to worship the Führer. The whole world was to shout "Heil Hitler" just so that he could stand there and hold his arm up a little longer with a hidden splint for support, of course. What a wonderful achievement to hold his arm up for a whole hour, surrounded by shouts of "Heil Hitler!" Sometimes I try to imagine what would have happened if he had won the war. He would still have been nothing more than a fiendishly clever gangster but in the eyes of the world he would have been a great man. As it is, he has Germany's decline and downfall on his conscience.[51]

But for many more Germans, with or without uniforms, Hitler continued to embody hope for a German victory until defeat. His rare public addresses tended to cause a spike in popular confidence and morale that then quickly dropped under the weight of disastrous news that now came almost without respite.[52] Two months before Germany's unconditional surrender, on March 13, 1945, a Wehrmacht propaganda officer reported from Nuremberg, "There is a strong current among broad segments of the population and especially among the heavily hit national comrades that shows absolute confidence and firm faith in the future. . . . They express particular faith in the Führer that he will master this situation like he did before. Among soldiers, too, the outlook is consistently positive."[53] While the veracity of this statement is unclear, it seems likely that even in the final war months, many Germans venerated Hitler's visions of the Greater Germanic Reich, even though nothing but ruins remained. A German airman maintained during interrogation,

> I don't see what faults one can find in our leadership. Germany has become larger under Hitler than she ever was before. One can, with justice, compare Hitler with Napoleon. . . . Alas for the good old days! Africa, Poland, Norway, and Russia . . . I suppose that one can't avoid having a few neutral states left. But we could have got away with taking Switzerland and Sweden. . . . I don't think that the Führer himself ever had any evil intentions toward the populace of countries that we occupied. We should have treated them a lot more harshly, a few more kicks in the bottom would have done them a bit of good.[54]

The crisis conditions of the final war period served as fertile ground for popular rumors, speculations, and conspiracy theories. Just as Germans fashioned dueling narratives of Hitler as Germany's savior and nemesis, they interpreted the unfolding events in increasingly polarized and paranoid terms. Popular speculations around the July plot, for instance, resurfaced with surprising vehemence. A March 1945 Wehrmacht intelligence report about conditions at the home front claimed, "Soldiers and civilians alike often proclaim that the Führer may try hard to bring the war to a victorious conclusion. [But people speculate that] perhaps the war could already have been won or could have taken a significant turn if there was not constant betrayal at work. The ghost of July 20th is ever present."[55]

The ghost was also present when another Wehrmacht propaganda officer filed a report on March 31, 1945, about popular responses to the US crossing of the Remagen Rhine Bridge earlier that month. Suspecting sabotage,

Hitler had ordered the execution of several officers who had failed to blow up this bridge. According to the report, the people in Berlin also suspected "sabotage" and discussed the events in "connection with July 20, 1944": "Broad segments of the population express the opinion that today's situation is the reverse from the situation of the First World War. [Today] the home front holds under tremendous strain while the front gives in."[56] A Wehrmacht propaganda officer reported from Hamburg on March 22, 1945: "2 workers were talking in a streetcar about the advance of the Bolsheviks and expressed the opinion that everything was treason and was connected to the coup of July 20, 1944. Said one of them: 'Every soldier from the East says the same. My son, too.'"[57]

While many Germans blamed the July conspirators for Germany's precipitous decline, some came to different conclusions. For instance, as one POW explained, "We've lost the war for certain. If only the attempt on Hitler's life of July 20 had been a success! Of course, when it happened I condemned the officers who tried it like every other German did, but now I understand that these were men who loved their country so deeply that they were prepared to die for it."[58] Even decades into the postwar era, this opinion remained taboo among the "war generation."

There is ample evidence that many Germans continued to believe in the legitimacy of their cause and the righteousness of a German victory well into 1945. At the same time, it is important to consider that the Third Reich in decline was a dictatorship marked by escalating terror and coercion against its own populace. As one mole observed, "[Even if German soldiers] have the possibility to surrender, they feel ashamed before fanatical Nazi members of their outfits who practically invariably are for continuing the fight at all odds."[59] In fact, these coercive dynamics extended even into German POW camps. OSS operative Levine described how a small minority of "active Nazis" could maintain control over the prisoner population. He believed them able to cow or sway others because they were "schooled in political and propaganda work." Their willingness to use threats and violence ensured that "the Nazi grip [held] good even in captivity." Levine described several ways in which these "die-hard Nazis" operated. For instance, they spread rumors that "selected active Nazis" used a "code ([the] first letter of each word in their letters home)" to "convey to Germany the names of prisoners" who in captivity were "not loyal to the Nazi creed." He continued, "Nothing would be further from the truth than to expect that after capture the anti-Nazis would get the upper hand in a group of German soldiers. For this [to occur] they are by far not strong enough numerically and they are not organized at all, or they don't agree with each other and they are poorly trained for indoctrination in comparison to the Nazis. Only a tendency to more open and frank discussions may be observed."[60]

Another mole corroborates Levine's account of inter-prisoner coercion. During a stay in a camp, he reported, "[I] did not meet any [POW] who dared to stand up as an honest anti-Nazi. . . . Only a few I met [dared] to criticize the Nazis, and this only after they had learnt what we ourselves were thinking."[61] This, of course, was prudent behavior for anyone familiar with the reality of the "endurance terror" (*Durchhalteterror*) that permeated the home front and the final battlefields.[62] In a conversation in January 1945, Captain Schmidt remarked, for instance, "Some people seem to think that there may be a revolution—but there won't be. A revolution is quite impossible in Germany. It's impossible in any dictatorship." His cellmate Corporal Pompe replied, "And they can't stop fighting at the front either, otherwise they're put before a 'Party Court.' In Germany the people often ask why the men at the front don't just stop fighting, they don't realize that we're in exactly the same position as they are at home."[63] Jessen-Schmidt had witnessed scenes of coercion and terror in Berlin just weeks before the German surrender. He reported,

> The continued reign of terror imposed [on] the German population since Hitler's ascendency to power proved so potent a force that even the day before the [party bigwigs] left the town and told, for instance, inmates of my own air raid shelter, that reserve troops would shortly be brought into Berlin by the Nazis to restore law and order and punish the traitors to the Nazi regime, a new wave of anxiety blossomed forth and brought panic to those who questioned the Thousand Year Reich. I saw several dead Nazi soldiers hanged on lanterns and trees with a placard on their breast bearing the following inscription[:] "I, Gefreiter Schulze, hang here because I refuse to defend my wife and child." On nearly every door there was a notice signed by Hitler saying that anyone who refused to defend the city would be hanged immediately.[64]

Under the combined onslaught of Allied violence and German-on-German terror during the final war months, Germans with or without uniforms came to identify as both heroes and victims of their war, even if specific details of their victim narratives varied widely. Some thought of themselves as victims of global injustice. Polz, for instance, believed himself a victim of a world so "unfairly . . . divided."[65] Some, like Reisiger, believed themselves victims of a Jewish world conspiracy against the Nordic races, much like the one outlined by Hitler in his political testament. Indeed, as many believed well into the final war period: "It was foolish to kill the Jews too early, before victory was secured. One ought to have made them work with dangerous war materials. Then, most of them would have been killed at work and the remainder of them could have been murdered after victory was achieved."[66] Another mole concurred that among German POWs, the "influence of antisemitism is simply devastating." He reported that the prisoners frequently agreed, "We should have postponed the extermination of the Jews till after the war because then we would have had less enemies and better chances of victory." Others feared that after a German defeat the Jews would "take their revenge." He concluded that "only very few" among the German POWs "were thinking normally about the Jews."[67]

As seen here, many Germans were not "thinking normally" about many things in the final period of the war. Their stories from the precipice of defeat are riddled with extreme contradictions, paranoia, and confusions. But even amid this toxic swirl, Levine believed that most Germans retained at least one core disposition amenable to reason. He said, "Practically all prisoners, regardless of their political shading, agree in their love for their beautiful Fatherland and in their desire to minimize the destruction of their towns and villages, brought upon by this war." He believed that Germans could be persuaded to lay down their weapons to save "a million lives" and prevent "enormous additional destruction." He thought that they would be amenable to the following appeal: "You are fighting on because Hitler has nothing more to lose: He lost already. You die not for victory or Germany but for Himmler's period of grace."[68]

As the nation lurched toward defeat, some Germans came to realize the truth of these assessments. Many others did not, their faith in the führer as ingrained as their belief in their cause and the righteousness of a German victory against all odds. This was true even when they considered that the history books might condemn them. As a German POW by the name of Hofmann reflected, "I suppose [the Allies] are writing a history of the war for the coming generation, and we Germans will be depicted as war criminals, and Hitler will be made a scapegoat for having started the war. No one will have anything to do with the German people anymore and everyone will hate us. But the German people will never forget Hitler." When his cellmate interjected that "Hitler will be hated by the German people as much as by the others," Hofmann maintained, "One can't judge that today at all, only history will be able to judge. Schopenhauer wasn't thought great by his contemporaries, either, and only the coming generations will be able to say whether the Führer was a genius or not."[69]

Conclusion

Understanding What National Socialism Is

World War II was the deadliest war in human history, a global calamity of proportions unprecedented then and unmatched since. In its quest for a Greater Germanic Reich, the Nazi regime unleashed waves of barbarism and destruction that wiped entire worlds off the map long before its own citizens experienced the full impact of the conflagration. Few Germans had welcomed the war when it began in 1939, but the ease and spectacle of the early conquests seduced many. Shocked when the tide turned in 1943, they reluctantly embarked on total mobilization while resenting the inequities of its burdens. By 1944, when the nation suffered a catastrophic bloodletting, many Germans considered the continuation of the war a matter of national self-preservation. Still waiting for the vaunted "miracle" or "turnaround," they were stunned when in 1945 defeat came instead.

This book is about the stories Germans told themselves to make sense of their world in crisis. While the Nazi regime orchestrated the epic of its self-destruction, Germans struggled to shape the narratives of their own wartime experiences. Increasingly distrustful of official propaganda, they nonetheless scoured domestic and foreign news reports for reliable indicators of the war effort. Most importantly, they talked and listened to each other, whether in extended conversations or in hushed remarks, overheard or shared. Germany's wartime rumor mill churned incessantly as people traded in stories, gossip, and speculations that ranged from the factual to the fabricated, from the mundane to the outlandish. Members of the civilian and military populations exchanged information with particular urgency to assess the true state of the war abroad and at home. This perpetual, multidirectional information transfer produced endless strands of popular commentary on the unfolding events. As Germans wove them into the often incongruous tapestry of their wartime discourse, they also fashioned early iterations of the "war generation's" collective memories, myths, and alibis that would persist for decades to come.

As Peter Hoffmann, a prolific scholar of the Nazi period, reminds us, "One of the most difficult tasks for students of history is to see historical events and persons as their contemporaries saw them. Students must attempt to know and understand what those of another time knew and understood."[1] This was the goal of this book: to know and understand some of what Germans at war knew and understood or, perhaps more precisely, what they thought they knew and understood. I take seriously the historian's responsibility to contextualize and annotate voices from the past, particularly voices from an era that wrought such devastation. At the same time, my primary aim was not to assess the veracity of the individual accounts featured in this book. The wartime rumors and stories relayed here, with all the unwitting errors and deliberate corruptions they entail, offer glimpses into people's attempts to assign order and meaning to a world upended. They serve as portals in the mental landscapes inhabited by Germans at war and the values, beliefs, and prejudices embedded therein.

There is no single story of Germans at war, and I did not aim to forge one out of the chorus of voices captured here. Instead, this book serves as an examination of a range of experiences, interpretations, and attitudes that were commonly and frankly expressed by select members of the German military and civilian populations and that transcended the divisions of German wartime society and reverberated beyond the small sample under examination. We know that time and place mattered in how Germans experienced the prolonged dissolution of the Third Reich. Choice and contingency, too, accounted for dramatically different wartime experiences in the many theaters of war over time, including the home front. However, no matter where they lived and fought, German civilians and combatants increasingly perceived their experiences as comparable and their contributions to the war effort as equally critical. This was due in part to the dynamic and intentional information exchange between the various segments of Germany's wartime society, which molded shared perceptions of the Nazi regime in the later war years and generated common reactions to impending defeat.

Between 1943 and 1945, German civilians and military combatants increasingly reimagined themselves as the war's heroes and victims simultaneously, struggling for the very survival of their nation against a global enemy coalition. The collective inversion of the war's aggressor and victim roles resulted in popular expressions of bewilderment and self-pity that seem ludicrous in hindsight. This was of course most pronounced among Germans like Reisiger who harbored "firm loyalties to Nazi principles" and who believed that the war had been instigated by "the Jews" for the destruction of "the Nordic people." As late as January 1945, he fretted, "In a way, everyone is to blame for these misfortunes that have befallen us. If one were to think about it all properly, it would break one's heart."[2] But Germans along a moral and ideological spectrum revealed a similar mix of confusion, self-absorption, anger, and resignation about their personal and national fate. How else to explain the German letter writer who, genuinely shocked, stated in September 1944, "We Germans have nothing but enemies in the entire world, and one has to wonder why we are so hated"? Another letter writer professed confusion about the source of their enemies' "hatred" given that the "German is such an industrious and decent person." And a third mused, "It can't be because of the Nazis because they did not exist in 1918 and back then the entire world hated us too."[3] These reflections suggest that few Germans questioned the legitimacy of their war well into defeat.

"The war" constituted the mental landscape that framed many Germans' observations and perceptions regardless of their specific circumstances. Not surprisingly, this had a decisive impact on the nature and endurance of popular support for the Nazi regime. In their reflections on the world at war, contemporaries vigorously contested the efficacy of the Nazi regime in decline. Indeed, a wealth of evidence suggests that many Germans disengaged from the Nazi movement even before the strains of a long war exacerbated their disillusionment. People openly resented the uneven realization of the vaunted Nazi "social revolution" and its failure to eradicate old privileges in

German society. Worse, in the eyes of many, the regime had introduced new inequities by promoting a class of brazen usurpers, deserving neither by birth nor by merit. Germans' near unanimous loathing of petty party functionaries was a powerful indicator of a long-standing popular discontent. Not surprisingly, such resentments were amplified as the spoils of war dwindled and its burdens grew. The diatribes of Lieutenant Metzenthien against the greed and callousness of Nazi administrators were indicative of a widespread animus against the party apparatus.[4]

Many Germans were quick to impugn all levels of the Nazi hierarchy, including the very top, at every military setback. After the final defeat, they used their earlier critiques to bolster their credentials, cast off their incriminating past, and position themselves advantageously for the future in the post-Nazi era. Victor Klemperer, who observed the waning years of the Third Reich from the periphery of the persecuted, bemoaned this trend already discernible in the final months of the war. Together with his ailing wife, he had spent the spring months of 1945 on an odyssey across southern Germany, making his way from bombed-out Dresden to Lower Bavaria. It was an act of tenacity and defiance, an attempt to outrun the violent crescendo of war and a regime intent on his destruction even as it self-destructed. As he had vowed years earlier, Klemperer continued to "bear witness, precise witness!" while the "everyday calamities" of life in wartime continued until the very end.[5]

In his search for reliable information about the unfolding collapse, Klemperer not only chronicled his own reflections but also captured the thoughts and observations of the countless friends, acquaintances, and strangers he encountered along the way. Though rarely conclusive, his diary is a collage of their voices from the final weeks of the world at war, rendered in vivid detail. On May 4, 1945, with peace so close, Klemperer chronicled a long conversation with two young Wehrmacht soldiers the previous day. He noted that the men, both Sudeten Germans in their early twenties, had served in the army for five years before their unit disbanded in Bavaria, and they were trying to make their way home. Klemperer recounted their reflections:

> They had frequently passed Americans, finally some were riding along the railway track on a trolley, so far unmolested. Yesterday they had listened to a radio, *everything* including Berlin, had capitulated, and Hitler was dead. The student declared: "If anyone had told me that, even four weeks ago, I would

have shot him down—but now I don't believe anything anymore. . . ." [The Nazis] had wanted too much, they had overdone things, there had been atrocities, the way people had been treated in Poland and Russia, inhuman![6]

With his customary acuity, Klemperer captured a seeming paradox frequently found in the stories many Germans told themselves about defeat. They claimed to have retained their trust in the Nazi regime and had fought bravely until the bitter end only to see their profound loyalty evaporate totally and irrevocably in defeat. In this telling, then, popular "faith" in the regime was faith in the regime's ability to achieve victory. When Germany's unconditional surrender made the reality of defeat undeniable, popular allegiances allegedly vanished. Some, like the young Wehrmacht soldiers, added perfunctory critiques of the Nazi regime's crimes and atrocities to account for their disillusionment. However, they rarely reckoned with the implicit fact that they had accepted such conditions as part of the war as long as a German victory seemed attainable. Nor did they reckon with the now inconvenient truth that even their tacit acceptance of Nazi occupation policies and genocidal violence bound them closely to the regime that had subjugated an entire continent to enact a horrendously brutal vision of German greatness.

Another encounter recorded by Klemperer on May 11, 1945, three days after Germany's unconditional surrender, adds to this picture. He asked a woman, "young, not unintelligent," who had returned from Munich "if she had heard anything about Hitler and the other Nazi bosses": "*No*, she had no time to ask about that: in other words: it no longer interested her. The 3rd Reich is already almost as good as forgotten, everyone was opposed to it, 'always' opposed to it; and the people have the most absurd ideas about the future. And patriotism?"[7] Klemperer went on to recount an argument he had overheard between a local woman and two wartime refugees over who had borne the greatest sacrifices for the war effort. The woman was adamant that the peasants like herself had contributed the most. She claimed that they "had worked, were the most important people, etc." Meanwhile, one of the refugees insisted that industrial workers had shouldered not only the burdens of the home front but those of the entire war effort. She proclaimed, "*We* worked in the armaments factories." In his diary, Klemperer confessed that, like the refugees, he, too, harbored resentments toward Germany's peasants. On the whole, he believed the rural populations had been "better off" and sheltered from the war's dangers. And now, in the immediate postwar era they continued to be "incomparably better off than the rest."[8] If popular Nazi loyalties could evaporate overnight, the same was clearly not true for popular resentments over the unequal burdens of the war.

The ubiquity of "turncoats" in the general population and their brazen, expedient erasure of the inconvenient Nazi past led Klemperer to lament, "The populace is absolutely without history, in every respect."[9] Was National Socialism so ephemeral and contingent a phenomenon that it vanished alongside the wartime landscapes that had framed the internal and external lives of Germans for so many years? Was it already forgotten at the war's end? The answer is bound to be complicated. The myth of the war's end as a German zero hour has long been unmasked as such. But although too many of the Third Reich's defining structures and mentalities endured beyond defeat, contemporaries frequently described their experience of the final war years as belonging to a world that vanished in 1945. What endured were stories of their own suffering and hardships that would come to define the "war generation's" collective "memory" of World War II. It left little room for a reckoning with the suffering that Germans had wrought onto others.

The threads of popular opportunism and expediency run through the pages of Klemperer's diaries as they do through the pages of this book, though they alone cannot explain popular support for twelve years of Nazism, including nearly six years of war. Many ordinary Germans were deeply invested in National Socialism's twin projects of racial imperialism and homogenization that found their devastating, genocidal expression in the war. Metzenthien had hinted at this in his discussion of the "political attitude of the German" in the fall of 1944. He had brushed aside as mere semantics the question of how the ideology of "National Socialism" differed from "communism" or "socialism." To him, National Socialism was not a substantive belief system rooted in German politics or culture but a banner under which Hitler had reached for German global supremacy. In achieving what "no-one else could," Hitler had made "every German a Nazi."[10] Metzenthien's reflections suggest that, even late in the war, many Germans remained committed to National Socialism in hopes that the movement would deliver on its early promises. Popular loyalty endured despite the regime's much-lamented flaws and contradictions. Germans complained incessantly about the system's corruptions, its failures and pathologies, and the strains of total war. Still, many continued to believe that the Nazi regime was capable of redeeming itself even as evidence of its self-destruction mounted.

Metzenthien's assertion notwithstanding that "a Müller or a Schubert" could have led Germany in continental conquest, Hitler held a central position in the public imagination of Germans at war. Indeed, the story of Germans' enduring investment in National Socialism cannot be told without their relationship to the führer. Among the Nazi elite, Hitler alone commanded the ardent love and devotion that withstood even the military catastrophes of the final war years. Popular expressions of adulation liberally and indiscriminately mixed religious, mythical, and ideological elements, as was the case in a tortured letter written by Fräulein A. Helms in late August 1944, in which she explained Hitler's central role in the future Reich that would be built on the ruins of the "sacrificial offering of our nation":

> All those who have failed will not partake in the fruits and the joy [that is ours once we] overcome the crisis. Those are not for them. But thankfully they are just a few while the majority is decent and has enough of a sense of honor to not get misled but do something! *And we must continue to believe that all sacrifices for the nation are worth it.* There was a time when I was so silly to believe that [all sacrifices were] worth it for the Führer and for the Fatherland [alone], for the Idea of it rather than for the people. . . . Today I know that that is not right because the Führer, the Idea and the Fatherland would be merely an illusion without the Volk which [is the center of] everything. *And that is why I won't be led astray and will continue to believe in the Volk,* [which means I believe] *in the Führer as my embodiment and in our holy Germany.*[11]

Popular faith in Hitler endured even the violent end phase of the war. In his conversation with the two German soldiers mere days before the German surrender, Klemperer noted their stubborn insistence that "the Führer probably knew nothing about" the crimes and atrocities committed in the German name. Klemperer concluded that Hitler "undoubtedly had a religious effect" on the populace.[12] The reflections of many other contemporaries point to the fact that Nazism's foundational myth was broadly accepted as fact and endured in the popular imagination until defeat. For instance, as late as October 1944, Lieutenant Ahlers reasoned: "From a religious point of view one has got to admit that the German people are *the* people in the world, obviously, and when Providence has given us a man like the Führer, and this man is a genius, the kind that is only born once every few hundred years, a man with a sixth sense, who has lifted the German people out of the mess they were in, do you think that was just in order to let them sink back again to where they were before?"[13]

Throughout the 1930s, Hitler had promised the German people a national revival, greatness, and purpose.[14] They had believed him, and his early successes suggested that he would deliver on these promises even more spectacularly in war. Hitler remained the embodiment of Germans' hopes and aspirations even after the war effort deteriorated. That is not to say that he was immune from criticism. Germans from all walks of life complained of Hitler's failures during the years of increasing hardship. But every German military success—whether real or perceived—also elicited popular expressions of gratitude to the führer and renewed faith that he would soon produce the longed-for "miracle" or "turnaround." Indeed, the depth of people's faith in Hitler is evident in the common belief that his continuation of the war was proof of the inevitability of a German victory. Many Germans could not conceive that a leader, *their* leader, intentionally pursued the policy of personal and national self-annihilation that had been announced after the defeat at Stalingrad. Even in a world at war, where anything could and indeed did happen, this notion remained unthinkable. At the very least, popular expressions of doubt about Hitler's capabilities and intentions remained a social taboo even among those who otherwise "grumbled and complained." As Herr Engelkrug put it in an intercepted letter from Barkhausen to the eastern front in September 1944, "There are people here especially in our neighborhood who think differently, but I really let them have it. No one can take away my faith in the Führer and in the final victory."[15] Hence, many Germans experienced Hitler's suicide as a shocking act of betrayal that in their eyes dwarfed his many other crimes. Indeed, his abandonment of the German people in defeat led many to assume the role of victim at war's end.

Hitler held a powerful sway over the German imagination because many believed that he alone could produce the "miracle" needed to turn the course of the war once again in Germany's favor. Plied by incessant propaganda with decidedly religious and mystical overtones, many Germans imagined the "miracle" as a sudden but definitive blow against the Allies and that would ultimately deliver a German final victory. The "miracle" was essentially an act of redemption and that would provide compensation for the sacrifices and disappointments of the final war years. It kept hope for a victory alive and allowed them to discount evidence of Nazi Germany's catastrophic unraveling. It opened spaces for people to vent their doubts about the Nazi leadership they nonetheless thought capable of self-redemption. As they waited for the return on their hopes invested in National Socialism, Germans forged themselves into the mobilized national community of Nazi lore. In the later war years, they did so increasingly despite the Nazis.

Many also did so despite themselves. The stories that Germans told themselves frequently chronicled their relentless efforts to weed out "truth" from misinformation, whether in official or personal accounts. They condemned clumsy propaganda and prided themselves on their critical faculties and independent reason, clearly unaware of their own ideological conversion. For instance, few people explicitly acknowledged that the very notion of the "miracle" was a figment of Nazi propaganda. Nor did they accede that the longed-for "miracle" as a harbinger of geopolitical supremacy and a racially homogenous social order was firmly rooted in the Nazi worldview.

What do we know and understand about what the Germans of the waning Third Reich knew and understood? We know that "ordinary Germans" expended tremendous energies to make sense of their world at war. They clamored for "facts." They demanded to know the "truth," and when the truth proved too hard to bear, they blended fact and fiction seamlessly. Nazi ideology provided many of the ingredients that papered over the cracks in their worldview. Under escalating crisis conditions, Germans frequently described their world in binaries of good and evil, strength and weakness, dominance and annihilation. And, once again accustomed to the experience of German supremacy, they long refused to contemplate defeat as a real possibility. They deemed the undesirable unthinkable and the unthinkable impossible. And they convinced themselves that somehow, someday—with and even without the Nazis—they would achieve their destined personal and national fulfillment.

Scholars have argued that the seemingly disjointed, incoherent, and virulent aspects of Nazi ideology were an asset, not a liability.[16] This seems particularly true in the later war years, when the Nazi regime orchestrated the existential struggle that lay at the very heart of its philosophy. As their world plunged into extreme upheaval, Germans struggled to make sense of the preposterous events that unfolded daily, including the mass slaughter of civilians, be it of Jewish civilians in the killing fields or of German civilians in cities turned to rubble by Allied bombers. Nazi ideology provided some of the vocabulary and concepts that helped them analyze and explain these events. Few seemed aware, however, that Nazi ideology did not just mirror the world around them, but had driven its destruction.

The fragmented stories of the final war years as told by the principal actors are testament to the fact that ordinary people's worldviews can be malleable and tenacious at once and that reason and moral scruples can be suspended with ease. They are a reminder that under extreme conditions, extreme acts and rationalizations are not only possible but can become the norm. This is what truly set the world at war apart. Still, many Germans eschewed the part that Nazi leadership assigned them in the epic of dissolution. They were not blind believers, and theirs was not a suicidal fanaticism. Most fought to live, not die. They fought to see a future in which they would be compensated for their own sacrifices and shielded from the consequences of their crimes. From its inception, the Nazi movement and its ideology had been aspirational. It had promised grand visions for the future and few blueprints for the now. That is why the strains of war never fully discredited the regime. In fact, the opposite is true. Crisis conditions obscured Nazism's shortcomings in the now while promising true realizations in the far-off future. As the regime's failures compounded, so did the aspiration of many Germans for personal and national fulfillment in a far-off postwar era. Their faith in the self-redemptive power of Nazism only died in total defeat, but by then they were well accustomed only to look forward and never back.

Notes

Introduction

1. CSDIC (CMF), X 70, information received October 9–13, 1944, RG 226, Entry 109, Box 9, Folder 62, 4, NARA.

2. Ibid., 3.

3. Ibid., 2.

4. Ibid.

5. Ibid., 3.

6. Ibid.

7. Ibid., 4.

8. Ibid., 1.

9. Ibid., 7.

10. RH 13/49, Wehrmacht Field Post Censorship Digest from September 1944, 22, BA-MA. The censorship digest is based on analysis of more than twenty thousand pieces of mail to and from the front.

11. CSDIC (CMF), X 70, information received October 9–13, 1944, RG 226, Entry 109, Box 9, Folder 62, 3, NARA.

12. Ibid., 4.

13. Ibid., 7.

14. For an introduction to the rich German-language literature on the violence and crimes of the war's "end phase," see Sven Keller, *Volksgemeinschaft am Ende: Gesellschaft und Gewalt 1944/45* (Munich: Oldenbourg Verlag, 2013).

15. Wolfram Wette, "Zwischen Untergangspathos und Überlebenswillen: Die Deutschen im letzten halben Kriegsjahr 1944/45," in Wolfram Wette, Ricarda Bremer, and Detlef Vogel, eds., *Das letzte halbe Jahr: Stimmungsberichte der Wehrmachtpropaganda 1944/45* (Essen: Klartext Verlag, 2001), 10.

16. Michael H. Kater, *The Nazi Party: A Social Profile of Members and Leaders, 1919–1945* (Cambridge, MA: Harvard University Press, 1983), 159.

17. Wette, "Zwischen Untergangspathos und Überlebenswillen," 12.

18. Nicholas Stargardt, *The German War: A Nation under Arms, 1939–1945; Citizens and Soldiers* (New York: Basic Books, 2015), 1.

19. RH 13/49, letter dated September 8, 1944, excerpt in Wehrmacht Field Post Censorship Digest from September 1944, 24, BA-MA.

20. My sample of transcripts covers the period under examination and draws from the different branches of the German armed forces quite evenly. Of the 2,370 transcripts used here, 880 were generated in 1943, 1,075 in 1944, and 415 in the first four months of 1945. Furthermore, 402 of the transcripts cover conversations between rank-and-file members of the Luftwaffe, 555 between members of the Wehrmacht, and 348 between members of the German navy; 307 are mixed conversations between members of different branches; and 709 detail conversations among German generals.

21. For a brief overview of the origin and organization of the CSDIC, see Stephen Tyas, "Allied Intelligence Agencies and the Holocaust: Information Acquired from German Prisoners of War," *Holocaust and Genocide Studies* 22, no. 1 (Spring 2008): 1–24.

22. Sönke Neitzel, *Abgehört: Deutsche Generäle in britischer Kriegsgefangenschaft 1942–1945* (Berlin: Ullstein Taschenbuchverlag, 2007), 13.

23. This topic list was quoted by Tyas from a 1944 War Office report. Tyas, "Allied Intelligence," 2–3.

24. Neitzel, *Abgehört*, 14–15.

25. Tyas, "Allied Intelligence," 2.

26. CSDIC (CMF), X 70, information received October 9–13, 1944, RG 226, Entry 109, Box 9, Folder 62, 4, NARA.

27. Many prisoners may have suspected that they were being monitored. Many may have been guarded even in their seemingly "private" conversations, but conversations that were noticeably guarded or reticent were unlikely to be recorded and transcribed. A close reading of the transcripts and other intelligence materials suggests that the level of personal or ideological affinity between cellmates was the most important factor determining how freely and extensively prisoners spoke about sensitive subject matters.

28. While the names of those involved in atrocities were collected by British authorities for the Central Registry of War Criminals and Security Suspects, Tyas has found no indication that CSDIC records had been used to investigate or prosecute war criminals. Instead, after the end of the war Britain's Joint Intelligence Sub-Committee decided to protect their sources and methods by classifying the reports as top secret. See Tyas, "Allied Intelligence," 15–16.

29. The US War Department oversaw a monitoring operation run jointly by the US Army and the US Navy at Camp Tracy in California and Fort Hunt in Virginia. Though they worked with a smaller pool of about three thousand German POWs, they created more substantive intelligence files, which included extensive interrogation records, social profiles, biographical sketches, questionnaires, and longitudinal tracking of attitudes and opinions. See Felix Römer, *Kameraden: Die Wehrmacht von innen* (Munich: Piper Verlag, 2012). There is also evidence that the Soviet Union and Germany may have taped or otherwise documented interviews and interrogations of select prisoners. Neitzel, *Abgehört*, 12.

30. I am greatly indebted to the pioneering analyses of CSDIC transcripts in Neitzel, *Abgehört*; Sönke Neitzel and Harald Welzer, *Soldaten: Protokolle vom Kämpfen, Töten und Sterben* (Frankfurt am Main: S. Fischer Verlag, 2011); and Harald Welzer, Sönke Neitzel, and Christian Gudehus, eds., *"Der Führer war wieder viel zu human, viel zu gefühlvoll": Der Zweite Weltkrieg aus der Sicht deutscher und italienischer Soldaten* (Frankfurt am Main: S. Fischer Verlag, 2011). These and other related titles have been expertly analyzed by Robert Gellately in his review published in the *Journal of Modern History* 86, no. 2 (June 2014): 479–485.

31. CSDIC (CMF), X 70, information received October 9–13, 1944, RG 226, Entry 109, Box 9, Folder 62, 4, NARA.

32. RH 13/49, letter dated September 18, 1944, excerpt in Wehrmacht Field Post Censorship Digest from September 1944, 44, BA-MA.

33. In fact, the Nazi regime tried to utilize German civilians' trust in soldiers as a source of "truthful" information for its own propaganda and surveillance purposes. Between October 1944 and April 1945, it began a new campaign in several major cities that aimed to boost morale and gauge public opinion. Soldiers were deployed to start whisper campaigns among the general population and report back their impressions. Wette, "Zwischen Untergangspathos und Überlebenswillen," 18.

34. RH 13/49, letter dated September 17, 1944, excerpt in Wehrmacht Field Post Censorship Digest from September 1944, 42, BA-MA. (Jansen is from page 42; Lakowsky from page 47; both letters have the same date.)

35. Ibid.

36. In fact, more than five hundred thousand German women served as Wehrmacht helpers (Wehrmachthelferinnen) over the course of the war in a number of different capacities. While most were deployed to the home front, others served in occupied Poland and France, as well as in Yugoslavia, Greece, and Romania. See Karen Hagemann, "Mobilizing Women for War: The History, Historiography, and Memory of German Women's War Service in the Two World Wars," *Journal of Military History* 75 (2011): 1055–1094.

37. On "linguistic landscape," see Frederick Corney, *Telling October: Memory and the Making of the Bolshevik Revolution* (Ithaca, NY: Cornell University Press, 2004), 201.

38. RH 13/49, letter dated August 22, 1944, excerpt in Wehrmacht Field Post Censorship Digest from September 1944, 78, BA-MA. The line of verse originates from "Men and Boys," a poem of the Napoleonic War era by Carl Theodor Körner. It frequently

appeared in Nazi propaganda, most famously in Joseph Goebbels's 1943 Sport Palace speech, in which he called for total mobilization.

39. RH 13/49, letter dated September 22, 1944, excerpt in Wehrmacht Field Post Censorship Digest from September 1944, 40, BA-MA.

40. RH 13/49, Wehrmacht Field Post Censorship Digest from September 1944, 22, BA-MA.

41. Ibid., 21.

42. RH 13/49, Wehrmacht Field Post Censorship Digest from September 1944, 20, BA-MA.

43. RH 13/49, letter dated September 14, 1944, excerpt in Wehrmacht Field Post Censorship Digest from September 1944, 38, BA-MA.

44. RH 13/49, letter dated September 10, 1944, excerpt in Wehrmacht Field Post Censorship Digest from September 1944, 62–63, BA-MA.

1. Stalingrad

1. Joseph Goebbels, head of the Nazi Party's propaganda staff, "Guidelines for the Speech by Party Leaders to the Party Membership," January 29, 1943, German Propaganda Archive, Calvin University, https://research.calvin.edu/german-propaganda-archive/30jan1943.htm#speech, accessed August 24, 2020.

2. Aristotle A. Kallis, "Die Talsohle der Stimmungslage: Stalingrad," in *Die Deutsche Kriegsgesellschaft 1939 bis 1945*, Bd. 9, T. 2, *Ausbeutung, Deutungen, Ausgrenzung*, ed. Jörg Echternkamp (Munich: Deutsche Verlags-Anstalt, 2005), 231–233.

3. Speech quoted from Max Domarus, ed., *Hitler, Speeches and Proclamations 1932–1945 and Commentary by a Contemporary: The Chronicle of a Dictatorship*, vol. 4, *1941–1945* (Wauconda, IL: Bolchazy-Carducci Publishers, 1987), 2745–2746.

4. Heinz Boberach, ed. *Meldungen aus dem Reich 1938–1945* (Herrsching: Pawlak Verlag, 1984), Nr. 356, February 4, 1943, 4751.

5. Victor Klemperer, *I Will Bear Witness: A Diary of the Nazi Years, 1942–1945* (New York: Modern Library, 2001), 357.

6. Ibid., 231–233.

7. Kallis, "Die Talsohle der Stimmungslage," 231.

8. Klemperer, *I Will Bear Witness*, 150.

9. Letter quoted in Richard J. Evans, *The Third Reich at War, 1939–1945* (New York: Penguin, 2009), 410.

10. SRN1338, information received December 11, 1942, WO 208/4144, TNA.

11. SRN1238, information received December 2, 1942, WO 208/4144, TNA.

12. SRN1338, information received December 11, 1942, WO 208/4144, TNA.

13. Victor Klemperer, *The Language of the Third Reich: LTI—Lingua Tertii Imperii; A Philologist's Notebook* (New York: Continuum, 2006), 40.

14. Michael Geyer, "*Endkampf* 1918 and 1945: German Nationalism, Annihilation, and Self-Destruction," in *No Man's Land of Violence: Extreme Wars in the 20th Century*, ed. Alf Lüdtke and Bernd Weisbrod (Göttingen: Wallstein Verlag, 2006), 52.

15. *Meldungen*, Nr. 356, February 4, 1943, 4751.

16. *Meldungen*, Nr. 370, March 25, 1943, 5002.

17. *Meldungen*, Nr. 365, March 8, 1943, 4902.

18. SRA1275, information received June 28, 1943, WO 208/4130, TNA.

19. Ibid.

20. Ibid.

21. SRA4799, information received January 9, 1944 (my translation from the German), TNA.

22. Ibid.

23. Peter Fritzsche, *Life and Death in the Third Reich* (Cambridge, MA: Belknap Press of Harvard University Press, 2008), 282.

24. SRA4105, information received June 20, 1943, WO 208/4130, TNA.

25. SRM411, information received November 9, 1943 (translated from the German), WO 208/4137.

26. SRN1845, information received May 26, 1943, WO 208/4130, TNA.

27. Ibid.

28. SRA3945, information received April 17, 1943, WO 208/4130, TNA.

29. Ibid.

30. SRN1468, information received February 21, 1943, WO 208/4144, TNA.

31. Ibid.

32. SRM292, information received June 20, 1943, WO 208/4136, TNA.

33. SRA3956, information received April 18, 1943, WO 208/4130, TNA.

34. SRX1424, information received December 26, 1942, WO 208/4162, TNA.

35. SRM202, information received June 20, 1943, WO 208/4136, TNA.

36. SRN1468, information received February 21, 1943, WO 208/4144, TNA.

37. SRA4805, information received January 9, 1944, WO 208/4132, TNA.

38. *Meldungen*, Nr. 356, February 4, 1943, 4751.

39. SRX1876, information received October 10, 1943, WO 208/4137, TNA.

40. SRX1428, information received December 28, 1942, WO 208/4162, TNA.

41. SRA4791, information received January 6, 1944, WO 208/4132, TNA.

42. *SD-Berichte zu Inlandsfragen*, August 19, 1943 (Rote Serie), 5646.

43. SRA4054, information received June 3, 1943, WO 208/4130, TNA.

44. Ibid.

45. SRM419, information received December 19, 1943, WO 208/4137, TNA.

46. SRA4566, information received November 23, 1943, WO 208/4131, TNA.

47. Ibid.

48. SRM253, information received October 19, 1943, WO 208/4137, TNA.

49. SRM253, information received July 6, 1943, WO 208/4130, TNA.

50. Ibid.

51. Ibid.

52. SRN242, information received September 2, 1943, WO 208/4137, TNA.

53. *Meldungen*, Nr. 357, April 8, 1943, 5081.

54. Ibid.

55. *Meldungen*, Nr. 370, March 25, 1943, 5002.

56. *SD-Berichte zu den Inlandsfragen*, December 27, 1943 (Weisse Serie), 6206.

57. Ibid., 5062.

58. *Meldungen*, Nr. 363, March 1, 1943, 4869.

59. *Meldungen*, Nr. 376, April 15, 1943, 5124.

60. SRA4805, information received January 9, 1944, WO 208/4132, TNA.

61. *Meldungen*, June 25, 1943, 5402.

62. SRA4283, information received August 13, 1943, WO 208/4130, TNA.

63. Ibid.

64. Ibid.

65. *SD-Berichte zu Inlandsfragen*, November 11, 1943 (Grüne Serie), 5995.

66. *Meldungen*, Nr. 373, April 5, 1943, 5061.

67. *Meldungen*, Nr. 374, April 8, 1943, 5080–5081.

68. SRA4109, information received June 21, 1943, WO 208/4130, TNA.

69. Ibid.

70. *SD-Berichte zu Inlandsfragen*, November 11, 1943 (Grüne Serie), 5990.

71. Ibid.

72. *Meldungen*, Nr. 368, March 18, 1943, 4967.

73. *SD-Berichte zu Inlandsfragen*, August 12, 1943 (Rote Serie), 5595.

74. Ibid., 5595–5596.

75. Ibid., 6112.

76. Ibid. (emphasis mine).

77. *Meldungen*, Nr. 374, April 8, 1943, 5081.

78. *Meldungen*, Nr. 368, March 18, 1943, 4966.

79. *Meldungen*, Nr. 365, March 8, 1943, 4902.

80. *Meldungen*, Nr. 368, March 18, 1943, 4966.

81. Fritzsche, *Life and Death*, 280–281.

82. Ibid., 10.

83. Ibid.

84. SRM363, information received October 31, 1943, WO 208/4137, TNA.

85. Klemperer, *I Will Bear Witness*, 54.

86. Ibid., 357.

87. Ibid., 198.

88. Ibid., 357.

89. As Peter Fritzsche explains, "Thousands of loyal Nazis killed themselves and their families in April and May 1945." Fritzsche, *Life and Death*, 282.

2. Mobilizing the National Community

1. Willi A. Boelcke, ed., *"Wollt Ihr den totalen Krieg?" Die geheimen Goebbels Konferenzen 1939–1943* (Munich: Deutsche Verlags-Anstalt, 1969), 414.

2. Joseph Goebbels, "People, Rise Up, and Storm, Break Loose," in *Landmark Speeches of National Socialism*, ed. Randall L. Bytwerk (College Station: Texas A&M University Press, 2008), 114.

3. Ibid., 138–139.

4. Albert Speer, *Inside the Third Reich* (New York: Simon & Schuster, 1970), 257.

5. Goebbels, "People, Rise Up," 136.

6. Peter Longerich, *Joseph Goebbels: Biographie* (Munich: Siedler Verlag, 2010), 539–545.

7. SRA4105, captured on April 7, 1943, WO 208/4130, TNA.

8. A4130, information received June 13, 1943, WO 208/4130, TNA.

9. SRN1799, information received May 13, 1943, WO 208/4145, TNA.

10. SRA4427, captured on August 27, 1943, WO 208/4131, TNA.

11. SRM435, captured in Italy on October 7, 1943, WO 208/4137, TNA.

12. SRA4148, information received July 13, 1943, WO 208/4130, TNA.

13. SRM435, captured on October 18, 1943, WO 208/4137, TNA.

14. SRN1799, captured on April 17, 1943, WO 208/4130, TNA.

15. SRA4185, information received January 19, 1944, WO 208/4131, TNA.

16. SRA4843, information received June 3, 1945, WO 208/4145, TNA.

17. Ibid.

18. Ibid.

19. SRN1875, information received May 13, 1945, WO 208/4145, TNA.

20. SRN1799, captured on May 11, 1943, WO 208/4243, TNA.

21. Ibid.

22. SRA4243, captured on May 23, 1943, WO 208/4145, TNA.

23. SRN1857, captured on November 12, 1942, WO 208/4144, TNA.

24. SRN1304, captured on September 19, 1943, WO 208/4132, TNA.

25. *Meldungen*, Nr. 361, February 22, 1943, 831.

26. *Meldungen*, Nr. 362, February 25, 1943, 4844.

27. Martin Pöppel, *Heaven and Hell: The War Diaries of a German Paratrooper* (Staplehurst, Kent: Spellmount, 1988), 101.

28. *Meldungen*, Nr. 362, February 25, 1943, 4844.

29. *Meldungen*, Nr. 364, March 4, 1943, 4893.

30. Ibid.

31. Sven Oliver Müller, *Deutsche Soldaten und ihre Feinde: Nationalismus an Front und Heimatfront im Zweiten Weltkrieg* (Frankfurt am Main: S. Fischer Verlag, 2007), 87–95.

32. *Aus deutschen Urkunden 1935–1945*, Nr. 32, IWM.

33. *Meldungen*, Nr. 361, February 22, 1943, 4831.

34. Ibid.

35. RH 13/49, Wehrmacht Field Post Censorship Digest from September 1944, 21, BA-MA.

36. Goebbels, "People, Rise Up," 130.

37. Ibid., 127–130.

38. Ibid., 130.

39. Wolfgang Michalka, ed., *Das Dritte Reich: Dokumente zur Innen- und Außenpolitik* (Munich: Deutscher Taschenbuch Verlag, 1985), 294.

40. Longerich, *Joseph Goebbels*, 544–548.

41. Ibid., 556.

42. *Meldungen*, Nr. 357, February 8, 1943, 4765.

43. Ibid.

44. SRM423, information received December 23, 1943, WO 208/4137, TNA.

45. SRA3945, information received April 17, 1943, WO 208/4130, TNA.

46. SRN1799, captured on April 17, 1943, WO 208/4145, TNA.

47. SRA4791, information received January 6, 1944, WO 208/4132, TNA.

48. SRA4858, information received January 23, 1944, WO 208/4132, TNA.

49. SRA4791, information received January 6, 1944, WO 208/4132, TNA.

50. SRM385, information received November 16, 1943, WO 208/4137, TNA.

51. Ibid.

52. SRA4819, information received January 12, 1943, WO 208/4132, TNA.

53. SRN1888, information received June 8, 1943, WO 208/4145, TNA.

54. SRN1878, information received January 8, 1943, WO 208/4145, TNA.

55. *Meldungen*, Nr. 356, February 4, 1943, 4756.

56. SRN1294, captured on November 21, 1942, WO 208/4144, TNA.

57. Ibid.

58. SRN1304, captured on November 21, 1942, WO 208/4145, TNA.

59. SRN1294, captured on November 21, 1942, WO 208/4144, TNA.

60. SRN1799, captured on April 17, 1943, WO 208/4145, TNA.

61. SRA4433, information received September 28, 1943, WO 208/4131, TNA.

62. SRA4183, captured on April 17, 1943, WO 208/4130, TNA.

63. Gitta Sereny, *Albert Speer: His Battle with Truth* (New York: Vintage Books, 1995), 387–390.

64. Elke Fröhlich, ed., *Die Tagebücher von Joseph Goebbels*, Teil II, *Diktate 1941–1945*, Bd. 10, *Oktober–Dezember 1943* (Munich: K. G. Saur, 1994), 69–70.

65. SRN1799, captured on April 17, 1943, WO 208/4145, TNA.

66. SRN1845, captured on April 17, 1943, WO 208/4145, TNA.

67. *Meldungen*, Nr. 381, March 6, 1943, 5235.

68. SRN1799, information received May 13, 1943, WO 208/4145, TNA.

69. SRX1424, information received December 26, 1942, WO 208/4162, TNA.

70. Ibid.

71. SRA4181, information received July 12, 1943, WO 208/4130, TNA.

72. SRA4805, information received January 9, 1943, WO 208/4132, TNA.

73. SRM410, information received December 16, 1943, WO 208/4137, TNA.

74. SRN434, information received December 29, 1943, WO 208/4137, TNA.

75. SRA4433, information received September 28, 1943, WO 208/4131, TNA.

76. SRA4818, information received January 12, 1944, WO 208/4132, TNA.

77. SRA4266, information received August 9, 1943, WO 208/4130, TNA.

78. Ibid.

79. SRA4182, information received July 13, 1943, WO 208/4130, TNA.

80. Ibid.

81. Ibid.

82. Ibid.

83. Ibid.

84. Ibid.

85. SRA4435, information received September 29, 1943, WO 208/4131, TNA.

86. Ibid.

87. *Meldungen*, Nr. 381, March 6, 1943, 5236–5237.

88. RH 13/49, letter dated September 17, 1944, excerpt in Wehrmacht Field Post Censorship Digest from September 1944, 47, BA-MA.

89. *Meldungen*, Nr. 381, March 6, 1943, 5236–5237.

90. In particular, see Götz Aly, *Hitler's Beneficiaries: Plunder, Racial War, and the Nazi Welfare State* (New York: Metropolitan Books, 2007).

91. Evans, *The Third Reich at War*, 427.

92. *Meldungen*, Nr. 379, April 29, 1943, 5202.

93. SRM435, captured on October 7, 1944, WO 208/4137, TNA.

94. SRN1294, captured on November 21, 1942, WO 208/4144, TNA.

95. SRA4182, captured on April 17, 1943, WO 208/4130, TNA.

96. M217, captured on May 7, 1943, WO 208/4136, TNA.

97. SRA4182, captured on April 17, 1943, WO 208/4130, TNA.

98. A1385, captured on May 12, 1943, WO 208/4132, TNA.

3. Genocide and Mass Atrocities

1. Richard Breitman, *The Architect of Genocide: Himmler and the Final Solution* (Hanover, NH: Brandeis University Press, 1991), 241–243.

2. Ibid., 242–243.

3. Bradley F. Smith and Agnes F. Peterson, eds., *Heinrich Himmler: Geheimreden 1933 bis 1945* (Frankfurt am Main: Propyläen Verlag, 1974), 169–171.

4. Quoted in Sereny, *Albert Speer*, 392.

5. Peter Longerich, *"Davon haben wir nichts gewusst!": Die Deutschen und die Judenverfolgung 1933–1945* (Munich: Siedler Verlag, 2006).

6. David Bankier, *The Germans and the Final Solution: Public Opinion under Nazism* (Cambridge, MA: Blackwell Publishers, 1992), 102.

7. Smith and Peterson, *Heinrich Himmler*, 13.

8. SRA4373, information received September 13, 1943, WO 208/4131, TNA.

9. *Die Juden*, Nr. 701, 529.

10. SRA4561, information received October 16, 1943, WO 208/4131, TNA.

11. *Die Juden*, Nr. 701, 529.

12. SRN1309, information received December 3, 1942, WO 208/4144, TNA.

13. SRA3948, information received April 16, 1943, WO 208/4130, TNA.

14. SRN1680, information received March 20, 1943, WO 208/4162, TNA.

15. Ibid.

16. SRM210, information received June 25, 1943, WO 208/4136, TNA.

17. Ibid.

18. SRA3966, information received April 26, 1943, WO 208/4130, TNA.

19. SRA4166, information received July 7, 1943, WO 208/4130, TNA.

20. SRA4216, information received July 20, 1943, WO 208/4130, TNA.

21. SRA2966, information received April 26, 1943, WO 208/4130, TNA.

22. SRA4174, information received July 14, 1943, WO 208/4130, TNA.

23. SRA4373, information received September 13, 1943, WO 208/4131, TNA.

24. SRN1680, information received March 20, 1943, WO 208/4162, TNA.

25. SRA4030, information received May 25, 1943, WO 208/4130, TNA.
26. SRA3964, information received April 23, 1943, WO 208/4130, TNA.
27. Ibid.
28. SRA2528, information received December 19, 1943, WO 208/4148, TNA.
29. Ibid.
30. Ibid.
31. SRA4174, information received July 14, 1943, WO 208/4130, TNA.
32. Information received December 19, 1943, WO 208/4148, TNA.
33. SRA2528, information received December 19, 1943, WO 208/4148, TNA.
34. Ibid.
35. SRA4604, information received October 27, 1943, WO 208/4131, TNA.
36. SRA4427, information received September 26, 1943, WO 208/4231, TNA.
37. SRA4604, information received October 27, 1943, WO 208/4131, TNA.
38. Ibid.
39. Ibid.
40. Ibid.
41. SRX1837, information received October 10, 1943, WO 208/4137, TNA.
42. Quoted and translated from "Rede des Reichsführers SS bei der SS-Gruppenführertagung in Posen am 4. Oktober 1943," available at *100(0) Schlüsseldokumente zur deutschen Geschichte im 20. Jahrhundert*. Accessed August 24, 2020, https://www.1000dokumente.de/pdf/dok_0008_pos_de.pdf.
43. SRA4604, information received October 27, 1943, WO 208/4131, TNA.
44. SRX1837, information received October 10, 1943, WO 208/4137, TNA.
45. Ibid.
46. Sönke Neitzel and Harald Welzer have shown that the topic appeared in only up to 0.2 percent of the available materials. However, according to the authors, the quality and tone of such conversations "do reveal that practically everybody knew or suspected that Jews were being murdered." Neitzel and Welzer, *Soldaten*, 146.
47. SRX1876, information received October 10, 1943, WO 208/4137, TNA.
48. SRA4030, information received May 25, 1943, WO 208/4130, TNA.
49. SRA3964, information received April 23, 1943, WO 208/4130, TNA.
50. SRA3948, information received April 16, 1943, WO 208/4130, TNA.
51. ARM4137, information received November 18, 1943, WO 208/4137, TNA.
52. SRA4373, information received September 26, 1943, WO 208/4231, TNA.
53. SRA4820, information received January 13, 1944, WO 208/4132, TNA.
54. SRA4243, information received August 1, 1943, WO 208/4130, TNA.
55. SRM426, information received December 28, 1943, WO 208/4137, TNA.
56. SRA4820, information received January 13, 1944, WO 208/4132, TNA.
57. SRA4604, information received October 27, 1943, WO 208/4131, TNA.
58. SRA4174, information received July 14, 1943, WO 208/4130, TNA.
59. Neitzel and Welzer, *Soldaten*, 146.
60. SRA3948, information received April 16, 1943, WO 208/4130, TNA.
61. *Die Juden*, Nr. 664, 510.
62. *Die Juden*, Nr. 696, 527.
63. Document IIIC4-Wi/Gi, SD Stuttgart, November 6, 1944, in *Aus deutschen Urkunden 1935–1945*, IWM.

64. Richard Breitman, *Official Secrets: What the Nazis Planned, What the British and Americans Knew* (New York: Hill and Wang, 1998), 88–92.

65. Longerich, *"Davon haben wir nichts gewusst!,"* 240–242. As Peter Longerich has pointed out, based on his analysis of the remnants of British propaganda material from this period, including radio and leaflets, while the murder of Jews was mentioned repeatedly and in increasingly specific terms, it rarely constituted the focus of this coverage but was generally presented as part of other Nazi atrocities. Longerich, *"Davon haben wir nichts gewusst!,"* 246–247.

66. SRN1387, information received December 24, 1942, WO 208/4144, TNA.

67. *BBC Surveys of European Audiences, Germany*, May 22, 1943, RG 208, Entry 367, Box 255, File E92, Series IF, NARA.

68. As per Goebbels's instructions to newspaper publishers, journalists were to sensationalize British atrocities in particular, "be it in India, in the Near East, in Iran, Egypt, etc., anywhere where there are Englishmen." There were a few attempts, but the campaign never really got off the ground, and there is little evidence to suggest that the German readership paid any attention to it. Longerich, *"Davon haben wir nichts gewusst!,"* 257.

69. Longerich, *Joseph Goebbels*, 542–573.

70. *BBC Surveys of European Audiences, Germany*, May 22, 1943, RG 208, Entry 367, Box 255, File E92, Series IF, NARA.

71. Goebbels, "People, Rise Up," 121.

72. Klemperer, *I Will Bear Witness*, 202.

73. Ibid.

74. *Die Juden*, Nr. 668, 513.

75. *Die Juden*, Nr. 667, 512–513.

76. *Die Juden*, Nr. 669, 513–514.

77. *Die Juden*, Nr. 691, 525.

78. *Die Juden*, Nr. 709, 532.

79. *Die Juden*, Nr. 689, 524.

80. *Die Juden*, Nr. 721, 536.

81. *Die Juden*, Nr. 664, 510.

82. *Die Juden*, Nr. 709, 532.

83. *Die Juden*, Nr. 700, 529.

84. *Die Juden*, Nr. 668, 510.

85. *Die Juden*, Nr. 679, 519–520.

86. *Die Juden*, Nr. 682, 521.

87. Ibid. See also Longerich, *"Davon haben wir nichts gewusst!,"* 283–285.

88. *Die Juden*, Nr. 684, 521–522.

89. Longerich, *"Davon haben wir nichts gewusst!,"* 263–264.

90. *Die Juden*, Nr. 709, 532.

91. *Die Juden*, Nr. 675, 527.

92. *Die Juden*, Nr. 701, 529.

93. *Die Juden*, Nr. 707, 531.

94. *Die Juden*, Nr. 711, 533.

95. *Die Juden*, Nr. 682, 521.

96. *Die Juden*, Nr. 705, 530.

97. *Die Juden*, Nr. 698, 528.

98. *Die Juden*, Nr. 694, 526.

99. *Die Juden*, Nr. 688, 523–524.

100. Ibid.

101. Longerich, *"Davon haben wir nichts gewusst!,"* 267–269.

102. *BBC Surveys of European Audiences: Germany*, May 22, 1943, RG 208, Entry 367, Box 255, File E92, Series IF, NARA.

103. *Die Juden*, Nr. 674, 515–516.

104. *Die Juden*, Nr. 678, 519.

105. Ibid.

106. *Die Juden*, Nr. 674, 515–516.

107. *Die Juden*, Nr. 675, 518.

108. *Die Juden*, Nr. 676, 518.

109. Yehuda Bauer, "Holocaust Rescue Revisited," *Israel Journal of Foreign Affairs* 7, no. 3 (2013): 142.

4. Enemies Within and Without

1. Peter Hoffmann, *The History of the German Resistance 1933–1945* (Montreal: McGill-Queen's University Press, 1996), 404.

2. Ibid., 507–523. The failed assassination and coup attempt of July 20, 1944, have been examined in great detail. In addition to Hoffmann's study, see also Peter Hoffmann, ed., *Behind Valkyrie: German Resistance to Hitler; Documents* (Montreal: McGill-Queen's University Press, 2011).

3. Evans, *The Third Reich at War*, 638–639.

4. Stargardt, *The German War*, 452.

5. Adolf Hitler, "Rundfunkansprache zum Attentat vom 20. Juli 1944, 21. Juli 1944, 1.00 Uhr.," *100(0) Schlüsseldokumente zur deutschen Geschichte im 20. Jahrhundert*. Accessed September 4, 2020, https://www.1000dokumente.de/index.html?c=dokument _de&dokument=0083_ahr&object=translation&l=de.

6. Klemperer, *I Will Bear Witness*, 337–338.

7. Jörg Echternkamp, ed., *Germany and the Second World War*, vol. 9, pt. 1, *German Wartime Society 1939–1945: Politicization, Disintegration, and the Struggle for Survival* (New York: Oxford University Press, 2008), 648–649.

8. RH 13/48, letter dated September 3, 1944, excerpt in Wehrmacht Field Post Censorship Digest from September 1944, 66–67, BA-MA.

9. RH 13/48, letter dated August 1, 1944, excerpt in Wehrmacht Field Post Censorship Digest from September 1944, 120, BA-MA.

10. RH 13/48, letter dated August 17, 1944, excerpt in Wehrmacht Field Post Censorship Digest from September 1944, 121, BA-MA.

11. RH 13/48, letter dated September 11, 1944, excerpt in Wehrmacht Field Post Censorship Digest from September 1944, 63, BA-MA.

12. SRA4781, information received January 5, 1944, WO 208/4132, TNA.

13. RH 13/48, Wehrmacht Field Post Censorship Digest from September 1944, 36, BA-MA.

14. RH 13/48, letter dated September 13, 1944, excerpt in Wehrmacht Field Post Censorship Digest from September 1944, 47–48, BA-MA.

15. RH 13/48, letter dated September 12, 1944, excerpt in Wehrmacht Field Post Censorship Digest from September 1944, 47–48, BA-MA.

16. RH 13/48, letter dated August 13, 1944, excerpt in Wehrmacht Field Post Censorship Digest from September 1944, 122, BA-MA.

17. RH 13/48, letter dated August 9, 1944, excerpt in Wehrmacht Field Post Censorship Digest from September 1944, 120, BA-MA.

18. CSDIC, SRGG1134 (C), information received January 3, 1945, RG 226, Entry 109, Box 9, Folder 61, NARA.

19. Ian Kershaw, *The End: The Defiance and Destruction of Hitler's Germany, 1944–1945* (New York: Penguin, 2011), 67–70.

20. CSDIC, SRM1010, information received February 27, 1945, RG 226, Entry 109, Box 9, Folder 61, NARA.

21. RH 13/49, undated letter, excerpt in Wehrmacht Field Post Censorship Digest from September 1944, 157–158, BA-MA.

22. CSDIC, SRGG 1125, information received January 27, 1945, RG 226, Entry 109, Box 9, Folder 61, 2, NARA.

23. RH 13/49, undated letter, excerpt in Wehrmacht Field Post Censorship Digest from September 1944, 157, BA-MA.

24. RH 13/49, letter dated September 8, 1944, excerpt in Wehrmacht Field Post Censorship Digest from September 1944, 120, BA-MA.

25. RH 13/49, letter dated September 16, 1944, excerpt in Wehrmacht Field Post Censorship Digest from September 1944, 38, BA-MA.

26. RH 13/49, letter dated September 16, 1944, excerpt in Wehrmacht Field Post Censorship Digest from September 1944, 39, BA-MA.

27. RH 13/49, letter dated September 15, 1944, excerpt in Wehrmacht Field Post Censorship Digest from September 1944, 29, BA-MA.

28. RH 13/49, letter dated September 11, 1944, excerpt in Wehrmacht Field Post Censorship Digest from September 1944, 63, BA-MA.

29. Stargardt, *The German War*, 450–456.

30. Jürgen Förster, "The Totalness of National Socialism after 20 July 1944," in Echternkamp, *Germany and the Second World War*, vol. 9, pt. 1, 648.

31. RH 13/48, Wehrmacht Field Post Censorship Digest from September 1944, 141, BA-MA.

32. RH 13/48, letter dated September 16, 1944, excerpt in Wehrmacht Field Post Censorship Digest from September 1944, 40, BA-MA.

33. RH 13/48, letter dated September 15, 1944, excerpt in Wehrmacht Field Post Censorship Digest from September 1944, 38, BA-MA.

34. RH 13/48, letter dated September 7, 1944, excerpt in Wehrmacht Field Post Censorship Digest from September 1944, 141, BA-MA.

35. RH 13/48, letter dated July 31, 1944, excerpt in Wehrmacht Field Post Censorship Digest from August 1944, 54, BA-MA.

36. RH 13/48, Wehrmacht Field Post Censorship Digest from September 1944, 141, BA-MA.

37. RH 13/48, letter dated September 20, 1944, excerpt in Wehrmacht Field Post Censorship Digest from September 1944, 42, BA-MA.

38. RH 13/48, letter dated September 19, 1944, excerpt in Wehrmacht Field Post Censorship Digest from September 1944, 42, BA-MA.

39. RH 13/48, letter dated September 15, 1944, excerpt in Wehrmacht Field Post Censorship Digest from September 1944, 44–45, BA-MA.

40. RH 13/48, letter dated September 21, 1944, excerpt in Wehrmacht Field Post Censorship Digest from September 1944, 43, BA-MA.

41. RH 13/48, letter dated September 16, 1944, excerpt in Wehrmacht Field Post Censorship Digest from September 1944, 43, BA-MA.

42. RH 13/48, letter dated September 16, 1944, excerpt in Wehrmacht Field Post Censorship Digest from September 1944, 43, BA-MA.

43. Stargardt, *The German War*, 469.

44. RH 13/48, Wehrmacht Field Post Censorship Digest from September 1944, 22, BA-MA.

45. Hans Uhle, "The Party Overcomes Terror," trans. Randall L. Bytwerk, German Propaganda Archive, Calvin University. Accessed August 24, 2020, http://research.calvin .edu/german-propaganda-archive/terror1944.htm. The article was published as "Die Partei überwinden den Terror," *Die Auslese*, July 1944, reprinted from the *Deutschen Illustrierte*, May 23, 1944. *Die Auslese* was a monthly periodical akin to the *Reader's Digest*.

46. CSDIC, SRN4649, information received February 27, 1945, RG 226, Entry 109, Box 9, Folder 61, NARA.

47. CSDIC, SRM1161, information received January 3, 1945, RG 226, Entry 109, Box 9, Folder 61, NARA.

48. CSDIC, SRA5692, information received December 29, 1944, RG 226, Entry 109, Box 9, Folder 61, NARA.

49. CSDIC, SRA5768, information received January 26, 1945, RG 226, Entry 109, Box 9, Folder 61, NARA.

50. CSDIC, SRN4464, information received December 21, 1944, RG 226, Entry 109, Box 9, Folder 61, NARA.

51. CSDIC (CMF), X 70, information received October 9–13, 1944, RG 226, Entry 109, Box 9, Folder 62, 1, NARA.

52. RH 13/48, letter dated September 11, 1944, excerpt in Wehrmacht Field Post Censorship Digest from September 1944, 141, BA-MA.

53. Dokument 81, reprinted in Jörg Echternkamp, ed., *Kriegsschauplatz Deutschland 1945: Leben in der Angst, Hoffnung auf den Frieden; Feldpost aus der Heimat und von der Front* (Paderborn: Ferdinand Schöningh, 2006), 189–190.

54. RH 13/49, letter dated September 7, 1944, excerpt in Wehrmacht Field Post Censorship Digest from September 1944, 39, BA-MA.

55. RH 13/49, letter dated September 4, 1944, excerpt in Wehrmacht Field Post Censorship Digest from September 1944, 70, BA-MA.

56. *Die Juden*, Nr. 733, 540.

57. *Die Juden*, Nr. 738, 541–542.

58. Dokument 82, reprinted in Echternkamp, *Kriegsschauplatz Deutschland 1945*, 190–191.

59. Ibid.

60. RH 13/48, letter dated September 9, 1944, excerpt in Wehrmacht Field Post Censorship Digest from September 1944, 167, BA-MA.

61. CSDIC, SRM1120, information received December 14, 1944, RG 226, Entry 109, Box 9, Folder 61, NARA.

62. CSDIC, SRM1110, information received December 8, 1944, RG 226, Entry 109, Box 9, Folder 61, NARA.

63. *Die Juden*, Nr. 725, 537.

64. *Die Juden*, Nr. 728, 538.

65. CSDIC, SRN4536, information received January 3, 1945, RG 226, Entry 109, Box 9, Folder 62, NARA.

66. CSDIC, SRX2080, information received January 2, 1945, RG 226, Entry 109, Box 9, Folder 61, NARA.

67. CSDIC (CMF), X 70, information received October 9–13, 1944, RG 226, Entry 109, Box 9, Folder 62, 4, NARA.

68. Toward the end of the war the regime tried to utilize German civilians' thirst for "true information" and their trust in soldiers as a source of truth for its own propaganda and surveillance purposes. Between October 1944 and April 1945, it began a new campaign in several major cities to boost morale and gather information about public attitudes. Soldiers were deployed to start whisper campaigns among the population and report back their impressions. Limited in scope, the operation nevertheless generated a few dozen surveillance reports illuminating public "mood and attitude" for a thinly documented period. See Wette, "Zwischen Untergangspathos und Überlebenswillen," *Das letzte halbe Jahr*, 18.

5. Dissolution

1. "Report of Birch, Chief Organizer of Operation Tissue," April 16, 1945, RG 226, Entry 210, Box 53, Folder 4, NARA.

2. CSDIC, "Nazi Philosophers, 1945," conversation held on January 16, 1945, RG 226, Entry 109, Box 9, Folder 61, NARA.

3. Ibid.

4. "What the Germans Are Saying," infantry private and ex-librarian, RG 263, ZZ17, Box 8, NARA.

5. CSDIC (UK), GRGG263, "Report on Information Obtained from Senior Officer PW on February 21–23, 1945," RG 165, Entry 179, Box 649, NARA.

6. "Certificate of Marriage, Private Will, and Political Testament of Adolf Hitler," translated digital copy, DocsTeach, NARA. Accessed 24, 2020, https://www.docsteach.org/documents/document/marriage-certificate-private-will-and-political-testament-of-adolf-hitler.

7. Fritzsche, *Life and Death*, 282.

8. CSDIC (CMF), X 70, information received October 9–13, 1944, RG 226, Entry 109, Box 9, File 62, 3, NARA.

9. As Wette explains, between 1944 and 1945, 10 million soldiers fought in the Wehrmacht. Between the summer of 1944 and May 1945, more Germans died than in the previous years of the war combined. During this period, between 300,000 and 400,000

German soldiers were killed per month. Altogether, some 2.6 million German soldiers died during this period. See Wette, "Zwischen Untergangspathos und Überlebenswillen," in Wette, Bremer, and Vogel, eds., *Das letzte halbe Jahr* (Essen: Klartext Verlag, 2001), 9–13.

10. RH 13/49, letter dated September 21, 1944, excerpt in Wehrmacht Field Post Censorship Digest from September 1944, 41, BA-MA.

11. Corporal Ernst M., Dokument 46, printed in Echternkamp, *Kriegsschauplatz Deutschland 1945*, 157.

12. CSDIC, "Nazi Philosophers, 1945," RG 226, Entry 109, Box 9, Folder 61, NARA.

13. CSDIC (Main), X 106, December 28, 1944, RG 226, Entry 109, Box 9, Folder 61, NARA.

14. RH 13/49, letter dated October 15, 1944, excerpt in Wehrmacht Field Post Censorship Digest from September 1944, 44, BA-MA.

15. RH 13/49, letter dated September 19, 1944, excerpt in Wehrmacht Field Post Censorship Digest from September 1944, 41, BA-MA.

16. RH 13/49, letter dated September 16, 1944, excerpt in Wehrmacht Field Post Censorship Digest from September 1944, 41, BA-MA.

17. RH 13/49, letter dated September 21, 1944, excerpt in Wehrmacht Field Post Censorship Digest from September 1944, 47, BA-MA.

18. RH 13/49, letter dated September 21, 1944, excerpt in Wehrmacht Field Post Censorship Digest from September 1944, 43–44, BA-MA.

19. Frau U., Angelsdorf, January 16, 1945, reprinted in Echternkamp, *Kriegsschauplatz Deutschland 1945*, 121.

20. RH 13/48, letter dated September 20, 1944, excerpt in Wehrmacht Field Post Censorship Digest from September 1944, 41, BA-MA.

21. Corporal Erwin S., November 14, 1944, Dokument 1, reprinted in Echternkamp, *Kriegsschauplatz Deutschland 1945*, 113–114.

22. CSDIC (CMF), XS 135, information received February 10, 1945, RG 226, Entry 109, Box 9, Folder 61, NARA.

23. Klemperer, *I Will Bear Witness*, 390.

24. "Report of Birch," April 16, 1945, RG 226, Entry 210, Box 53, Folder 4, NARA.

25. Gerhard Levine, "A Report on Contacts with German Prisoners of War," January 3, 1945, RG 226, Entry 210, Box 291, NARA.

26. Corporal Paul-Diedrich N., Holland, November 18, 1944, Dokument 2, reprinted in Echternkamp, *Kriegsschauplatz Deutschland 1945*, 114.

27. Corporal Ernst M., Gotenhafen, March 18, 1945, Dokument 49, reprinted in Echternkamp, *Kriegsschauplatz Deutschland 1945*, 113–114.

28. "Report of Birch," April 16, 1945, RG 226, Entry 210, Box 53, Folder 4, NARA.
29. Ibid.

30. RH 13/48, letter dated September 19, 1944, excerpt in Wehrmacht Field Post Censorship Digest from September 1944, 39, BA-MA.

31. "What the German PWs Think about the War," undated, RG 226, Entry 210, Box 175, NARA.

32. This report is not dated but appears to have been generated on or after January 23, 1945. The report's author provides a list of four potentially friendly German

POWs in the cages, dated January 23, 1945. See "Report about One Week's Life and Experiences in a P.W. Camp," RG 226, Entry 210, Box 175, NARA.

33. CSDIC, "Nazi Philosophers, 1945," RG 226, Entry 109, Box 9, Folder 61, NARA.

34. "Report about a Stay in a P.W. Camp," undated, RG, 226, Entry 210, Box 175, NARA.

35. CSDIC, "Nazi Philosophers, 1945," conversations held on January 16, 1945, RG 226, Entry 109, Box 9, Folder 61, NARA.

36. "Report of Birch," June 7, 1945, RG 226, Entry 210, Box 53, Folder 4, NARA.

37. Corporal Paul-Diedrich N., Holland, November 18, 1944, Dokument 2, reprinted in Echternkamp, *Kriegsschauplatz Deutschland 1945*, 114–115.

38. Levine, "A Report on Contacts with German Prisoners of War," January 3, 1945, RG 226, Entry 210, Box 291, NARA.

39. "Report of Birch," April 1, 1945, RG 226, Entry 210, Box 53, Folder 4, NARA.

40. Ibid.

41. "Report about a Stay in a P.W. Camp," 1945, RG 226, Entry 210, Box 175, NARA.

42. Levine, "A Report on Contacts with German Prisoners of War," January 3, 1945, RG 226, Entry 210, Box 291, NARA.

43. RH 13/48, Wehrmacht Field Post Censorship Digest from September 1944, 32, BA-MA.

44. CSDIC, SRX2033, information received October 26, 1944, RG 226, Entry 109, Box 9, Folder 61, NARA.

45. Dokument 65, "Bericht des Wehrmacht-Propaganda-Offiziers des Wehrkreiskommandos III, Berlin, Oberstleutnant Wasserfall, über den 'Sondereinsatz Berlin,'" 20. November 1944–26. November 1944, BA-MA, RW 4/v. 266, S. 133, reprinted in Wette, Bremer, and Vogel, *Das letzte halbe Jahr*, 159–160.

46. Klemperer, *I Will Bear Witness*, 390.

47. "What the Germans Are Saying," German prisoner of war captured in mid-October 1944 at Paros, Greece, RG 263, ZZ17, Box 8, NARA.

48. CSDIC (Main), X 90, November 28, 1944, RG, 226, Entry 109, Box 9, Folder 61, NARA.

49. CSDIC (Main), X 107, December 28, 1944, RG, 226, Entry 109, Box 9, Folder 61, NARA.

50. Levine, "A Report on Contacts with German Prisoners of War," January 3, 1945, RG 226, Entry 210, Box 291, NARA.

51. "What the Germans are Saying," an intelligent German corporal, captured near Forli, Italy, December 1944, RG 263, ZZ17, Box 8, NARA.

52. Ian Kershaw, *The "Hitler Myth": Image and Reality in the Third Reich* (New York: Oxford University Press, 1987), 181–184.

53. Dokument 85, "Bericht des Wehrmacht-Propaganda-Offiziers des Wehrkreiskommandos XIII, Nürnberg, Oberstleutnant Wasserfall, über den 'Sondereinsatz Berlin,'" 1. März 1945–15. März 1945, BA-MA, RW 4/v. 266, S. 202b–221, reprinted in Wette, Bremer, and Vogel, *Das letzte halbe Jahr*, 158

54. "What the Germans are saying. Conversation between a Brigadier General and a Colonel," September 1944, RG 263, ZZ17, Box 8, NARA.

55. Dokument 65, "Bericht des Wehrmacht-Propaganda-Offiziers des Wehrkreis-kommandos III, Berlin, Oberstleutnant Wasserfall, über den 'Sondereinsatz Berlin,'" 20. November 1944–26. November 1944, BA-MA, RW 4/v. 266, S. 133, reprinted in Wette, Bremer, and Vogel, *Das letzte halbe Jahr*, 158–159.

56. Dokument 81, "Bericht des Wehrmacht-Propaganda-Offiziers des Wehrkreis-kommandos III, Berlin, Oberstleutnant Wasserfall, über den 'Sondereinsatz Berlin,'" 23. März 1945–29. März 1945, BA-MA, RW 4/v. 266, S. 43–52, reprinted in Wette, Bremer, and Vogel, *Das letzte halbe Jahr*, 309–310.

57. Dokument 88, "Bericht des Wehrmacht-Propaganda-Offiziers des Wehrkreis-kommandos X, Hamburg, Hauptmann Schubert, 15. März 1945–22. März 1945, BA-MA, RW 4/v. 266, S. 179–183, reprinted in Wette, Bremer, and Vogel, *Das letzte halbe Jahr*, 232

58. "What the Germans Are Saying," sergeant major captured on the Fifth Army Front, November 19, 1944, RG 263, ZZ17, Box 8, NARA.

59. Levine, "A Report on Contacts with German Prisoners of War," January 3, 1945, RG 226, Entry 210, Box 291, NARA.

60. Ibid.

61. "Report about a Stay in a P.W. Camp," undated, RG, 226, Entry 210, Box 175, NARA.

62. See Wette, "Zwischen Untergangspathos und Überlebenswillen," in Wette, Bremer, and Vogel, eds., *Das letzte halbe Jahr*, 12.

63. CSDIC (CMF), X 130, conversation held on January 9, 1945, RG 226, Entry 109, Box 9, Folder 61, NARA.

64. "Report of Birch," June 7, 1945, RG 226, Entry 210, Box 53, Folder 4, NARA.

65. CSDIC (CMF), X 145, conversation held on March 15, 1945, RG 226, Entry 109, Box 8, NARA.

66. "What the German PWs Think about the War," undated, RG 226, Entry 210, Box 175, NARA.

67. "Report about a Stay in a P.W. Camp," undated, RG 226, Entry 210, Box 175, NARA.

68. Levine, "A Report on Contacts with German Prisoners of War," January 3, 1945, RG 226, Entry 210, Box 291, NARA.

69. CSDIC (CMF), XS 135, information received February 10, 1945, RG 226, Entry 109, Box 9, Folder 61, NARA.

Conclusion

1. Hoffmann, *Behind Valkyrie*, 3.

2. CSDIC, "Nazi Philosophers, 1945," RG 226, Entry 109, Box 9, Folder 61, NARA.

3. RH 13/49, Wehrmacht Field Post Censorship Digest from September 1944, 36, BA-MA.

4. CSDIC (CMF), X 70, information received October 9–13, 1944, RG 226, Entry 109, Box 9, File 62, 3, NARA.

5. Klemperer, *I Will Bear Witness*, 479 (entry from May 13, 1945).

6. Ibid., 472–473.

7. Ibid., 477–478.

8. Ibid., 478.

9. Ibid.

10. CSDIC (CMF), X 70, information received October 9–13, 1944, RG 226, Entry 109, Box 9, File 62, 7, NARA.

11. RH 13/49, letter dated August 31, 1944, excerpt in Wehrmacht Field Post Censorship Digest from September 1944, 63–64, BA-MA.

12. Klemperer, *I Will Bear Witness*, 472–473. Other contemporaries, too, argued that Nazism was best understood as a "political religion" in a secular age in which regimes tried to achieve political cohesion through popular ideologies of blood and class, among others. Eric Voegelin, *Die politischen Religionen* (Paderborn: Wilhelm Fink, 1993).

13. CSDIC (CMF), X 70, information received October 9–12, 1944, RG 226, Entry 109, Box 9, File 62, 5, NARA.

14. Claudia Koonz, *The Nazi Conscience* (Cambridge, MA: Belknap Press of Harvard University Press, 2003), 2.

15. RH 13/49, letter dated September 15, 1944, excerpt in Wehrmacht Field Post Censorship Digest from September 1944, 39, BA-MA.

16. Koonz, *The Nazi Conscience*, 2.

BIBLIOGRAPHY

Archival Sources

Bundesarchiv-Militärarchiv, Freiburg, Germany (BA-MA)

RH 13/48.
RH 13/49.

Imperial War Museum, Department of Documents, London,
United Kingdom (IWM)

Aus deutschen Urkunden 1935–1945.

The National Archives, Kew, United Kingdom (TNA)

FO 371/34426–34440: *Foreign Office: Political Departments: General Correspondence from*
1906–1966.
WO 208/3699–5018: *War Office: Directorate of Military Operations and Intelligence, and*
Directorate of Military Intelligence; Ministry of Defence, Defence Intelligence Staff.

National Archives and Records Administration (II), College Park, Maryland, United States (NARA)

Record Group 165, Entry 179, Box 649, NARA: *Records of the War Department General and Special Staffs.*

Record Group 208, Entry 367, Box 255, File E92, Series If: *Records of the Office of War Information.*

Record Group 226, Entry 109, Boxes 8 and 9: *Records of the Office of Strategic Services.*

Record Group 226, Entry 210, Box 53: *Records of the Office of Strategic Services.*

Record Group 263, ZZ17, Box 8: "What the Germans Are Saying."

Published Primary Sources

Boberach, Heinz, ed. *Meldungen aus dem Reich 1938–1945.* Bd. 12–17. Herrsching: Pawlak Verlag, 1984.

Boelcke, Willi A., ed. *"Wollt Ihr den totalen Krieg?" Die geheimen Goebbels Konferenzen 1939–1943.* Munich: Deutsche Verlags-Anstalt, 1969.

Buchbender, Ortwin, and Reinhold Sterz, eds. *Das andere Gesicht des Krieges: Deutsche Feldpostbriefe 1939–1945.* Munich: Verlag C. H. Beck, 1982.

Fröhlich, Elke, ed. *Die Tagebücher von Joseph Goebbels.* T. II, *Diktate 1941–1945*, Bd. 10, *Oktober–Dezember 1943.* Munich: K. G. Saur, 1994.

Humburg, Martin, ed. *Das Gesicht des Krieges: Feldpostbriefe von Wehrmachtssoldaten aus der Sowjetunion 1941–1944.* Opladen, Wiesbaden: Westdeutscher Verlag, 1998.

Klemperer, Victor. *I Will Bear Witness: A Diary of the Nazi Years, 1942–1945.* New York: Modern Library, 2001.

Kulka, Otto Dov, and Eberhard Jäckel, eds. *Die Juden in den geheimen Stimmungsberichten 1933–1945.* Düsseldorf: Droste, 2004.

Michalka, Wolfgang, ed. *Das Dritte Reich: Dokumente zur Innen- und Außenpolitik.* Munich: Deutscher Taschenbuch Verlag, 1985.

Pöppel, Martin. *Heaven and Hell: The War Diaries of a German Paratrooper.* Staplehurst, Kent: Spellmount, 1988.

Smith, Bradley F., and Agnes F. Peterson, eds. *Heinrich Himmler: Geheimreden 1933 bis 1945.* Frankfurt am Main: Propyläen Verlag, 1974.

Published Secondary Sources

Aly, Götz. *Hitler's Beneficiaries: Plunder, Racial War, and the Nazi Welfare State.* New York: Metropolitan Books, 2007.

Ansbacher, H. L. *Attitudes of German Prisoners of War: A Study of the Dynamics of National-Socialist Followership.* Psychological Monographs: General and Applied, vol. 62. Washington, DC: American Psychological Association, 1948.

Arendes, Cord, Edgar Wolfrum, and Jörg Zedler, eds. *Terror nach Innen: Verbrechen am Ende des Zweiten Weltkrieges.* Göttingen: Wallstein Verlag, 2006.

Arendt, Hannah. *The Origins of Totalitarianism.* New York: Meridian, 1969.

Bajohr, Frank. *Massenmord und schlechtes Gewissen: Die deutsche Bevölkerung, die NS-Führung und der Holocaust.* Frankfurt am Main: S. Fischer Verlag, 2008.

———. *Parvenüs und Profiteure: Korruption in der NS-Zeit.* Frankfurt: S. Fischer, 2001.

Bajohr, Frank, and Dieter Pohl. *Der Holocaust als offenes Geheimnis: Die Deutschen, die NS-Führung und die Alliierten.* Munich: Beck, 2006.

Bankier, David. *The Germans and the Final Solution: Public Opinion under Nazism.* Cambridge, MA: Blackwell, 1992.

———, ed. *Probing the Depths of German Antisemitism: German Society and the Persecution of the Jews, 1933–1941.* New York: Berghahn Books, 2000.

———. *Secret Intelligence and the Holocaust.* New York: Enigma Books, 2006.

Bartov, Omer. *The Eastern Front, 1941–1945: German Troops and the Barbarization of Warfare.* London: Macmillan, 1985.

———. *Hitler's Army: Soldiers, Nazis, and War in the Third Reich.* New York: Oxford University Press, 1992.

———. *Mirror of Destruction: War, Genocide, and Modern Identity.* New York: Oxford University Press, 2002.

Bauer, Yehuda. "Holocaust Rescue Revisited." *Israel Journal of Foreign Affairs* 7, no. 3 (2013): 127–142.

Bergen, Doris. *War and Genocide: A Concise History of the Holocaust.* 3rd ed. New York: Rowman & Littlefield, 2016.

Bessel, Richard. *Germany 1945: From War to Peace.* New York: HarperCollins, 2009.

———. *Nazism and War.* New York: Modern Library, 2004.

Blair, Clay. *Hitler's U-Boat War: The Hunted, 1942–1945.* New York: Modern Library, 2000.

Breitman, Richard. *The Architect of Genocide: Himmler and the Final Solution.* Hanover, NH: Brandeis University Press, 1991.

———. *Official Secrets: What the Nazis Planned, What the British and Americans Knew.* New York: Hill and Wang, 1998.

Broszat, Martin. *Der Staat Hitlers.* Munich: DTV, 1969.

Browning, Christopher R. *Ordinary Men: Reserve Police Battalion 101 and the Final Solution in Poland.* New York: Harper Perennial, 1992.

Bytwerk, Randall L., ed. *Landmark Speeches of National Socialism.* College Station: Texas A & M University Press, 2008.

Childers, Thomas. *The Nazi Voter: The Social Foundations of Fascism in Germany, 1919–1933.* Chapel Hill: University of North Carolina Press, 1983.

Chodoff, Elliot P. "Ideology and Primary Groups." *Armed Forces and Society* 9 (Summer 1983): 569–593.

Corney, Frederick. *Telling October: Memory and the Making of the Bolshevik Revolution.* Ithaca, NY: Cornell University Press, 2004.

Danker, Uwe, and Astrid Schwabe, eds. *Die NS-Volksgemeinschaft: Zeitgenössische Verheißung, analytisches Konzept und ein Schlüssel zum historischen Lernen?* Göttingen: Vandenhoeck & Ruprecht, 2017.

Davis, Natalie Zemon. *Pardon Tales and Their Tellers in Sixteenth-Century France.* Stanford, CA: Stanford University Press, 1990.

Domarus, Max, ed. *Hitler, Speeches and Proclamations 1932–1945 and Commentary by a Contemporary: The Chronicle of a Dictatorship.* Vol. 4, *1941–1945.* Wauconda, IL: Bolchazy-Carducci Publishers, 1987.

Echternkamp, Jörg, ed. *Die Deutsche Kriegsgesellschaft 1939 bis 1945*. Bd. 9, T. 1, *Politisierung, Vernichtung, Überleben*. Munich: Deutsche Verlags-Anstalt, 2004.

———, ed. *Die Deutsche Kriegsgesellschaft 1939 bis 1945*. Bd. 9, T. 2, *Ausbeutung, Deutungen, Ausgrenzung*. Munich: Deutsche Verlags-Anstalt, 2005.

———, ed. *Germany and the Second World War*. Vol. 9, pt. 1, *German Wartime Society 1939–1945: Politicization, Disintegration, and the Struggle for Survival*. New York: Oxford University Press, 2008.

———, ed. *Kriegsschauplatz Deutschland 1945: Leben in der Angst, Hoffnung auf den Frieden; Feldpost aus der Heimat und von der Front*. Paderborn: Ferdinand Schöningh, 2006.

Evans, Richard J. *The Third Reich at War, 1939–1945*. New York: Penguin, 2009.

Fest, Joachim. *Speer: The Final Verdict*. New York: Harcourt, 1999.

Förster, Jürgen. "The Totalness of National Socialism after 20 July 1944." In *Germany and the Second World War*, vol. 9, pt. 1, *German Wartime Society 1939–1945: Politicization, Disintegration, and the Struggle for Survival*, edited by Jörg Echternkamp, 648–670. New York: Oxford University Press, 2008.

Friedrich, Carl J., ed. *Totalitarianism*. New York: Grosset & Dunlap, 1964.

Frieser, Karl-Heinz, ed. *Das Deutsche Reich in der Defensive: Die Ostfront 1943–1945; Der Krieg im Osten und an den Nebenfronten*. Munich: Deutsche Verlags-Anstalt, 2007.

Fritz, Stephen G. *Frontsoldaten: The German Soldier in World War II*. Lexington: University Press of Kentucky, 1997.

———. "'We Are Trying . . . to Change the Face of the World'—Ideology and Motivation in the Wehrmacht on the Eastern Front: The Views from Below." *Journal of Military History* 60, no. 4 (October 1996): 683–710.

Fritzsche, Peter. *Germans into Nazis*. Cambridge, MA: Harvard University Press, 1999.

———. *An Iron Wind: Europe under Hitler*. New York: Basic Books, 2016.

———. *Life and Death in the Third Reich*. Cambridge, MA: Belknap Press of Harvard University Press, 2008.

Gannon, Michael. *Black May: The Epic Story of the Allies' Defeat of the German U-Boats in May 1943*. New York: Dell, 1999.

Gellately, Robert. *Backing Hitler: Consent and Coercion in Nazi Germany*. New York: Oxford University Press, 2001.

———. *The Gestapo and German Society: Enforcing Racial Policy, 1933–1945*. New York: Oxford University Press, 1991.

———. Review of *Tapping Hitler's Generals: Transcripts of Secret Conversations, 1942–1945*, by Sönke Neitzel; *"Der Führer war wieder viel zu human, viel zu gefühlvoll": Der Zweite Weltkrieg aus der Sicht deutscher und italienischer Soldaten*, edited by Harald Welzer, Sönke Neitzel, and Christian Gudehus; *Soldaten: Protokolle vom Kämpfen, Töten, und Sterben*, by Sönke Neitzel and Harald Welzer; and *Kameraden: Die Wehrmacht von innen*, by Felix Römer. *Journal of Modern History* 86, no. 2 (June 2014): 479–485.

Geyer, Michael. "*Endkampf* 1918 and 1945: German Nationalism, Annihilation, and Self-Destruction." In *No Man's Land of Violence: Extreme Wars in the 20th Century*, edited by Alf Lüdtke and Bernd Weisbrod, 35–53. Göttingen: Wallstein Verlag, 2006.

Goda, Norman J. W. "Allied Intelligence, German Prisoners, Nazi Murderers." In *Secret Intelligence and the Holocaust*, edited by David Bankier, 157–170. New York: Enigma Books, 2006.

Goebbels, Joseph. "People, Rise Up, and Storm, Break Loose." In *Landmark Speeches of National Socialism*, edited by Randall L. Bytwerk, 112–140. College Station: Texas A & M University Press, 2008.

Goldhagen, Daniel Jonah. *Hitler's Willing Executioners: Ordinary Germans and the Holocaust*. New York: Vintage, 1997.

Groß, Sebastian. *Gefangen im Krieg: Frontsoldaten der Wehrmacht und ihre Weltsicht*. Berlin: be.bra wissenschaft verlag, 2012.

Groth, Alexander J. "Demonizing the Germans: Goldhagen and Gellately on Nazism." *Political Science Review* 32 (2003): 118–158.

Hagemann, Karen. "Mobilizing Women for War: The History, Historiography, and Memory of German Women's War Service in the Two World Wars." *Journal of Military History* 75 (2011): 1055–1094.

Hamburger Institut für Sozialforschung. *Krieg ist ein Gesellschaftszustand: Reden zur Eröffnung der Ausstellung "Vernichtungskrieg. Verbrechen der Wehrmacht 1941–1945."* Hamburg: Hamburger Edition, 1998.

Hartmann, Christian. *Wehrmacht im Ostkrieg: Front und militärisches Hinterland 1941–42*. Quellen und Darstellungen zur Zeitgeschichte, Bd. 75. Oldenbourg: Oldenbourg Wissenschaftsverlag, 2010.

Herf, Jeffrey. *The Jewish Enemy: Nazi Propaganda during World War II and the Holocaust*. Cambridge, MA: Belknap Press of Harvard University Press, 2006.

Heyen, Franz J. *Nationalsozialismus im Alltag: Quellen zur Geschichte des Nationalsozialismus vornehmlich im Raum Mainz-Koblenz-Trier*. Boppart: Harald Boldt Verlag, 1967.

Hillmann, Jörg, ed. *Kriegsende 1945 in Deutschland*. Munich: R. Oldenbourg Verlag, 2002.

Hoffmann, Peter, ed. *Behind Valkyrie: German Resistance to Hitler; Documents*. Montreal: McGill-Queen's University Press, 2011.

———. *The History of the German Resistance, 1933–1945*. Montreal: McGill-Queen's University Press, 1996.

———. *Widerstand, Staatsstreich, Attentat: Der Kampf der Opposition gegen Hitler*. Munich: R. Piper, 1969.

Kallis, Aristotle A. "Die Talsohle der Stimmungslage: Stalingrad." In *Die Deutsche Kriegsgesellschaft 1939 bis 1945*, Bd. 9, T. 2, *Ausbeutung, Deutungen, Ausgrenzung*, edited by Jörg Echternkamp, 231–233. Munich: Deutsche Verlags-Anstalt, 2005.

Kater, Michael H. *Hitler Youth*. Cambridge, MA: Harvard University Press, 2004.

———. *The Nazi Party: A Social Profile of Members and Leaders, 1919–1945*. Cambridge, MA: Harvard University Press, 1983.

Kautz, Fred. *The German Historians: Hitler's Willing Executioners and Daniel Goldhagen*. Montreal: Black Rose Books, 2003.

Kay, Alex, Jeff Rutherford, and David Stahel, eds. *Nazi Policy on the Eastern Front, 1941: Total War, Genocide and Radicalization*. Rochester, NY: University of Rochester Press, 2012.

Keller, Sven. *Volksgemeinschaft am Ende: Gesellschaft und Gewalt 1944/45*. Munich: R. Oldenbourg Verlag, 2013.

Kershaw, Ian. *The End: The Defiance and Destruction of Hitler's Germany, 1944–1945*. New York: Penguin, 2011.

———. *Hitler: 1936–1945, Nemesis*. New York: W. W. Norton, 2001.

———. *The "Hitler Myth": Image and Reality in the Third Reich.* New York: Oxford University Press, 1987.

———. *The Nazi Dictatorship: Problems and Perspectives of Interpretation.* New York: Oxford University Press, 2000.

———. *Popular Opinion and Political Dissent in the Third Reich: Bavaria 1933–1945.* New York: Oxford University Press, 2002.

Klemperer, Victor. *The Language of the Third Reich: LTI—Lingua Tertii Imperii; A Philologist's Notebook.* New York: Continuum, 2006.

Klotzbach, Kurt. *Gegen den Nationalsozialismus: Widerstand und Verfolgung in Dortmund 1933–1945.* Hannover: Verlag für Literatur und Zeitgeschehen, 1969.

Koonz, Claudia. *The Nazi Conscience.* Cambridge, MA: Belknap Press of Harvard University Press, 2003.

Latzel, Klaus. *Deutsche Soldaten—nationalsozialistischer Krieg? Kriegserlebnis—Kriegserfahrung 1939–1945.* Paderborn: Ferdinand Schöningh, 1998.

Longerich, Peter. *"Davon haben wir nichts gewusst!": Die Deutschen und die Judenverfolgung 1933–1945.* Munich: Siedler Verlag, 2006.

———. *Joseph Goebbels: Biographie.* Munich: Siedler Verlag, 2010.

Lotfi, Gabriele. *KZ der Gestapo: Arbeitserziehungslager im Dritten Reich.* Stuttgart: Deutsche Verlags-Anstalt, 2000.

Lüdtke, Alf, and Bernd Weisbrod, eds. *No Man's Land of Violence: Extreme Wars in the 20th Century.* Göttingen: Wallstein Verlag, 2006.

Mason, Timothy W. *Arbeiterklasse und Volksgemeinschaft: Dokumente und Materialien zur deutschen Arbeiterpolitik 1936–1939.* Opladen: Westdeutscher Verlag, 1975.

Müller, Rolf-Dieter, ed. *Die Wehrmacht: Mythos und Realität.* Munich: R. Oldenbourg Verlag, 1999.

Müller, Sven Oliver. *Deutsche Soldaten und ihre Feinde: Nationalismus an Front und Heimatfront im Zweiten Weltkrieg.* Frankfurt am Main: S. Fischer Verlag, 2007.

Neitzel, Sönke. *Abgehört: Deutsche Generäle in britischer Kriegsgefangenschaft 1942–1945.* Berlin: Ullstein Taschenbuchverlag, 2007.

Neitzel, Sönke, and Harald Welzer. *Soldaten: Protokolle vom Kämpfen, Töten und Sterben.* Berlin: Fischer Taschenbuchverlag, 2012.

Pendas, Devin, Mark Roseman, and Richard Wetzell, eds. *Beyond the Racial State: Rethinking Nazi Germany.* New York: Cambridge University Press, 2017.

Peukert, Detlev J. K. *Inside Nazi Germany: Conformity, Opposition, and Racism in Everyday Life.* London: B. T. Batsford, 1987.

Pohl, Dieter. *Die Herrschaft der Wehrmacht: Deutsche Militärbesatzung und einheimische Bevölkerung in der Sowjetunion 1941–1944.* Frankfurt am Main: Fischer Taschenbuch Verlag, 2011.

———. *Verfolgung und Massenmord in der NS-Zeit 1933–1945.* Darmstadt: Wissenschaftliche Buchgesellschaft, 2003.

Rass, Christoph. *"Menschenmaterial": Deutsche Soldaten an der Ostfront; Innenansichten einer Infanteriedivision 1939–1945.* Paderborn: Schöningh, 2003.

Read, Anthony. *The Devil's Disciples: Hitler's Inner Circle.* New York: W. W. Norton, 2006.

Reeken, Dietmar, and Malte Thiessen. *"Volksgemeinschaft" als soziale Praxis: Neue Forschungen zur NS-Gesellschaft vor Ort.* Paderborn, Schöningh, 2013.

Römer, Felix. *Kameraden: Die Wehrmacht von innen*. Munich: Piper Verlag, 2012.

Schmidt, Matthias. *Albert Speer: Das Ende eines Mythos*. Berlin: NZ Netzeitung, 2005.

Schmidt, Rainer F. *Rudolf Hess: "Bootgang eines Toren?" Der Flug nach Grossbritanien vom 10. Mai 1941*. Düsseldorf: Econ, 1997.

Schmiechen-Ackermann, Detlef. *"Volksgemeinschaft": Mythos, wirkungsmächtige soziale Verheißung oder soziale Realität im "Dritten Reich"? Zwischenbilanz einer kontroversen Debatte*. Paderborn: Schöningh, 2012.

Schüddekopf, Carl. *Krieg: Erzählungen aus dem Schweigen; Deutsche Soldaten über den Zweiten Weltkrieg*. Reinbek bei Hamburg: Rowohlt Verlag, 1997.

Sebald, W. G. *On the Natural History of Destruction*. New York: Modern Library Classics, 2004.

Sereny, Gitta. *Albert Speer: His Battle with Truth*. New York: Vintage Books, 1995.

Shandley, Robert R. *Unwilling Germans? The Goldhagen Debate*. Minneapolis: University of Minnesota Press, 1998.

Speer, Albert. *Inside the Third Reich*. New York: Simon & Schuster, 1970.

Stahel, David. "The Wehrmacht and National Socialist Military Thinking." *War in History* 24, no. 3 (2017): 336–361.

Stargardt, Nicholas. *The German War: A Nation under Arms, 1939–1945; Citizens and Soldiers*. New York: Basic Books, 2015.

Steber, Martina, and Bernhard Otto, eds. *Visions of Community in Nazi Germany: Social Engineering and Private Lives*. Oxford: Oxford University Press, 2014.

Steinberg, Hans-Josef. *Widerstand und Verfolgung in Essen 1933–1945*. Hannover: Verlag für Literatur und Zeitgeschehen, 1969.

Steinert, Marlis G. *Hitler's War and the Germans: Public Mood and Attitudes during the Second World War*. Athens: Ohio University Press, 1997.

Tooze, Adam. *The Wages of Destruction: The Making and Breaking of the Nazi Economy*. New York: Viking Penguin, 2007.

Tyas, Stephen. "Allied Intelligence Agencies and the Holocaust: Information Acquired from German Prisoners of War." *Holocaust and Genocide Studies* 22, no. 1 (Spring 2008): 1–24.

Voegelin, Eric. *Die politischen Religionen*. Paderborn: Wilhelm Fink, 1993.

Vollmer, Bernhard. *Volksopposition im Polizeistaat: Gestapo- und Regierungsberichte 1934–1936*. Stuttgart: Deutsche Verlags-Anstalt, 1957.

Weitz, Eric. *Century of Genocide: Utopias of Race and Nation*. Princeton, NJ: Princeton University Press, 2003.

Welzer, Harald, Sönke Neitzel, and Christian Gudehus, eds. *"Der Führer war wieder viel zu human, viel zu gefühlvoll": Der Zweite Weltkrieg aus der Sicht deutscher und italienischer Soldaten*. Frankfurt am Main: S. Fischer Verlag, 2011.

Wette, Wolfram. *Die Wehrmacht: Feindbilder, Vernichtungskrieg, Legenden*. Frankfurt am Main: S. Fischer Verlag, 2002.

Wette, Wolfram, Ricarda Bremer, and Detlef Vogel, eds. *Das letzte halbe Jahr: Stimmungsberichte der Wehrmachtpropaganda 1944/45*. Essen: Klartext Verlag, 2001.

Zierenberg, Malte. *Stadt der Schieber: Der Berliner Schwarzmarkt 1939–1950*. Göttingen: Vandenhoeck & Ruprecht, 2008.

INDEX

Figures are indicated by f in page number.